CONSTITUTION 3.0

CONSTITUTION

Freedom and Technological Change

3.0

Jeffrey Rosen

Benjamin Wittes

EDITORS

BROOKINGS INSTITUTION PRESS

Washington, D.C.

Library of Congress Cataloging-in-Publication data
Constitution 3.0 : freedom and technological change / Jeffrey Rosen and Benjamin Wittes, editors.
    p.   cm.
    Includes bibliographical references and index.
    Summary: "Explores the challenges to constitutional values posed by sweeping technological changes such as social networks, brain scans, and genetic selection and suggests ways of preserving rights, including privacy, free speech, and dignity in the age of Facebook and Google"—Provided by publisher.
    1. Constitutional law—United States.   2. Technology and law—United States.
3. Civil rights—United States.   4. Information technology—Law and legislation—United States.   5. Freedom of expression—United States.   6. Privacy, Right of—United States.   I. Rosen, Jeffrey, 1964–   II. Wittes, Benjamin.
    KF4550.C569 2011
    342.7308'5—dc23 2011040988

9 8 7 6 5 4 3 2 1

Printed on acid-free paper

Typeset in Minion

Composition by R. Lynn Rivenbark
Macon, Georgia

Printed by R. R. Donnelley
Harrisonburg, Virginia

Contents

Acknowledgments

This project would not have been possible without the assistance of a great many people whom we cannot thank enough. Let us start with the remarkable group of authors who contributed to this volume, all of whom attempted something extremely difficult: not only to imagine the future but to imagine its Constitution. Each of them brought to the project a different sensibility, expertise, and set of concerns. Each of them produced something that enriched the larger undertaking and that, individually and cumulatively, illustrates the richness and complexity of the ongoing process of constitutional adaptation.

Launching a broad Brookings project on technological development and its implications for the future of the Constitution was the brainchild of our colleague Pietro Nivola, who read an article Jeffrey Rosen had written in the *New York Times* magazine and immediately saw in it the sort of governance challenges in which the Governance Studies department at Brookings specializes. Throughout the project, he has served as sounding board, booster, and counselor for our thoughts and plans.

A special word of thanks goes out to the folks at James Madison's Montpelier, who hosted a wonderful seminar on some of the draft papers, which benefited a great deal from audience feedback. At Brookings, the team at Governance Studies has been invaluable. Darrell West, vice president for Governance Studies, made this project a feature of his new Center for Technology Innovation. And Courtney Dunakin, Ashley Bennett, Ellen Higgins, Robert Brier, John Seo, and Ritika Singh each made critical gears turn at just the right times. The Brookings Institution Press worked its unusual magic on an unruly and diverse manuscript. Chris Kelaher, Janet Walker, Katherine Kimball, Larry Converse, and Susan Woollen shepherded the book to publication. Rich Pottern designed its beautiful cover. Without all of these people, the pages of this volume would be blank.

Finally, we are very grateful for the generous support this project has received from a variety of entities and individuals. The Brookings Institution is a private nonprofit organization. Its mission is to conduct high-quality, independent research and, based on that research, to provide innovative, practical recommendations for policymakers and the public. The conclusions and recommendations of any Brookings publication are solely those of its authors and do not reflect the views of the institution, its management, or its other scholars.

This project was produced with the financial support of the Markle Foundation, the Ewing Marion Kauffman Foundation, Google, Gerry Ohrstrom, and an additional foundation that prefers not to be identified. Brookings recognizes that the value it provides to any supporter is in its commitment to quality, independence, and impact. Activities supported by its donors reflect this commitment and the analysis and recommendations are not determined by any donation.

JEFFREY ROSEN

1

Introduction: Technological Change and the Constitutional Future

At the beginning of the twenty-first century, changes in technology are posing stark challenges to our legal and constitutional values. From free speech to privacy, from liberty and personal autonomy to the privilege against self-incrimination, from the definition of personhood to the state's authority to protect security, basic constitutional principles are under stress from technological advances unimaginable even a few decades ago, let alone in the founding era. Consider a few cases that might plausibly confront the Supreme Court in the year 2025:

—In response to popular demand, Facebook decides to post live feeds from public and private surveillance cameras so they can be searched online. After Facebook grants the request, anyone in the world can log onto the Internet, select a particular street view on Facebook, and zoom in on a particular individual. The user can then back-click to retrace that person's steps since she left the house in the morning or forward-click to see where she is headed. With facial recognition technology, a user can click on an image of a stranger, plug the image into a Facebook or Google database to identify her by name, and then follow her movements from door to door. Imagine that this ubiquitous surveillance is challenged as a violation of the Fourth Amendment, which prohibits unreasonable searches and seizures of our "persons, houses, papers, and effects." Under existing doctrine, the Fourth Amendment may not be construed to regulate Facebook, a private corporation, and even if there were enough state action to trigger the Constitution, the Court has come close to saying that we have no expectations of privacy in public places.

—As genetic selection becomes more advanced, couples who use in vitro fertilization are increasingly selecting embryos on the basis of sex, height, sexual

1

orientation, and even intelligence. In response to concerns about the new eugenics, several states enact laws banning genetic screening for nontherapeutic purposes. These laws are then challenged before the Supreme Court as a violation of the personal liberty and autonomy protected by the due process clause of the Constitution. Existing case law, however, offers little guidance about whether the right to have offspring, recognized in cases such as *Roe* v. *Wade,* includes an unlimited right to select the characteristics of those offspring.

—As brain scans become increasingly sophisticated, they are becoming de rigueur in death penalty trials, where defense lawyers routinely seek to introduce functional magnetic resonance imaging (fMRI) scans to prove that their clients were unable to control their violent impulses—a kind of "my brain made me do it" defense. Under the relaxed evidentiary standards for capital sentencing, this evidence is usually admitted, and lawyers predict that "neurolaw" evidence will increasingly transform the legal system, calling into question traditional ideas of moral responsibility. Some scholars already claim that neuroscience should lead the legal system to jettison retribution as a goal of criminal punishment, since it's unfair to hold people responsible for actions that are predetermined by their brains rather than chosen by their free will. Imagine that in 2025 scans can predictably identify people with dangerous propensities to violence. And imagine that a state predicates a civil commitment on the results of scans. Should the Supreme Court strike down efforts to hold people responsible for their propensities rather than their actions as an unconstitutional bill of attainder, or is punishment for propensity different from the procedure that concerned the framers of the Constitution—namely, laws that outlawed specific persons, rather than actions, without the benefit of a judicial trial?

As these examples show, a series of constitutional provisions—including the First, Fourth, Fifth, and Fourteenth Amendments—provide no clear answers, at least as currently interpreted, to the question of how we can preserve American values in the face of dramatic and rapid technological change. Part of the challenge arises from a world in which private corporations have more power over free speech and privacy than any president, king, or Supreme Court justice; part arises from gaps in the Supreme Court's constitutional doctrine itself, which arose in response to very different challenges in the pre-Internet age.

Of course, the project of keeping the Constitution technologically current is not new. The most creative constitutional thinkers have long struggled to adapt constitutional values to changes in technology. Justice Louis Brandeis offers the paradigmatic example. As early as 1928, in a case called *Olmstead* v. *United States*, the Supreme Court first encountered the constitutionality of wiretaps. When the federal government began to tap phones in an effort to enforce prohibition, a bootlegger named Roy Olmstead protested that the wiretaps violated his rights under the Fourth Amendment. In a literal-minded majority opinion, Chief Justice William Howard Taft disagreed. The Fourth Amendment, he said, was originally understood to forbid only searches or seizures accompanied by physical trespass. The agents had not trespassed on Olmsted's property when they placed wiretaps on the phone lines in the streets near his house, Taft held, and conversations were not tangible "effects" that could be searched or seized.

In a visionary dissenting opinion, Brandeis grappled with the issue of translating late-eighteenth-century values in a twentieth-century world. As private life had begun to be conducted over the wires in the age of radio, he observed, telephone conversations contained even more intimate information than sealed letters, which the Supreme Court had held in the nineteenth century could not be opened without a warrant. To protect the same amount of privacy that the framers of the Fourth and Fifth Amendments intended to protect, Brandeis concluded, it had become necessary to translate those amendments into the twentieth century, extending them to prohibit warrantless searches and seizures of conversations over the wires, even if the violations occurred without physical invasions.

In a remarkably prescient passage, Brandeis then looked forward to the age of cyberspace, predicting that technologies of surveillance were likely to progress far beyond wiretapping. "Ways may someday be developed by which the Government, without removing papers from secret drawers, can reproduce them in court, and by which it will be enabled to expose to a jury the most intimate occurrences of the home," he wrote. In anticipation of those future innovations, Brandeis challenged his colleagues to translate the Constitution once again to take account of the new technologies, or else risk protecting less privacy and freedom in the twenty-first century than the framers of the Constitution expected in the eighteenth century.

The technologies that Brandeis imagined have now come to pass—and they do not only affect privacy; they affect a broad range of constitutional values. At the same time, these new technologies are having an impact on vastly greater numbers of people than Brandeis could have imagined possible. In the late 1890s, in the most famous article on the right to privacy ever written, Brandeis had worried about new technologies—the Kodak camera and the tabloid press—that were threatening the privacy of aristocrats and celebrities by spreading idle gossip. Today, in an age when 500 million members share billions pieces of content on Facebook each month, all of us face a kind of scrutiny through gossip and ill-advised photos and videos that Brandeis's celebrities could not have imagined.

Yet judges today are generally reluctant to take up Brandeis's challenge to translate legal and constitutional doctrines in light of new technologies. Furthermore, the task of doing so should not be left exclusively to judges or to constitutional doctrine. Sometimes, Congress has kept constitutional values current with legislation. The hard work of applying the Fourth Amendment to wiretapping was ultimately done not by judges but by the U.S. Congress, which in 1968 passed the federal wiretapping law and, a decade later, passed the Foreign Intelligence Surveillance Act. Sometimes, regulatory agencies have taken the lead, such as the Federal Communication Commission's embrace of the principal of network neutrality—namely, the idea that Internet service providers must treat all data equally and may not block or delay any content or applications. And sometimes, keeping the Constitution up to date may require amendments that update the constitutional text itself.

The Brookings Project on Technology and the Constitution was set up to identify, in a nonpartisan and nonideological manner, the range of options for constitutional translation—from courts and legislatures to regulators and new technologies. We asked leading thinkers to imagine the concrete threats that different technologies would pose to constitutional and legal values in the year 2025 and then invited them to select the balance of regulatory, legal, and technological responses that they thought could best preserve the values they considered most important. We chose contributors from very different philosophical and ideological backgrounds in the hope of discovering whether contemporary ideological disputes would map onto the futuristic scenarios. (In some areas, they did; in others, they did not.) This volume is testament both to the possibility of creative thinking about constitutional translation and to the difficulty of ensuring that the most promising solutions are adopted in practice.

The book proceeds in four parts. The first focuses on surveillance, data mining, and the Fourth Amendment. The second looks at the future of free expression and privacy. The third examines the constitutional implications of brain scan technologies. And the fourth explores various aspects of genetic engineering.

The first part, "The Future of Surveillance," begins with Christopher Slobogin's envisioning a future in which the police increasingly use global positioning system (GPS) tracking and other virtual searches. Slobogin argues that the Supreme Court's interpretation of the Fourth Amendment has failed to anticipate virtual searches and investigative techniques that do not require physical access to premises, people, papers, or effects. Slobogin argues that the Supreme Court, rather than focusing on individuals' expectations of privacy, should instead adopt a proportionality principle: for every state action that implicates the Fourth Amendment, he says, the government should demonstrate cause—a level of certainty that evidence of wrongdoing will be found—more or less proportionate to the intrusiveness of the search.

Orin Kerr also imagines the increasing use of surveillance and data-mining technologies; he speculates that the government in the future might monitor all subway riders as they enter and exit the station by collecting their fingerprints. Although this MONITOR system might help to foil terrorist plots by preventing people on watch lists from entering the station, he says, it might also be misused, allowing criminal investigators to track people in an effort to solve low-level crimes. Kerr says that rather than restricting the collection of data, legislators should pay greater attention to the use of data after they are collected.

Jack Goldsmith describes an even more ambitious monitoring program to meet the threat of a cyber attack. Sometime in the near future, he says, the government might mandate the use of a government-coordinated intrusion-prevention system throughout the domestic network that would electronically monitor all communications, including private ones. Although the program would be controversial, Goldsmith argues that massive government snooping in the network can be made lawful and constitutional if Congress and the president adopt credible safeguards, including independent scrutiny by the Foreign Intelligence Surveillance Court, privacy-protecting "minimization" procedures, oversight mechanisms, and sunset provisions.

My chapter begins part 2 of the book, "The Future of Free Expression and Privacy." I argue that in the twenty-first century, lawyers for Google and Facebook have more control over free speech and privacy than any president, judge, or king. I begin by imagining Open Planet, a decision by Facebook to link all public and private surveillance cameras and to put them live and online. Under existing Supreme Court case law, Open Planet might not violate the Fourth Amendment, but there are a series of other arguments for restricting ubiquitous surveillance. I then examine three other technologies—body scanners at airports, a web that never forgets, and controversial YouTube videos—and argue that in each case, political activism and federal regulations may be as important as constitutional doctrine in translating and preserving values of privacy and free speech.

Tim Wu argues that anyone who wants to understand free speech in the twenty-first century needs to know how the concept has expanded over time. The first free speech tradition focused on threats from government; the second, he argues, focuses on threats from private intermediaries, such as radio and broadcast networks and Internet platforms such as Google and Facebook. Wu imagines a merger between Google and AT&T, followed by an effort to crush its political opponents and favor its political supporters. Now that the future of free speech will be determined by concentrated, private intermediaries, he argues, regulatory agencies such as the Federal Communications Commission have more influence over speech than Supreme Court justices, and he urges the commission to use this power to prevent content discrimination by the private actors who control the lines.

In his "Mutual Aid Treaty for the Internet," Jonathan Zittrain notes that today, most people have direct access to the web, but that their online lives are controlled by consolidating search engines, content providers, and social networking sites. Greater online centralization means greater vulnerability to cyber attacks and threats to free speech: for example, Zittrain notes, a world where all of the world's books are stored in a centralized online Google depository means that a court order to delete a particular book because it infringes copyright would cut off access to all the world's readers. Zittrain argues that the key to solving this centralization problem, which he calls the "Fort Knox" problem, is to make the current decentralized web a more robust one by reforging the technological relationships between sites and services. Zittrain's model is mutual aid treaties among states, which create redundancy and security.

In part 3, "The Future of Neurolaw," Stephen Morse reflects on how neuroscience is attempting to transform legal notions of personal responsibility. Functional imaging and genetic evidence, he says, may be introduced more often, in coming years, in criminal cases outside of capital sentencing. Morse begins by imagining a young man who kills a fellow driver in an expression of road rage and, at trial, is found to have a predisposition to violent behavior. Morse considers and rejects neuroscience's radical challenge to responsibility, which treats people as victims of neuronal circumstances. If this view of personhood is correct, say Morse, it would indeed undermine all ordinary conceptions of responsibility and even the coherence of law itself.

In a similar vein, O. Carter Snead argues that advances in cognitive neuroscience have resurrected old arguments about human agency, moral responsibility, and the proper ends of criminal punishment. He begins by imagining that neuroimaging evidence of a predisposition to antisocial behavior, introduced at the sentencing phase of a capital trial, might be invoked to argue more frequently for the death penalty. Once retributive justice is off the table, Snead says, juries may be urged to execute criminals for the sole purpose of preventing them from committing the crimes to which they are neurologically predisposed. Like Morse, Snead wants to resist the radical conceptual challenge that neuroscience poses for criminal punishment in the United States.

Part 4 of the book, "Genetic Engineering and the Future of Constitutional Personhood," focuses on genetic engineering and the future of constitutional personhood. John Robertson begins with an examination of the coming legal challenges facing the constitutional doctrine of procreative liberty. He imagines a futuristic setting in which a gay couple, eager to have a male child who shares the sexual orientation of both parents, arranges to have "gay gene" sequences inserted into embryos created through in vitro fertilization. Robertson writes that by 2030, the logic of procreative freedom should lead courts to recognize a broad constitutional right of prospective parents to use the available technologies to have the family they choose.

Eric Cohen and Robert George imagine a future in which people could engineer genetic replicas of themselves or in which individuals could know what diseases they will suffer in the decades ahead. The new genetics, they argue, are rooted in a desire for self-understanding, new medical therapies, genetic engineering, the prediction of disease, and efforts to choose some lives and reject others. But each of these desires for personal autonomy presents profound moral and ethical questions about what it means to be human, raising the specter of a new eugenics. Instead of endorsing a constitutional solution to the potential excesses of genetic autonomy, Cohen and George prefer legislative solutions, including a national ban on human cloning and the patenting of human embryos, state-level prohibitions on the destruction of embryos for research, and a new regulatory body that monitors the safety of new reproductive technologies and has the power to restrict them in the interest of protecting children.

James Boyle hypothesizes that in the next century, it is likely that constitutional law will have to classify artificially created entities that have some but not all of the attributes we associate with human beings. Boyle imagines two entities with human attributes—Hal, a computer with artificial intelligence, and Vanna, a genetically engineered sex doll. Treating Hal and Vanna as full constitutional persons, Boyle argues, might have implications for the debates over fetal and corporate personhood that could discomfit liberals and conservatives alike. Instead of protecting Hal and Vanna with broad expansions of constitutional rights, and instead of trying to legislate the problem out of existence, Boyle argues, it may make more sense to muddle through with less abstract constitutional and statutory regulation.

Benjamin Wittes imagines that in coming years, biothreats—especially those emanating not from governments but from individuals—will present a profound challenge to the Constitution and the nation's basic assumptions about security. Imagining a genetically engineered small pox virus designed by a suicidal grad student terrorist, Wittes examines the continued proliferation of bioterrorism technologies and speculates that it will lead to a significant erosion of the federal government's monopoly over security policy. Rather than intrusive government monitoring that might cripple legitimate research, Wittes argues, the most effective defenses against bioterrorism may come from technological developments and from encouraging alert researchers, companies, and citizens to take on security responsibilities.

Finally, in a forward-looking epilogue, Lawrence Lessig argues that predicting the future in constitutional law is difficult because constitutional meaning comes just as much from what everyone knows to be true (both in the past and today) as from what the framers actually wrote. Yet "what everyone knows is true" changes over time, and in ways that are impossible to predict, even if quite possible to affect. To translate and protect values such as privacy and security in the face of unknown threats that will confront us in the future, Lessig says, we should adopt technologies today that will increase our range of choices tomorrow—such as an identity layer built into the Internet that would allow dangerous individuals to be identified but only with a court order. If we wait until after the threat has materialized, Lessig warns, adopting these thoughtful technologies of balance may not be politically feasible.

The contributors to this volume, in short, suggest a broad range of options for translating constitutional and legal values in light of new technologies. For some contributors—such as Slobogin and Robertson—courts should take the lead in constitutional translation; for others—Kerr, Goldsmith, and Cohen and George, for example—the most important actors will be legislators, not judges. Wu points to the importance of administrative regulation; Wittes and Zittrain emphasize voluntary cooperation; I stress the importance of political activists, working in conjunction with courts, legislators, and administrators. And Lessig describes how technological choices can shape the contours of the constitutional debate.

There is no question that the Constitution will change in response to developing technology in the future, as it has always changed in the past. But as the chapters in this volume suggest, it is far from clear how that change will take place, what form it will take, and how effective the changes will be. Citizens disagree vigorously and plausibly about whether judges should take the lead in adapting constitutional values to changing technologies or whether the more effective and democratically legitimate responses should come from the political branches or the private sector. Instead of endorsing a single approach, contributors to this volume have identified a range of options that judges, technologists, and legislators have as they struggle to respond to technological change. The result, we hope, is a provisional blueprint for translating constitutional and legal values into the twenty-first century.

PART I

The Future of Surveillance

CHRISTOPHER SLOBOGIN

2

Is the Fourth Amendment Relevant in a Technological Age?

The year is 2015. Officer Jones, a New York City police officer, stops a car because it has a broken taillight. The driver of the car turns out to be a man named Ahmad Abdullah. Abdullah's license and registration check out, but he seems nervous, at least to Jones. Jones goes back to his squad car and activates his Raytheon electromagnetic pulse scanner, which can scan the car for weapons and bombs. Nothing shows up on the screen. Nonetheless, he attaches a GPS (global positioning system) device known as a Q-ball underneath the rear bumper as he pretends to be looking at Abdullah's license plate.

Over the next several weeks, New York police use the GPS device to track Abdullah's travels throughout the New York City area. They also observe him taking walks from his apartment, relying on public video cameras mounted on buildings and light poles. When cameras cannot capture his meanderings or he takes public transportation or travels in a friend's car, the police use drone cameras, powerful enough to pick up the numbers on a license plate, to monitor him. Police interest is piqued when they discover that he visits not only his local mosque but several other mosques around the New York area. They requisition his phone and Internet service provider records to ascertain the phone numbers and e-mail addresses of the people with whom he communicates. Through digital sources, they also obtain his bank and credit card records. For good measure, the police pay the data collection company Choicepoint for a report on all the information about Abdullah that can be gleaned from public records and Internet sources. Finally, since Abdullah tends to leave his windows uncurtained, police set up a Star-Tron—binoculars with night vision capacity—in a building across the street from Abdullah's apartment so they can watch him through his window.

11

These various investigative maneuvers might lead to discovery that Abdullah is consorting with known terrorists. Or they might merely provide police with proof that Abdullah is an illegal immigrant. Then there is always the possibility that Abdullah has not committed any crime.

The important point for present purposes is that the Constitution has nothing to say about any of the police actions that take place in Abdullah's case once his car is stopped. The constitutional provision that is most likely to be implicated by the government's attempts to investigate Abdullah is the Fourth Amendment, which prohibits unreasonable searches of houses, persons, papers, and effects and further provides that if a warrant is sought authorizing a search, it must be based on probable cause and describe with particularity the place to be searched and the person or thing to be seized. This language is the primary constitutional mechanism for regulating police investigations. The courts have held that when police engage in a search, they must usually have probable cause—about a 50 percent certainty—that the search will produce evidence of crime, and they must usually also have a warrant, issued by an independent magistrate, if there is time to get one. As construed by the U.S. Supreme Court, however, these requirements are irrelevant to many modern police practices, including all of those involved in Abdullah's case.

The Fourth Amendment's increasing irrelevance stems from the fact that the Supreme Court is mired in precedent decided in another era. Over the past two hundred years, the Fourth Amendment's guarantees have been construed largely in the context of what might be called "physical searches"—entry into a house or car, stopping and frisking a person on the street, or rifling through a person's private papers. But today, with the introduction of devices that can see through walls and clothes, monitor public thoroughfares twenty-four hours a day, and access millions of records in seconds, police are relying much more heavily on what might be called "virtual searches," investigative techniques that do not require physical access to premises, people, papers, or effects and can often be carried out covertly from far away. As Abdullah's case illustrates, this technological revolution is well on its way to drastically altering the way police go about looking for evidence of crime. To date, the Supreme Court's interpretation of the Fourth Amendment has failed to anticipate this revolution and continued to ignore it.

The Supreme Court's Fourth Amendment

The Fourth Amendment's protections—warrants sworn under oath, particular descriptions of sought-after evidence, and cause requirements—are not triggered unless the government is carrying out a "search." The Supreme

Court has never defined this word the way a layperson would, as an act of looking for or into something. Rather, it has looked to either property law or privacy values in fleshing out the concept.

Initially, the Court defined Fourth Amendment searches in terms of property interests. A search occurred only when government engaged in some type of trespass.[1] Thus, for instance, wiretapping a phone was not a search because the surveillance involved accessing only outside lines. By contrast, the use of a spike mike that touched the baseboard of a house did implicate the Fourth Amendment.[2]

Then, in 1967, came the Court's famous decision in *Katz* v. *United States,* which held that covert interception of communications counts as a Fourth Amendment search.[3] Acting without a warrant, FBI agents bugged the phone booth Charlie Katz was using to place illegal bets. The government sought to justify the absence of a warrant by arguing that a phone booth is not a "constitutionally protected area" (because it is not a house, person, paper, or effect) and that planting and listening to the bugging device on a public booth worked no trespass. Justice Black also argued, in dissent, that conversations like those intercepted in *Katz* were intangibles that "can neither be searched nor seized" and in any event did not fit into the Fourth Amendment's foursome of houses, persons, papers, and effects.[4] All of these arguments were consistent with the traditional, property-based approach to the Fourth Amendment. But the majority stated that the Fourth Amendment "protects people, not places" and concluded that "what [a person] seeks to preserve as private, even in an area accessible to the public, may be constitutionally protected."[5] Justice Harlan's concurring opinion elaborated on the latter idea by recognizing that while the Fourth Amendment's protection of people still usually "requires reference to a place," places should receive that protection if they are associated with "an expectation . . . that society is prepared to recognize as 'reasonable.'"[6] It was this latter language that became the focal point for the Supreme Court's treatment of the Fourth Amendment's threshold.

Although it still defined *search* more narrowly than a layperson would, *Katz* was hailed as a long-overdue expansion of Fourth Amendment protection that was needed in an increasingly technological age. That celebration was premature. Supreme Court case law since *Katz* has pretty much limited that decision to its facts. While nonconsensual interception of the contents of one's communications over the phone or via computer remains a Fourth Amendment search, all other government efforts to obtain evidence of wrongdoing are immune from constitutional regulation unless they involve some type of physical intrusion. The Court has arrived at this intriguing result relying on four variations of the search-as-physical-intrusion theme: the knowing-exposure doctrine, the general-public-use doctrine, the contraband-specific doctrine, and the assumption-of-risk doctrine. All four doctrines have the effect of enabling the government to conduct most technologically aided, virtual searches without having to worry about the Fourth Amendment.

Katz itself said that while conversations over a public phone can be private for Fourth Amendment purposes, "what a person knowingly exposes to the public, even in his own home or office, is not a subject of Fourth Amendment protection."[7] This notion was first applied to government monitoring of activities in public spaces. In *United States* v. *Knotts*, the police lost visual sighting of the defendant's car as it traveled the streets but were able to use a tracking device affixed to the car to locate its eventual whereabouts.[8] Although the police would have been unable to find the defendant without the beeper, the Court held that its use was not a Fourth Amendment search because "a person travelling in an automobile on public thoroughfares has no reasonable expectation of privacy in his movements from one place to another."[9] Thus, after *Knotts*, police can use technology to spy on public activities without worrying about the Fourth Amendment.

In three later decisions, sometimes called the "flyover cases," the Court held that the knowing-exposure doctrine also sanctions suspicionless police viewing of activities on *private* property—even those that take place on the curtilage (the area immediately surrounding the premises)—so long as the police do not physically enter that area but rather view it from the air.[10] To the argument that the curtilage should be protected by the Fourth Amendment, at least when it is surrounded by a fence, the Court fancifully responded that "any member of the public" flying in navigable airspace could have seen what the police saw.[11] In one of the flyover cases, Chief Justice Burger, apparently recently returned from a trip to London, opined that even someone on a double-decker bus could have seen over the defendant's fence, thus rendering unreasonable any privacy expectation harbored by the defendant.[12]

The implications of this take on the knowing-exposure doctrine for technological surveillance should be fairly clear. As long as the police are located on a lawful vantage point, they can use technology to spy on anything occurring in public spaces or on private property outside the home without worrying about the Fourth Amendment. Governments have been quick to recognize how significantly this rule enhances investigations in an era of technological innovation. Putting a cop on every street corner around the clock is expensive and not cost effective. But video cameras of the type used to track Abdullah are increasingly seen as a good investment, especially since 9/11 has triggered federal funding for such projects. For instance, Chicago trains more than twenty-two hundred cameras, many equipped with zoom and night viewing capacity, on its urban populace day and night, every day of the week, some operating openly, others covertly; all of them are patched into the city's $43 million operations center.[13] Where cameras do not exist, satellite photography or drone cameras might be available.[14] The holding in *Knotts* ensures that the Fourth Amendment will not get in the way of these surveillance systems, at least if they are trained on venues outside the home.

Similar developments are occurring with tracking technology. Today it is both technologically and economically feasible to outfit every car with a radio frequency identification device that communicates current and past routes to an intelligent transportation system (ITS) computer.[15] Cell phones can be used to track anyone who has one within feet of his or her location; in the past several years, police have made over 8 million requests to phone companies for help in carrying out cell phone GPS tracking.[16] Again, in light of *Knotts*, most courts hold that the Fourth Amendment has nothing to say about such programs, even when they catalog weeks of travel.[17] The flyover cases also make clear that tracking onto private property, short of entry into the home, does not implicate the Fourth Amendment as long as, during that process, no government agent physically intrudes on curtilage.

One of the flyover cases also introduced the second Court doctrine limiting the definition of *search*—the concept of general public use. In *Dow Chemical v. United States*, the government relied on a $22,000 mapmaking camera to spy on Dow Chemical's fenced-in business property from an airplane. The Court had no problem with this use of technology because, it astonishingly asserted, such cameras are "generally available to the public."[18] According to the majority, because ordinary citizens can obtain such cameras and use them to view open fields and curtilage from airplanes, the government's actions in *Dow Chemical* did not infringe the Fourth Amendment.

Fifteen years later, the Court appeared to rethink this idea, at least with respect to technology used to spy on a home. In *Kyllo v. United States*, it held that a thermal imaging device is not in general public use—despite the fact that it cost a mere $10,000—and went on to hold that relying on such a device to detect heat differentials inside a house is a search.[19] In the end, however, *Kyllo* places few limitations on the use of technology to spy on the populace, for three reasons.

First, *Kyllo*'s ban on sophisticated technology applies only to viewing of the home. Thus, as already noted, government is able to use, without infringing

Fourth Amendment interests, any type of technology, generally available or not, if the target is located in a public space or on curtilage that is viewed from an area outside the curtilage.

Second, *Kyllo* expanded on *Dow Chemical's* holding by stipulating that even the home is not protected from surveillance with devices that are in "general public use." While thermal imagers may not cross that threshold, a wide array of technology is easily accessible by the public and thus can be used to peer inside the home. For instance, the lower courts have been willing to hold that police reliance on flashlights, binoculars, and zoom cameras to see inside premises does not implicate the Fourth Amendment.[20] Since telescopes can be bought at Wal-Mart for under $100, presumably they too fit in this category. Two courts have even held that night vision scopes of the type used in Abdullah's case are in general public use (which is not surprising, since they can be bought on eBay for under $2,000).[21]

A third reason *Kyllo* is little more than a pyrrhic victory for privacy advocates is that, in a bow to the knowing-exposure doctrine, the majority in that case stated that even very sophisticated technology may be used to view activities that take place in the home if it merely duplicates what a law enforcement officer could have seen with the naked eye from a lawful vantage point.[22] That idea, taken literally, could mean that government can rely on images from public camera systems or even satellites to see through un-curtained windows without infringing Fourth Amendment interests, as long as those windows are situated near a public street or sidewalk.

Even those parts of the home that are curtained and walled off may not be protected from sophisticated technological surveillance if the technology is contraband specific, meaning that it detects only items that are evidence of criminal activity. The Supreme Court broached this third limiting doctrine in a case involving a drug-sniffing dog, where it concluded, as a majority of the justices later put it, that "government conduct that can reveal whether [an item is contraband] and no other arguably 'private' fact compromises no legitimate privacy interest."[23] As anyone who has visited an airport knows, scientists have developed "mechanical dogs" that can sniff out weapons or contraband. Most of these instruments, particularly if based on x-ray technology, are not weapon or contraband specific; they expose other items as well. But as contraband-specific surveillance devices are developed, such as the Raytheon instrument the state police officer aimed at Abdullah's car, they will allow police to cruise the streets scanning vehicles, people, and homes for illicit items without in any way infringing on Fourth Amendment interests, because that type of virtual search would reveal only contraband.[24]

The three doctrines discussed to this point provide law enforcement officials with a wide array of options that allow technology to play an important, if not a dominant, role in their investigative pursuits, with no interference from the Fourth Amendment. The Supreme Court doctrine that most powerfully facilitates that role, however, is found in a series of cases holding that people assume the risk that information disclosed to third parties will be handed over to the government and thus cannot reasonably expect it to be private.

The two most important decisions in this regard are *Miller* v. *United States* and *Smith* v. *Maryland.* In *Miller,* the Court held that an individual "takes the risk, in revealing his affairs to another, that the information will be conveyed by that person to the government . . . even if the information is revealed on the assumption that it will be used only for a limited purpose and the confidence placed in the third party will not be betrayed."[25] That reasoning might make sense when the other person is an acquaintance, who can decide for his or her own reasons to reveal a friend's secrets to others.[26] But in *Miller* the third party was a bank. The Court held that even here one assumes the risk of a breach of confidence and therefore that depositors cannot reasonably expect that information conveyed to their banks will be protected by the Fourth Amendment. In *Smith*, the Court similarly held that a person who uses the phone "voluntarily" conveys the phone number to the phone company and "assume[s] the risk that the company would reveal to police the numbers he dialed."[27] As a result of *Miller* and *Smith*, the Fourth Amendment is irrelevant when government agents obtain personal information from third-party record holders, at least when the subject of that information knows or should know that the third party maintains it.

These decisions, which came at the dawn of the Information Age in the mid-1970s, have enormous implications for law enforcement investigation today. Traditionally, gathering documentary evidence required physically traveling to the relevant repository and asking for the appropriate records or, in somewhat more modern times, arranging for a fax transmission. That has all changed in the past couple of decades. The quantity of the world's recorded data has doubled every year since the mid-1990s. Computing power necessary to store, access, and analyze data has also increased geometrically since that time, and at increasingly cheaper cost.[28] Because of *Miller* and *Smith*, government can access free and clear of Fourth Amendment constraints all of this information, as well as the other types of data the police gathered in Abdullah's case, either directly or through the many private companies that today exist for the sole purpose of collecting and organizing personal transactions.

As Abdullah's case illustrates, not only is personal information now easier to obtain, but it is also much easier to aggregate. In the old days accumulation of data from disparate sources involved considerable work. Today it can often occur at the touch of a button, with the result that private companies as well as governments now excel at creating "digital dossiers" from public and quasi-private records.[29]

The scope of the government's technologically driven data-gathering efforts is staggering. A program tellingly called REVEAL combines information from sixteen government and private databases, including those maintained by the Internal Revenue Service and the Social Security Administration.[30] MATRIX, a federally funded data accumulation system that at one time catered to a number of state law enforcement agencies, claims that it allows clients to "search tens of billions of data records on individuals and businesses in mere seconds."[31] The best-known effort in this regard originally carried the discomfiting name Total Information Awareness (TIA), later changed to Terrorism Information Awareness. The brainchild of Admiral Poindexter and the Department of Defense's Defense Advanced Research Projects Agency, TIA was designed to access scores of information sources, including financial, travel, educational, medical, and even veterinary records, at which point terrorist profiles would help determine which individuals should receive special attention.[32] Although TIA was defunded in 2003, it continues to exist under other names and in other forms, including something called "fusion centers," which feature computer systems that "fuse" information from many different sources in an effort to assist law enforcement efforts.[33]

Total Information Awareness's original icon, a picture of an all-seeing eye surveying the globe accompanied by the maxim "Knowledge is Power," would seem to trigger the privacy protection meant to be provided by the Fourth Amendment. But the Supreme Court's assumption-of-risk doctrine has apparently exempted TIA-like programs from constitutional scrutiny. As a result, government may constitutionally construct personality mosaics on each of us, for no reason or for illicit ones, as long as all of the information comes from third parties.

Even if, because of its scope, the Total Information Awareness program were thought to be governed by the Fourth Amendment, other Supreme Court doctrines might well permit it to continue in relatively unrestricted fashion. The most important of these doctrines is implicated, in the words of a widely cited 1985 Supreme Court opinion, "in those exceptional circumstances in which special needs, beyond the normal need for law enforcement, make the warrant and probable cause requirements impracticable."[34] Lower courts have made clear that this special needs exception readily applies to antiterrorism efforts like TIA. For instance, courts have held that checkpoints established to detect terrorists are not focused on "normal" crime. As Judge Sotomayor stated in upholding a federal program that authorized routine suspicionless searches of passengers and cars on a New York ferry system in the wake of 9/11, "Preventing or deterring large-scale terrorist attacks presents problems that are distinct from standard law enforcement needs and indeed go well beyond them."[35]

Courts have also relied on special needs analysis to uphold programs that are not investigative in nature. For instance, in holding that a government plan to force prisoners to provide DNA samples is exempt from traditional Fourth Amendment rules, the Court of Appeals for the Fourth Circuit noted that the sampling was "not trying to determine that a particular individual has engaged in some specific wrongdoing."[36] Courts could easily decide that TIA and similar programs are designed primarily to collect intelligence about terrorism or other criminal activity and thus are special needs programs that, even if denominated "searches," do not have to meet the usual Fourth Amendment requirements.

Who Cares?

Under current law, most virtual searches are not Fourth Amendment searches or, if they are, they can usually be carried out on little or no suspicion if they do not involve interception of communication content. Given the huge amount of information that virtual searches provide about everyone's activities and transactions, traditional physical searches—with their cumbersome warrant and probable cause requirements—are much less necessary than they used to be. American citizens may eventually live, and indeed may already be living, in a world where the Fourth Amendment as currently construed is irrelevant to most law enforcement investigations. Technological developments have exposed the fact that the courts' view of the Fourth Amendment threatens the entire edifice of search and seizure law.

Some might react to all of this with a shrug of the shoulders. Think about Abdullah again. If he is a terrorist, technology has been a boon to our security. Even if he is merely an illegal immigrant, technology has enabled us to catch a miscreant who otherwise might not have been caught. And because the virtual searches in his case were carried out covertly, if he is innocent of wrongdoing he will probably never even find out he has been investigated. Indeed, given economic and other practical constraints on the government, most people who have done nothing wrong will never become targets at all. So why impose constitutional limitations on virtual searches?

One reason is that many people *are* bothered by technological surveillance. Studies that have asked people to rate the "intrusiveness" of various types of police investigative techniques show that the typical person views the techniques the government used in Abdullah's case to be more than a minor transgression.[37] On average, this research indicates, government accessing of bank, credit card, and phone records is thought to be more intrusive than search of a car, which requires probable cause under the Fourth Amendment.[38] Technological tracking of a vehicle is viewed, on average, to be nearly as intrusive as a frisk, which requires reasonable suspicion, a lesser level of certainty than probable cause but still something more than a hunch.[39] And public camera surveillance is considered, on average, to be much more intrusive than a roadblock, which is also regulated by the Fourth Amendment and in some situations requires individualized suspicion.[40]

Even programs designed to protect national security have sparked resistance. In 2006 reports surfaced that the National Security Agency had monitored the numbers of hundreds of millions of overseas and domestic phone calls to determine whether any communication patterns fit terrorist profiles. A subsequent poll indicated that while 63 percent felt that the program was an "acceptable way to fight terrorism," 37 percent disagreed.[41] The latter percentage would undoubtedly climb if this kind of surveillance were to spread from the National Security Agency to ordinary police departments and from national security investigations to investigations of ordinary crime.

Antipathy toward virtual searches could exist for a number of reasons. First, there is the prototypically American aversion to overweaning government power. As one opponent of the National Security Agency monitoring program inveighed, "Whether the next president is a Republican or a Democrat, there is nothing to prevent him from using this Executive Branch database for his own political purposes. That is a real threat to America. This database needs to be immediately and completely destroyed."[42] From J. Edgar Hoover's misuse of FBI files to Attorney General John Mitchell's illegal authorization of wiretaps on thousands of 1970s dissidents, from recent reports of the FBI's illicit use of National Security Letters to the Bush administration's attempts to access information about antiwar journalists and protesters, history confirms that, as TIA's icon proclaims, knowledge is power.[43] And power can be abused.

Even when government officials act in good faith in an effort to stomp out real crime, they can overstep their initial authority. The phenomenon of mission creep is well known in virtual search circles. For instance, fusion centers, initially designed as a replacement for TIA, now routinely come into play in ordinary investigations and collect all sorts of information about all sorts of individuals. One fusion center trainer put the point quite succinctly: "If people knew what we were looking at, they'd throw a fit."[44] Similarly, municipal cameras originally set up to deter violent crime and property theft are today more commonly used as a means of identifying "flawed consumers"—the homeless and vagrants—and removing them from community centers.[45] As Peter Swire has observed, "History . . . shows the temptation of surveillance systems to justify an ever-increasing scope of activity."[46]

Exacerbating the mission creep phenomenon is the inevitable fact that, just as with physical searches, virtual searches can lead to mistakes, sometimes serious ones. Based on record reviews conducted after 9/11, thousands of persons of Middle Eastern descent were subjected to interviews, and scores of them were detained as "material witnesses" for months on end on little or no suspicion, as evidenced by the fact that virtually none were prosecuted for terrorism-related crime and the vast majority were not prosecuted for any crime.[47] No-fly lists contain a notorious number of false positives, including the late senator Ted Kennedy and former assistant U.S. attorney general Jim Robinson.[48] Gun detection devices might sound the alarm for those who are legally, as well as illegally, carrying concealed weapons.[49] Methamphetamine profiles can lead to arrests of anyone who buys an abnormal amount of cold medicine.[50]

It does not take much imagination to compare the capacious intrusions technology facilitates to the general warrants that led to the inclusion of the Fourth Amendment in the Constitution. General warrants were abhorred by the colonists because they permitted ordinary officers to search any home and conveyance at their discretion.[51] As James Otis stated in the speech that John Adams later declared gave birth to the American Revolution, writs of assistance were obnoxious because they permitted entries of anyone's home or conveyance on "bare suspicion."[52] Under the Supreme Court's approach to virtual searches, even bare suspicion is not required when police monitor our transactions and public activities.

The ill effects of virtual searches do not stop with official misuse of information resulting from general searches. Less tangible, but arguably just as important, is the discomfort people feel when they are being watched or monitored even if, or perhaps especially when, they are not sure they are being targeted. In other words, for many individuals, privacy vis-à-vis the government has value in and of itself, regardless of whether there is evidence of government abuse, overstepping, or mistake. Thus when Daniel Solove asked people on his privacy blog how they would respond to someone who claims to be unconcerned about government surveillance because "I've got nothing to hide," he received numerous vigorous retorts: "If you've got nothing to hide, why do you have curtains?" and "If you've got nothing to hide, can I see your credit card bills for the last year?" and "If you've got nothing to hide, then you don't have a life."[53]

These sentiments may be associated with real-world impacts even when government makes no use of the surveillance product. Studies of the workplace indicate that panoptic monitoring makes employees, even completely "innocent" ones, more nervous, less productive, and more conformist.[54] And surveillance of public activities—whether via cameras, satellites, or visual means—clearly diminishes the anonymity people expect not only in the home but as they go about their daily activities in public spaces. As one court— unfortunately, an outlier that is not representative of the typical court on these issues—stated in describing the impact of a Q-ball GPS device of the type used in Abdullah's case,

> Disclosed in the data retrieved from the transmitting unit, nearly instantaneously with the press of a button on the highly portable receiving unit, will be trips the indisputably private nature of which takes little imagination to conjure: trips to the psychiatrist, the plastic surgeon, the abortion clinic, the AIDS treatment center, the strip club, the criminal defense attorney, the by-the-hour motel, the union meeting, the mosque, synagogue or church, the gay bar and on and on. What the technology yields and records with breathtaking quality and quantity, is a highly detailed profile, not simply of where we go, but by easy inference, of our associations—political, religious, amicable and amorous, to name only a few—and of the pattern of our professional and avocational pursuits.[55]

Most broadly, freedom from random governmental monitoring—of both public spaces and recorded transactions—might be an essential predicate for self-definition and development of the viewpoints that make democracy vibrant. This reason to be concerned about virtual searches, while somewhat amorphous, is important enough to have been remarked on by two Supreme Court justices. The first justice wrote, "Walking and strolling and wandering . . . have been in part responsible for giving our people the feeling of independence and self-confidence, the feeling of creativity. These amenities have dignified the right to dissent and have honored the right to be non-conformists and the right to defy submissiveness. They have encouraged lives of high spirits rather than hushed, suffocating silence."[56] The second justice wrote:

> Suppose that the local police in a particular jurisdiction were to decide to station a police car at the entrance to the parking lot of a well-patronized bar from 5:30 p.m. to 7:30 p.m. every day. . . . I would guess that the great majority of people . . . would say that this is not a proper police function. . . . There would be an uneasiness, and I think a justified uneasiness, if those who patronized the bar felt that their names were being taken down and filed for future reference. . . . This ought not be a governmental function when the facts are as extreme as I put them.[57]

The first passage comes, not surprisingly, from Justice William Douglas, a lion of civil rights. More surprising is the author of the second passage: William Rehnquist, writing soon after he joined the Court and began a long career of reducing Fourth Amendment protections.

None of this means that surveillance by the government should be prohibited. But it does suggest that it should be regulated under the Constitution, just as physical searches are. Furthermore, it suggests that back-end regulation of virtual searches, through provisions limiting information disclosure and use, will not be sufficient, because it will not prevent the subterranean abuse of information already collected, nor will it eradicate the feeling of being watched and the chilling effects occasioned by surveillance. Thus proposals advocating a trade-off between disclosure rules and collection rules (allowing the latter to be relaxed or eliminated if the former are strengthened) will probably greatly exacerbate these harms.[58] Restrictions on the extent to which covertly obtained information is revealed to the public are necessary, but they are not a panacea. Just as search of a house requires probable cause even when the occupant is not at home, the government should have to justify privacy-invading virtual searches even though no physical confrontation is involved.

A Technologically Sensitive Fourth Amendment

If reform of the Fourth Amendment were thought to be important as a means of responding to technological developments, the most obvious first step would be to conform the definition of search to its lay meaning of looking into, over, or through something in order to find somebody or something.[59] This move would immediately encompass virtual searches within the ambit of the Fourth Amendment's protections. Camera surveillance, tracking, targeting places or people with devices (whether or not they are in general public use or contraband specific), and accessing records via computer all involve searches under this definition.

Reform could not stop there, however. Current Fourth Amendment law also usually requires probable cause for a search. If police attempts to watch a person walk down the street, follow a car on the public highway, or acquire access to court records or utility bills all required probable cause, law enforcement would come to a screeching halt. Indeed, it may have been to avoid such a disaster that most justices on the Court, including many of its liberal members, have been willing simply to declare that these investigative techniques are immune from constitutional review.[60]

But there is a compromise position, suggested by the Fourth Amendment itself. After all, the Fourth Amendment requires only that searches and seizures be "reasonable." It does not require probable cause or any other particular quantum of suspicion.

I have argued elsewhere that the Fourth Amendment's reasonableness inquiry should adhere to a proportionality principle.[61] The idea of calibrating the justification for an action by reference to its impact on the affected party permeates most other areas of the legal system.[62] For instance, at the adjudication stage the law assigns increasingly heavier burdens of proof depending on the consequences: a mere preponderance of the evidence in civil litigation, the more demanding clear and convincing evidence standard for administrative law suits and civil commitment, and the most onerous requirement of proof beyond a reasonable doubt when the state deprives an individual of liberty through criminal punishment. Similarly, levels of scrutiny in constitutional litigation vary depending on whether the individual right infringed by the government is "fundamental."

The proportionality principle even has found its way into the Supreme Court's Fourth Amendment case law. It provides the best explanation, for example, of why arrests require probable cause while stops require only reasonable suspicion. As the Court stated in *Terry* v. *Ohio*, the case that established this particular hierarchy, "There can be 'no ready test for determining reasonableness other than by balancing the need to search against the invasion which the search entails.'"[63] Unfortunately, the Court has applied this principle only haphazardly and, when it does apply it, inconsistently.

A more formal adoption of the proportionality principle would state that for every government action that implicates the Fourth Amendment, government must demonstrate "cause"—defined as the level of certainty that evidence of wrongdoing will be found—roughly proportionate to the intrusiveness of the search.[64] Given the history of the Fourth Amendment, the baseline rule for application of the proportionality principle would be that searches of houses and similarly intrusive actions require probable cause. But less intrusive searches and seizures could be authorized on something less. For instance, the Court is clearly correct in its intuition that police viewing of public activities is generally less invasive than police entries into houses. Short-term camera surveillance and tracking of public movements, use of binoculars to look through a picture window, or perusal of a record of an individual's food purchases would not require probable cause under proportionality reasoning.

In contrast to the Supreme Court's jurisprudence, however, only the most minimal intrusions would be exempt from Fourth Amendment regulation in a proportionality-driven regime. Thus while randomly surveying the public streets with a camera might be untouched by the Fourth Amendment, using cameras to target an individual would trigger its guarantees (albeit perhaps only in the sense that an articulable reason for the targeting would be required).[65] In further contrast to the Supreme Court's approach, proportionality reasoning dictates that law enforcement demonstrate a high degree of cause for virtual searches determined to be as invasive or nearly as invasive as entry into the home. For instance, if the aforementioned empirical research on lay views is replicated—thus contradicting the Court's dismissive assertions about the expectation of privacy "society" associates with bank and phone records—*Miller* and *Smith* would be overturned, and police would have to demonstrate reasonable suspicion or perhaps even probable cause before gaining access to such information.

At least one exception to the proportionality principle should be recognized, however. When the purpose of a search is to prevent significant, specific, and imminent danger, society's interest in protecting itself is sufficiently strong that the justification normally required by proportionality reasoning should be relaxed. This danger exception is consistent with the clear and present danger exception in First Amendment jurisprudence as well as with *Terry* v. *Ohio*, which sanctioned preventive frisks when police have reasonable suspicion, rather than probable cause, that a person they have stopped is armed.[66]

Other exceptions might be necessary, especially if the search is of a large group, a topic taken up below. The important point for now is that proportionality reasoning should be the presumptive framework for Fourth Amendment analysis. The Court's Fourth Amendment jurisprudence—which, aside from the holding in *Katz* itself, is identical to the property-based regime that *Katz* supposedly discarded—opens the door wide to the extremely invasive investigative techniques that technological advances are providing the government at an increasing rate. By recognizing that some Fourth Amendment searches may take place on something less than probable cause, proportionality reasoning facilitates extension of the Fourth Amendment's protection beyond physical invasions and thus allows it to adapt to modern law enforcement.

Searches of Groups

A number of the technologically aided investigative techniques described in earlier pages—camera surveillance and Total Information Awareness, to name two—involve searches that affect large numbers of people. In effect they are search and seizure programs, not searches and seizures targeting a specific individual. The usual Fourth Amendment paradigm—sometimes said to focus on "individualized suspicion"—does not work well in these situations. At least four possible alternatives can be imagined, varying most prominently in terms of the degree to which courts have control over whether the program is constitutionally viable.[67]

The Supreme Court has usually dealt with group searches and seizures by invoking its special needs doctrine. Extremely deferential to legislative and executive decisionmaking, special needs jurisprudence usually upholds government programs that allow suspicionless searches and seizures of groups, based on two bald assertions. First, the Court proclaims that the government is confronted with a significant law enforcement problem involving something other than "ordinary criminal wrongdoing" of the type handled by the regular police force—such as illegal immigration, student drug use, or terrorism—and notes that the problem will be difficult to handle if individualized suspicion is required.[68] Second, the Court declares that the intrusions occasioned by the program will be relatively minimal (a brief stop at a roadblock) or will occur in an environment where expectations of privacy are already reduced (schools, the workplace).[69]

In carrying out this analysis, the Court rarely specifies the significance of the crime problem. And although the degree of intrusion may be somewhat mitigated by the group nature of the search or seizure, the Court's conclusion that this fact, by itself, justifies giving carte blanche to law enforcement is too facile. Programmatic investigations do raise special concerns, but they should not be exempt from the usual Fourth Amendment strictures simply because they are focused on "extraordinary" rather than ordinary crime or on groups rather than individuals.

A second, more judicially oriented approach to the large-scale search and seizure scenario is to adapt the proportionality principle—the idea that the justification should be proportionate to the intrusion—to group settings. As the Court sometimes suggests, a group search may be less intrusive precisely because of its group nature. For instance, the studies cited earlier found that when the government is accessing thousands of records as it looks for the proverbial needle in the haystack, its investigative efforts are viewed as less intrusive than when the records are sought with a specific target in mind.[70] Yet unless the intrusion is de minimis, proportionality reasoning would still require some concrete justification for these blunderbuss intrusions, beyond the type of broad pronouncements about law enforcement problems on which the Court usually relies. More specifically, instead of looking for what the courts have called "individualized suspicion," proportionality analysis in the group context could require what might be called "generalized suspicion."[71]

Generalized suspicion can be thought of as a measure of a program's success, or "hit rate," which under proportionality analysis must match its intrusiveness. A requirement of generalized suspicion proportionate to the intrusion visited on individuals in the group would force the government to produce concrete justification for its search and seizure programs. For instance, in *Edmond* v. *City of Indianapolis*, a roadblock case, police searches produced evidence of drug crime in 5 percent of the cars stopped.[72] Whether that potential hit rate would be sufficient to justify the intrusion associated with a roadblock would depend on how that intrusion compares with other police actions, such as arrests, which require probable cause (and might require a hit rate of about 50 percent, given the similarity of probable cause to a more-likely-than-not standard), and field investigation stops, which require reasonable suspicion (quantified at around 30 percent).[73] Assessment of hit rates might have to be speculative if a particular type of group search or seizure has never been attempted. But presumably a program instituted in good faith is motivated by the perception that a significant crime problem exists. In the absence of such facts (and assuming the danger exception does not apply), courts applying proportionality analysis would be leery of finding that a group investigation is justified.

The proportionality approach has at least two difficulties, however. As just mentioned, relevant hit rate information can be hard to come by. Second, proportionality analysis is unidimensional in that it looks only at hit rates, not at the deterrent effects of the search and seizure program, alternative means of achieving the government's ends, and so on. In the individual investigative context, this unidimensionality is not problematic because programmatic concerns are irrelevant. But where group searches and seizures conducted pursuant to statutes or executive policies are involved, more depth of analysis is possible.

Thus a third approach to regulation of group searches and seizures is to subject them to the type of judicial "strict scrutiny" analysis found in equal protection and First Amendment cases.[74] On the assumption that privacy from unwanted governmental intrusion is a fundamental right, the government could be required to show that such programs not only advance a compelling state interest but also are the least drastic means of doing so. Under this approach, courts would be even more active than under proportionality analysis in determining whether group searches and seizures are the best means of fighting the crime problem.

Unfortunately, strict scrutiny analysis encounters the same difficulties as proportionality reasoning, only magnified. Fighting crime—whether it is terrorism, illegal immigration, or drug possession—is either always a compelling government need (the Court's assumption in its special needs analysis) or compelling only when a quantifiable problem in the relevant locale exists (the generalized suspicion inquiry). If courts adopt the latter approach to defining what is compelling, as they probably should if they want to adhere to the spirit of strict scrutiny analysis, then the hit rate problem arises all over again. Regardless of how courts deal with this threshold issue, an even more confounding question, by a significant magnitude, is the remaining part of the strict scrutiny inquiry: whether a particular search and seizure program is necessary to achieve the government's interest. However competent courts may be at assessing, in First Amendment cases, whether time, place, and manner restrictions on speech are necessary, they are sorely ill equipped to analyze which law enforcement techniques work best.

Consider, for instance, how a court would apply strict scrutiny analysis to a public camera system. Assume that the area in which the government wants to set up cameras has a high crime rate and that research conducted in similar types of locations indicates that, through increased deterrence and apprehension, their presence can reduce property crime by as much as 25 percent and violent crime by as much as 5 percent (estimates based on the most optimistic studies).[75] In a proportionality regime, this information would be sufficient to allow the court to make its decision. In a strict scrutiny regime, however, even if the court found the government's interest compelling it would still have to inquire into whether the camera system was narrowly tailored to meet the government's objective.

That inquiry raises a number of imponderables. Alternatives to a camera system could include placing more police on the scene (presumably limited to watching people only when they have individualized suspicion), installing more street lights and greater pedestrian access to the area, and passing broader loitering laws that would allow police greater preventive authority.[76] Comparing the effectiveness, not to mention the expense, of these competing approaches is far from the typical judicial job. And although assessing the relative intrusiveness of these various techniques is within the usual judicial purview, balancing that assessment with these other variables and figuring out which technique most efficaciously deals with the crime problem in the least restrictive manner raises micromanaging quandaries that most judges would find daunting and that, for both political and institutional reasons, are probably inappropriate for courts to address in any event.[77]

That observation suggests a fourth approach to group searches and seizures, involving application of political process theory. As laid out by John Hart Ely, political process theory addresses the institutional tensions that arise when unelected judges review legislation enacted by popularly elected bodies under vague constitutional provisions such as the Fourteenth Amendment's prohibition on deprivations of life, liberty, and property "without due process of law."[78] In these situations, Ely argued, the appropriate division of labor should generally favor the legislature. Courts should strike down statutes passed by Congress or state representative bodies only if the legislative pronouncement is the result of a significant defect in the democratic process.

Ely did not focus on how this theory might apply to the amorphous reasonableness language of the Fourth Amendment. But Richard Worf has recently argued that it can apply in the latter context as well, at least where programmatic searches and seizures are involved. As Worf explains, "Where only groups are affected, very important, disputed questions can safely be left to the political process," because groups have access to that process.[79] Putting aside search and seizure programs that involve full-blown searches of houses or arrests (situations that the colonists clearly believed required individualized probable cause),[80] this approach is worth considering. In theory at least, groups—such as those subjected to the TIA program or public camera surveillance—can protect themselves through the political process in ways that individuals cannot. If the authorizing legislation applies evenly to the entire group (including its legislative representatives), the full costs of the program are likely to be considered in enacting it. And, as already noted, evaluation of search and seizure programs requires analysis of deterrent effects, resource expenditures, and other complicated interdisciplinary matters that legislatures are much better than judges at addressing.

While it does counsel deference to legislatures, political process approach is not simply special needs analysis dressed up in fancy theory. As conceptualized by Ely, judicial deference would be mandated only if the search and seizure program were established pursuant to legislation (as opposed to executive fiat), adequately constrained the executive branch (by, for instance, instructing police to search everyone, or everyone who meets predefined criteria), and avoided discriminating against a discrete and insular minority or any other group that is not adequately represented in the legislature. Irrational search and seizure programs—those that have no articulable rationale—would also be unconstitutional. Most of the group search and seizures addressed by the Court to date do not meet these requirements. Many were not even the product of legislative action.[81] And in most of the remaining special needs situations the Court has encountered, the authorizing legislation delegated too much power to executive branch law enforcement officials.[82]

In individual search and seizure situations proportionality analysis works well. But in the group search setting a combination of proportionality analysis and political process theory may be the best solution. The Supreme Court's special needs doctrine should be jettisoned because it is vacuous. Strict scrutiny analysis in the criminal law enforcement context is too dependent on judicial ability (or inability) to evaluate complicated law enforcement strategies. Instead, if a search and seizure program is authorized by legislation that is untainted by political process defects and is not irrational, courts should defer to it. If a process defect exists, the courts should apply proportionality reasoning using the generalized suspicion concept.

Consider how the foregoing framework would apply to a data-mining program such as TIA. First, it would have to be authorized by the legislature. This requirement would immediately disqualify TIA as a candidate for judicial deference, because it was the product of Admiral Poindexter's imagination and the executive branch, not Congress.[83] Assuming Congress could be persuaded to establish such a program, careful attention would still have to be paid to whether it circumscribed executive discretion by, for instance, requiring that the records of everyone, including members of Congress, be collected or by requiring a random records selection process (say, every fifth record). As Justice Jackson stated years ago, "There is no more effective practical guaranty against arbitrary and unreasonable government than to require that the principles of law which officials would impose upon a minority must be imposed generally."[84] A failure to follow this injunction, or a program that targeted an insular minority such as people of Middle Eastern descent, would subject the program to further judicial review.

If a court determined that sufficient discretion-limiting features were not present in the legislation, it would have to ascertain, under proportionality reasoning, whether the potential hit rate of the data-mining program justified the degree of intrusion involved. Assuming, as apparently was the case, that the TIA program contemplated obtaining and scrutinizing records describing financial information, credit card purchases, and phone and Internet contacts, a relatively high hit rate would be necessary. The required showing could only be reduced if human scrutiny were minimized through use of profiling technology or, consistent with the danger exception described earlier, a significant, imminent threat existed.[85]

Conclusion

Virtual searches are rapidly replacing physical searches of homes, cars, and luggage. Outdoor activities and many indoor ones as well can be caught on camera, monitored using tracking devices or documented using computers. Yet none of this technological surveillance can be challenged under the Fourth Amendment if its target could conceivably be viewed, with the naked eye or with common technology, by a member of the public, or could be detected using a contraband-specific device, or has been voluntarily surrendered to a human or institutional third party. And even those technological investigations that are considered searches will usually survive Fourth Amendment challenge, if they can be characterized as preventive or intelligence-gathering exercises rather than efforts to solve ordinary crime.

It is time to revert back to first principles. A search involves looking for something. Justification for a search should be proportionate to its intrusiveness except in the rare circumstances when the search is part of a large-scale program authorized by legislation that avoids political process defects or is aimed at preventing specific, imminent, and significant danger. These principles will restore the Fourth Amendment to its place as the primary arbiter of how government investigates its citizens, even when those investigations rely on technology that can be used covertly and from a distance.

Notes

1. See, for example, *Silverman* v. *United States*, 365 U.S. 505, 510 (1961).
2. Compare *Olmstead* v. *United States*, 277 U.S. 438 (1928), with *Silverman*, 365 U.S. 505.
3. *Katz* v. *United States*, 389 U.S. 347 (1967).
4. Id. at 365 (Black, J., dissenting).
5. Id. at 351.
6. Id. at 361 (Harlan, J., concurring).
7. *Katz*, 389 U.S. at 351.

8. *United States* v. *Knotts,* 460 U.S. 276 (1983).

9. Id. at 281.

10. *Ciraolo* v. *California,* 476 U.S. 207 (1986); *Riley* v. *Florida,* 488 U.S. 445 (1989); *Dow Chemical* v. *United States,* 476 U.S. 227 (1986).

11. *Riley,* 488 U.S. at 446.

12. *Ciraolo,* 476 U.S. at 211.

13. Fran Spielman, "Feds Give City $48 Million in Anti-Terrorism Funds," *Chicago Sun-Times,* December 4, 2004, 10.

14. See, for example, Katie Baker, "Houston Police Use Drone Planes," InfoWars. com, March 22, 2008 (www.truthnews.us/?p=973).

15. See Federal Trade Commission, *Radio Frequency Identification: Applications and Implications for Consumers* (March 2005), 3, 5; Smithsonian National Air and Space Museum, *How Does GPS Work?* (www.nasm.si.edu/exhibitions/gps/work.html).

16. Justin Elliott, "How Easy Is It for the Police to Get GPS Data from Your Phone?" TPM Muckraker, December 9, 2009 (http://tpmmuckraker.talkingpointsmemo.com/ 2009/12/cell_phone_surveillance_unpacking_the_legal_issues.php).

17. Kevin Keener, "Personal Privacy in the Face of Government Use of GPS," 3 *I/S: Journal of Law and Policy for the Information Society* (2007): 473 (describing cases permitting warrantless use of GPS for real-time tracking and to learn about previous travels and noting that only three jurisdictions require a warrant for either purpose). See also *In re Application of USA for Order Directing Provider of Electronic Communication Service to Disclose Records to Government,* 620 F.3d 304 (3d. Cir. 2010) (requiring only "specific and articulable facts" establishing that cell phone location information outside the home is "relevant" to an investigation). But see *United States* v. *Maynard,* 615 F.3d 544 (D.C. Cir. 2010).

18. *Dow Chemical,* 476 U.S. at 238.

19. *Kyllo* v. *United States,* 533 U.S. 37, 40 (2001).

20. *State* v. *Vogel,* 428 N.W.2d 272, 275 (S.D. 1988) (zoom cameras); *State* v. *Rose,* 909 P.2d 280, 286 (Wash. 1996) (flashlights); *Colorado* v. *Oynes,* 902 P.2d 880, 883 (Colo. Ct. App. 1996) (binoculars); *Oregon* v. *Carter,* 790 P.2d 1152, 1155 (1990) (binoculars).

21. *Baldi* v. *Amadon,* No. Civ. 02-3130-M, 2004 WL 725618, at *3 (D.N.H. Apr. 5, 2004); *People* v. *Katz,* No. 224477, 2001 WL 1012114, at *2 (Mich. App. Sept. 4, 2001).

22. *Kyllo,* 533 U.S. at 40 (concluding that if the police could have seen the details inside the home "without physical intrusion" then viewing them technologically is not a search).

23. *Jacobsen* v. *United States,* 466 U.S. 109, 122–23 (1984) (stating that this conclusion is "dictated" by *Place* v. *United States,* 462 U.S. 696 [1984], which held that a dog sniff of luggage is not a search).

24. See Paul Joseph Watson, "Fourth Amendment–Violating Mobile X-Ray Scanners Hit the Streets," PrisonPlant.com, August 25, 2010 (www.prisonplanet.com/4th-amendment-violating-mobile-x-ray-scanners-hit-the-streets.html) ("backscatter x-ray vision devices mounted on trucks are already being deployed inside the United States to scan passing individuals and vehicles").

25. *Miller* v. *United States*, 425 U.S. 435, 443 (1976).

26. See, for example, *Hoffa* v. *United States*, 385 U.S. 293 (1966).

27. *Smith* v. *Maryland*, 442 U.S. 735, 744 (1979).

28. Jeffrey W. Seifert, *Data Mining and Homeland Security: An Overview 2*, Congressional Research Service, January 18, 2007 (www.fas.org/sgp/crs/intel/RL 31798.pdf).

29. See Daniel Solove, *The Digital Person: Technology and Privacy in the Information Age* (New York University Press, 2004), chap. 2; Martha Neil, "Beyond Big Brother: Some Web Hosts Are Watching Your Every Keystroke," *ABA Journal* (August 2, 2010) (www.abajournal.com/news/article/some_web_hosts_are_watching_your_every_ key stroke/) ("Web hosts are watching what you read, what you say, what you buy and where you go online, via cookies and other tracking tools that enable them to assemble—and sell—detailed profiles to other companies").

30. Dalia Naamani-Goldman, "Anti-Terrorism Program Mines IRS' Records," *Los Angeles Times*, January 15, 2007, C1.

31. See Laura K. Donohue, "Anglo-American Privacy and Surveillance," 96 *Journal of Criminal Law and Criminology* (2006): 1059, 1151.

32. U.S. Department of Defense, Defense Advanced Research Projects Agency, *Report to Congress Regarding the Terrorism Information Awareness Program*, May 20, 2003, 3–9.

33. The TIA program was defunded by a voice vote. See 149 *Congressional Record*, daily ed., January 23, 2003, S1379-02: 1373, 1416. For a description of post-TIA programs, see Ellen Nakashima and Alec Klein, "Profiling Program Raises Privacy Concerns," *Washington Post*, February 28, 2007, B1; Shane Harris, "TIA Lives On," *National Journal*, February 25, 2006; and Lillie Coney, Electronic Privacy Information Center, statement to the Department of Homeland Security Data Privacy and Integrity Advisory Committee, September 19, 2007, 1, 4 (www.epic.org/privacy/fusion/fusion-dhs.pdf).

34. *T.L.O.* v. *New Jersey*, 469 U.S. 325, 353 (1985) (Blackmun, J., concurring).

35. *Cassidy* v. *Chertoff*, 471 U.S. 67, 82 (2d Cir. 2006).

36. *Nicholas* v. *Goord*, 430 F.3d 652, 668 (2005). See also *United States* v. *Pool*, 2010 WL 3554049 (upholding provision of federal Bail Reform Act requiring defendant to provide DNA sample as a condition of pretrial release).

37. See Christopher Slobogin, *Privacy at Risk: The New Government Surveillance and the Fourth Amendment* (University of Chicago Press, 2007), 112, 184 (tables reporting data).

38. *Carroll* v. *United States*, 267 U.S. 132 (1925).

39. *Terry* v. *Ohio*, 392 U.S. 1 (1968).

40. *Indianapolis* v. *Edmond*, 531 U.S. 32 (2000).

41. Karen Tumulty, "Inside Bush's Secret Spy Net," *Time*, May 22, 2006, 35.

42. Michael Stabeno, letter to the editor, *Portland Oregonian*, May 16, 2006, B09, available at 2006 WLNR (WestLaw News Resource) 8457654.

43. For a description of Hoover's abuses, see Solove, *Digital Person*, 175–87; for Mitchell's, see Frederick S. Lane, *American Privacy* (Boston: Beacon Press, 2009), xvii;

for recent abuses, including the use of National Security Letters by FBI special agents to obtain financial and other types of records, see Christopher Slobogin, "Distinguished Lecture: Surveillance and the Constitution," 55 *Wayne State Law Review* (2009): 1107, 1128–29, and William Fisher, "DoD Releases Records of Illegal Surveillance," Truthout, March 3, 2010 (http://archive.truthout.org/dod-releases-records-illegal-surveillance57329) (detailing Department of Defense collection of intelligence on Planned Parenthood, antiwar groups, and nonviolent Muslim conferences).

44. Quoted in Torin Monahan and Neal A. Palmer, "The Emerging Politics of DHS Fusion Centers," 40 *Security Dialogue* (2009): 617, 625.

45. Slobogin, *Privacy at Risk*, 96, 257–58n134.

46. Peter Swire, "The System of Foreign Intelligence Surveillance Law," 72 *George Washington Law Review* (2004): 1306, 1371.

47. See William Fisher, "Ashcroft's Post-9/11 Roundups Spark Lawsuit," Truthout, September 27, 2010 (http://archive.truthout.org/ashcrofts-post-911-roundups-spark-lawsuit63626).

48. Slobogin, "Distinguished Lecture: Surveillance and the Constitution," 1128.

49. In more than half the states, carrying a concealed weapon is legal. See National Rifle Association, Institute for Legislative Action, "Right-to-Carry" (2010) (www.nraila.org/Issues/FactSheets/Read.aspx?ID=18).

50. Brian Sullivan, "Silly Surveillance," *ABA Journal* (December 2009): 71.

51. Jacob B. Landynski, *Search and Seizure and the Supreme Court* (Johns Hopkins Press, 1966), 30–31.

52. Otis, quoted in *Legal Papers of John Adams,* edited by L. Kinvin Wroth and Hiller B. Zobel (Belknap Press of Harvard University Press, 1965), 142–44.

53. Daniel Solove, "'I've Got Nothing to Hide' and Other Misunderstandings of Privacy," 44 *San Diego Law Review* (2007): 745, 750.

54. Carl Botan, "Communication Work and Electronic Surveillance: A Model for Predicting Panoptic Effects," 63 *Communications Monographs* (1996): 293–313, 308–09. See Slobogin, *Privacy at Risk,* 257n129.

55. *People* v. *Weaver,* 12 N.Y.3d 433, 882 N.Y.S.2d 357, 909 N.E.2d 1195 (May 12, 2009). For a more recent case espousing the same views, see *United States* v. *Maynard,* 615 F.3d 544 (D.C. Cir. 2010).

56. *Papachristou* v. *Jacksonville,* 405 U.S. 156, 164 (1972).

57. William H. Rehnquist, "Is an Expanded Right of Privacy Consistent with Fair and Effective Law Enforcement?; or, Privacy, You've Come a Long Way, Baby," 23 *Kansas Law Review* (1974): 1, 9.

58. See William J. Stuntz, "Local Policing after the Terror," 111 *Yale Law Journal* (2002): 2137, 2181.

59. Of more than passing interest is the fact that in *Kyllo,* Justice Scalia felt prompted to note that this was also the definition of search at the time the Fourth Amendment was drafted. *Kyllo,* 533 U.S. at 32n1.

60. See Christopher Slobogin, "The Liberal Assault on the Fourth Amendment," 4 *Ohio State Journal of Criminal Law* (2007): 603, 605–11 (making this argument).

61. Slobogin, *Privacy at Risk.*

62. See generally Alice Ristroph, "Proportionality as a Principle of Limited Government," 55 *Duke Law Journal* (2005): 263 ("Principles of proportionality put the limits into any theory of limited government").

63. *Terry,* 392 U.S. at 21 (quoting *Camara* v. *Municipal Ct.*, 387 U.S. 523, 536–37 [1967]).

64. References to "intrusiveness" or "invasiveness" are found throughout the Court's Fourth Amendment case law with little or no attempt at definition. I have argued that the concept should be an amalgam of empirically determined views and positive law reflecting views about privacy, autonomy, freedom of speech and association, and, most generally (following the Fourth Amendment's language), security. Slobogin, *Privacy at Risk,* 23–37, 98–108. See also Christopher Slobogin, "Proportionality, Privacy, and Public Opinion: A Reply to Kerr and Swire," 94 *Minnesota Law Review* (2010): 1588, 1594–1608 (describing the concept of intrusiveness in detail).

65. For a more detailed description of this regime, see Slobogin, *Privacy at Risk,* chap. 5.

66. Ibid., 28. The exception would not, however, allow relaxation of justification requirements associated with investigating past crime; the intrusiveness associated with search of a house does not vary by the nature of the crime, just as the prosecution's burden of proof is not lessened simply because homicide is the charge. See Slobogin, "Proportionality, Privacy, and Public Opinion," 1611–14, for elaboration of this argument.

67. Much of this discussion is taken from Christopher Slobogin, "Government Dragnets," 73 *Journal of Law and Contemporary Problems* (2010): 107.

68. See discussion in *Edmond* v. *City of Indianapolis,* 531 U.S. 32, 37–40 (2000).

69. See *Vernonia School District 47J* v. *Acton,* 515 U.S. 646, 654–57 (1995).

70. See Slobogin, *Privacy at Risk,* 191–92.

71. Ibid., 40 (distinguishing generalized from individualized suspicion on the ground that the former is more explicitly based on profiles or statistical information).

72. *Edmond,* 531 U.S. at 450.

73. See C. M. A. McCauliff, "Burdens of Proof: Degrees of Belief, Quanta of Evidence, or Constitutional Guarantees?" 35 *Vanderbilt Law Review* (1982): 1293, 1325 (summarizing a survey of judges).

74. See, for example, Scott Sundby, "A Return to Fourth Amendment Basics: Undoing the Mischief of Camara and Terry," 72 *Minnesota Law Review* (1988): 383.

75. See Slobogin, *Privacy at Risk,* 84–88.

76. Compare Neal Katyal, "Architecture as Crime Control," 111 *Yale Law Journal* (2002): 1039, 1092–98 (exploring how city architecture might enhance crime control); *City of Chicago* v. *Morales,* 527 U.S. 41, 66 (1999) (O'Connor, J., concurring) (speaking of loitering statutes that might be "reasonable alternatives" to the loitering statute struck down by the majority).

77. Compare *Michigan Department of State Police* v. *Sitz,* 496 U.S. 444, 453–54 (1990) ("for purposes of Fourth Amendment analysis, the choice among such reasonable

alternatives remains with the governmental officials who have a unique understanding of, and a responsibility for, limited public resources, including a finite number of police officers").

78. John Hart Ely, *Democracy and Distrust: A Theory of Judicial Review* (Harvard University Press, 1980).

79. Richard C. Worf, "The Case for Rational Basis Review of General Suspicionless Searches and Seizures," 23 *Touro Law Review* (2007): 93, 117. William Stuntz broached a similar idea back in 1992. William Stuntz, "Implicit Bargains, Government Power, and the Fourth Amendment," 44 *Stanford Law Review* (1992): 553, 585–89.

80. See generally Daniel Steinberg, "Restoring the Fourth Amendment: Revisiting the Original Understanding," 33 *Hastings Constitutional Law Quarterly* (2005): 47 (arguing that the Fourth Amendment was meant to govern only searches of homes and arrests).

81. See, for example, *Michigan Dept. of State Police,* 496 U.S. 444, and *Edmond,* 531 U.S. 32, where roadblocks policies were promulgated by the local police department, and *Treasury Employees* v. *Von Raab,* 489 U.S. 656 (1989), where the policies were developed by federal officials.

82. See, for example, *New York* v. *Burger,* 482 U.S. 691 (1987) (statute allowed police to enter junkyards at will); *Skinner* v. *Railway Labor Executives' Assn.,* 489 U.S. 602 (1989) (statute simply directed the executive agency to promulgate rules); *United States* v. *Martinez-Fuerte,* 428 U.S. 543 (1976) (no statute and immigration agents given discretion to determine who should be sent to a secondary checkpoint).

83. John Markoff, "Pentagon Plans a Computer System That Would Peek at Personal Data of Americans," *New York Times,* November 9, 2002, A1 (www.nytimes.com/2002/11/09/politics/09COMP.html).

84. *Railway Express Agency, Inc.* v. *New York,* 336 U.S. 106, 112–13 (1949) (Jackson, J., concurring).

85. A procedure known as selective revelation, a process that allows humans to see records only after a computer applies a profile that generates the appropriate hit rate, might be useful here. See K. A. Taipale, "Data Mining and Domestic Security: Connecting the Dots to Make Sense of Data," 5 *Columbia Science and Technology Law Review* (2003): 2, 79–80.

ORIN S. KERR

3

Use Restrictions and the Future of Surveillance Law

The year 2030 was the year of the subway terror attack threat. As far back as the 2004 Madrid subway bombing, terrorists had seen how a single modest subway attack could wreak havoc on a busy city center. Sporadic attacks continued in the first three decades of the twenty-first century, including unsuccessful attacks on the New York subway in 2018 and the Washington, D.C., Metro system in 2023.

But 2030 changed everything. On January 1, 2030, Abdullah Omar, the leader of the Brotherhood, the reincarnation of the earlier al Qaeda network, made an ominous announcement: The Brotherhood had a dozen sleeper cells in the United States. In 2030 he would activate the cells. The cells would launch terror attacks on the transit systems of each of five major cities. Each system would be hit twice, and a few would be attacked more. Omar threatened that each attack would come with a "surprise."

Omar named the transit systems: the New York City subway, the Washington Metro, the Chicago 'L,' the San Francisco BART system, and the Boston T. The attacks would occur sometime during the year unless the United States agreed to withdraw all support from the state of Israel.

Some critics dismissed the threat as posturing. Others doubted the Brotherhood could pull it off. But in classified briefings, the director of national intelligence told President Booker that he thought the threat was extremely real. Omar's promised surprise was likely to be some kind of biological attack. Some attacks might fail. But others could work. The overall damage to life and to the economy amounted to a grave national threat, he explained, and the threat demanded a thorough response.

President Booker agreed. He set up a commission to advise him on how to respond. The commission, consisting of top intelligence and national security officials, recommended establishing a new federal surveillance system. The system would be known formally as the Minding Our National Interest Transit or Rail program. It would be known informally by its acronym: MONITOR. MONITOR worked by requiring that all subway passengers use a MONITOR card when they entered a subway system. Each card was activated by its owner's fingerprints. The fingerprints identified the user and kept records of where the user had entered and exited the system.

The Department of Homeland Security administered the MONITOR system out of a central office in downtown Washington, D.C. MONITOR's computers kept records of every entry into and exit from the subway, information that was then fed into the government's database in its central office. The system assigned each subway rider one of three colors. Green meant that the rider was authorized to ride the subway. Yellow indicated that the user was a "person of interest" whom the government wanted to follow (such as someone on a terrorist watch list). Yellow riders were allowed to enter the subway, but their progress was flagged by the MONITOR computers. Red riders were not allowed to enter the subway system at all.

MONITOR was up and running by late February, and it ran through the end of the year. By most accounts, it was a mixed success. Its most celebrated use was identifying a terror cell known as the South Loop Seven.

The South Loop Seven was a group of seven young Muslim men who attempted to enter the Chicago 'L' system within minutes of one another. Four of the seven men had been flagged as yellow because they were on a terrorist watch list. The entrance of all four yellow riders into the same station in a short period triggered an immediate response from the Department of Homeland Security. The four men were found minutes later with bomb-related materials in knapsacks. The 'L' trains were shut down immediately. A search of the station yielded the three other cell members, each of whom also had bomb materials in packages he was carrying.

To many observers, MONITOR's success in stopping the South Loop Seven justified the entire program. But other uses of MONITOR proved more controversial. For example, MONITOR's access to a fingerprint database drew the attention of the Federal Bureau of Investigation. The bureau sought to use the fingerprint database to crack unsolved crimes. MONITOR had not been intended to be used for criminal investigations, but President Booker eventually allowed MONITOR's data to be provided to the FBI with the proviso that they be used to solve only serious crimes. Hundreds of crimes were solved.

Some of these were serious, including murder and rape. Others were decidedly less serious, ranging from mail fraud to tax evasion.

Abuses occurred as well. For example, a few employees of the Department of Homeland Security were caught using MONITOR for personal reasons. One employee used the data to keep tabs on his wife, whom he suspected of having an affair. The employee flagged his wife's account yellow so he could watch her coming and going through the D.C. Metro system. In another case, an employee of Homeland Security lost a laptop computer that included a MONITOR database containing millions of datasets of fingerprints. The computer was never recovered. No one knows whether it was destroyed or if the information eventually made it into the hands of criminals or even foreign governments.

The Lessons of MONITOR

What are the lessons of MONITOR? In my view, MONITOR calls for a shift in our thinking about surveillance. In the past, the law has tried to regulate surveillance mostly by focusing on whether data can be created. The focus has been on the first stage of surveillance systems, the collection of data.

That must change. Computer surveillance uses widespread collection and analysis of less intrusive information to yield clues normally observable only through the collection of more intrusive information. To achieve those benefits, the law will need to allow relatively widespread collection of data but then give greater emphasis and attention to their use and disclosure.

In short, the future of surveillance calls for a shift in the legal system's focus—not merely a shift in how to regulate but a shift as well in what to regulate. Instead of focusing solely on the initial collection of information, we need to distribute regulation along the entire spectrum of the surveillance process. The future of surveillance is a future of use restrictions—rules that strictly regulate what the government can do with information it has collected and processed.

Of course, the law should still regulate the collection of evidence. But surveillance law should not end there. The shift to computerization requires renewed attention to regulation of both the use and disclosure of information and its collection. To see why, we need to understand the computerization shift and the stages of surveillance law. We can then see how use restrictions would be the key to protecting privacy while ensuring security in the case of the MONITOR system.

The Computerization Shift

In the past, information ordinarily was collected and shared using the human senses. We generally knew what we knew because we had either seen it directly or heard it from someone else. Knowledge was based on personal observation. If we wanted to know what was happening, we had to go out and take a look. We had to see it and observe it with our own eyes, or at least speak to those who had done so to get a second-hand account. The human senses regulated everything.

In that world, surveillance systems were simple. The "system" was really just a collection of individuals. They would listen or watch. If they saw something notable, they would tell others about it.

Computers change everything. More and more, our daily lives are assisted by and occur through computers. Computer networks are extraordinary tools for doing remotely what we used to have to do in person. We wake up in the morning and use the network to send and receive messages. We make our purchases online, using the network to select and order goods. Instead of hiring a person to watch our property, we use cameras to record what goes on in open places and to keep records of what occurred. All of these routine steps are facilitated by computers and computer networks.

The switch from people-based information to computer-based information means that knowing what's happening requires collecting and analyzing data from the networks themselves. The network contains information zipping around the world, and the only way to know what is happening is to analyze it. Specifically, some device must collect the information, and some device must manipulate it. The information must then go from the computer to a person, and in some cases, from a person to the public. The result is a substitution effect: work that used to be performed entirely by the human senses now must be done in part by tools.

The Four Stages of Computer Surveillance

The shift to computerization has profound consequences for how we think about surveillance law. A world of human surveillance involves a single step: a person who observes information then discloses it to others.

Computers complicate the surveillance process in a critical way. Instead of one step, there are now four: data collection, data manipulation by a machine, human disclosure, and public disclosure. A threshold problem faced by any system of surveillance law is which of these steps—or which combination of them—should be the focal points of regulation. Should the law focus on reg-

tion collected by MONITOR could not be disclosed to criminal investigators under any circumstances could minimize the risk that it might be used for less serious government interests.

The other uses of MONITOR were more obvious abuses. Employees misused the data for personal reasons; and data were disclosed inadvertently when an employee lost a laptop. Here the law should impose strict limitations on use and disclosure and ensure that they are enforceable. Data security is paramount, and remedies for violations should be harsh.

Courts or Congress?

The final question is what branch of government will create the use restrictions I have in mind. Can courts do this in the name of the Fourth Amendment, or is it up to Congress? In my view, Congress is the most likely regulator. The Fourth Amendment prohibits unreasonable searches and seizures. Use limitations are neither searches nor seizures, however. They are restrictions on what the government can do with information after it has searched for and seized it. There is little in the way of constitutional text, history, or precedent that supports recognizing use restrictions as part of Fourth Amendment protections.

Granted, it is possible to creatively reimagine Fourth Amendment law in ways that recognize use restrictions. As far back as 1995, Harold Krent made such an argument.[1] Krent reasoned that obtaining information is a seizure and that the subsequent use of the information—including downstream disclosures of it—could make the seizure "unreasonable." In other words, instead of saying that searches and seizures occur at a specific time, they could be deemed to occur over a period of time. All uses of information would be required to be reasonable, and courts could distinguish between acceptable and unacceptable uses of information according to their reasonableness.

The argument is creative, but I think it is too far a stretch from existing doctrine to expect courts to adopt it. In my view, there are two basic problems. First, most of the information collected by the government is not protected under current Fourth Amendment law. Collecting third-party records is neither a search nor a seizure (which is why they are frequently collected; information that is protected by the Fourth Amendment is collected only rarely). Under Krent's proposal, however, presumably we would need to overhaul that doctrine to make all evidence collection a seizure to enable courts to then pass on the reasonableness of the seizure. If we took that step, however, we would need an entirely new doctrine on what seizures are reasonable, quite apart from downstream uses. This would require a fairly dramatic overhaul of existing Fourth Amendment law, all to enable use restrictions.

Second, disclosures of information come in so many shapes and sizes that courts would have little basis on which to distinguish reasonable from unreasonable uses. Every database is different, every data point is different, and every disclosure is different. The kind of fine-grained reasonableness inquiry called for by Fourth Amendment law would leave judges with few clear guideposts or historical precedents on which to distinguish uses that violate the Fourth Amendment from those that do not. For both of these reasons, recognizing use restrictions in Fourth Amendment law may create more problems than it solves. At the very least, we should not expect courts to take such a leap any time soon. In contrast, legislatures are well equipped to enact use restrictions. They can promulgate bright-line rules concerning information collected under specific government powers, and they can explain the scope of the limitation and the contexts in which it is triggered. Furthermore, they can legislate use restrictions at the same time as they enact the statutes authorizing the evidence collection. That way, use restrictions can be a part of the original statutory design, rather than something imposed years later by the courts.

Note

1. Harold J. Krent, "Of Diaries and Data Banks: Use Restrictions under the Fourth Amendment," 74 *Texas Law Review* (1995): 49.

JACK GOLDSMITH

4

Cyberthreat, Government Network Operations, and the Fourth Amendment

Many corporations have intrusion prevention systems on their computers' connections to the Internet. These systems scan the contents and metadata of incoming communications for malicious code that might facilitate a cyber attack and take steps to thwart it. The U.S. government will have a similar system in place soon. But public and private intrusion prevention systems are uncoordinated, and most firms and individual users lack such systems. This is one reason why the national communications network is swarming with known malicious cyber agents, raising the likelihood of an attack on a critical infrastructure system that could cripple our economic or military security.

Imagine that to meet this threat, sometime in the near future the government mandates the use of a government-coordinated intrusion prevention system throughout the domestic network to monitor all communications, including private ones. Imagine, more concretely, that this system requires the National Security Agency (NSA) to work with private firms in the domestic communication network to collect, copy, share, and analyze the content and metadata of all communications for indicators of possible computer attacks and to take real-time steps to prevent such attacks.

This scenario, I argue in this chapter, is one end point of government programs that are already up and running. It is where the nation might be headed,

Thanks to Orin Kerr, Larkin Reynolds, and Jeffrey Rosen for conversations and comments, and Matthew Bobby, Keith Gerver, and Joshua Gruenspecht for research assistance and related help. This work was funded by the Office of Naval Research under award number N00014091059.

though perhaps not before we first suffer a catastrophic cyber attack that will spur the government to take these steps. Such a program would be controversial. It would require congressional approval and in particular require mechanisms that would credibly establish that the NSA was not using extraordinary access to the private network for pernicious ends. But with plausible assumptions, even such an aggressive program could be deemed consistent with the U.S. Constitution, including the Fourth Amendment.

The Threat

Our economy, our energy supply, our means of transportation, and our military defenses are dependent on vast, interconnected computer and telecommunications networks that are poorly defended and inherently vulnerable to theft, disruption, or destruction by foreign states, criminal organizations, individual hackers, and—potentially—terrorists. The number of public and private cyber attackers, spies, and thieves is growing rapidly. Their weapons are hidden inside the billions of electronic communications that traverse the world each day. And these weapons are becoming more potent relative to our defenses in an arena where offense already naturally dominates.[1]

With the current state of technology, computer system defenders cannot easily determine when the systems are being attacked—at least until the attack is under way or complete, and sometimes not even then. When defenders discover the attack, the attacker's identity usually cannot quickly or precisely be ascertained. Even when the computer or geographical source of the attacks is identified, it is hard to know whether some other computer in some other place launched the attack. Even if we have certain knowledge about which computer in which place was the ultimate source of the attack, we usually do not know whether the agent behind the attack is a private party or a state actor. And even if we know the actor's geographical location and precise identity, he is usually located beyond our borders, where our law enforcement capacities are weak and where we cannot use our military power except in the most extreme circumstances. And even if we could use military force, it might not be effective in thwarting the attack in any event.

And so the mature Internet, by eliminating the geographical and physical barriers that used to protect vital American assets, has empowered untold thousands of new actors to steal or destroy these assets; at the same time, it has made it difficult for the United States to find and punish, and thus deter, these actors. The result is that the U.S. government currently lacks the tools to stop the growing attacks on and theft of its vital economic and military assets. And the government is worried. President Obama thinks that the "cyber threat is one of the most serious economic and national security challenges we face as a nation." He declared in May 2009 that "our digital infrastructure—the networks and computers we depend on every day—will be treated as a strategic national asset" and the protection of this infrastructure "will be a national security priority."[2]

This most serious of national security threats presents a dilemma unique in American history. The U.S. government has access to and potential control over the channels of attack on the homeland from air, sea, land, and space. But it does not have legal access to, or potential control over, the channels of cyber attack on the homeland: the physical cables, microwave and satellite signals, computer exchange points, and the like. The private sector owns and controls these communication channels. This is a dangerous state of affairs because these private firms focus on profits, not national security, and thus tend to invest in levels of safety that satisfy their private purposes and not the national interest in cybersecurity. To make matters worse, between 90 and 95 percent of U.S. government military and intelligence communications travel over these privately owned systems—systems through which military and intelligence systems can themselves be attacked or exploited.

We have grown accustomed to thinking about computer and telecommunication systems as private communications infrastructure and about data storage media as presumptively immune from government scrutiny, vigorously protected by both the Fourth Amendment and an array of complex and demanding statutory restrictions. But in the coming decades, and probably much sooner, this understanding will change, perhaps radically, because these systems are also channels of attack on our nation's most valuable military, intelligence, and economic assets. Only the government has the incentive and the responsibility to maintain network security at levels appropriate for national security. And only with the government's heavy involvement will the United States have the resources and capacity to make the network secure.

The government will need to take many politically difficult and legally controversial steps to address the cybersecurity problem. One such step, and the focus of this chapter, involves the active monitoring of the private communications network. When someone enters the United States physically at the border (by air, sea, or land), or when someone physically enters a government building or a sports stadium, the government has the authority to inspect the visitor to ensure that he or she does not present a threat and to take steps, sometimes proactive ones, to ensure that a threatening visitor does not do harm. The government asserts similar authorities at airport screening stations and highway safety checkpoints. It also has the power to intercept air, sea, and land attacks on U.S. critical infrastructure components—such as the New York

Stock Exchange or a nuclear power plant. The cyberthreat is no less serious than these kinetic threats, and indeed may be more serious in our wired society. Citizens will demand that the government keep these systems secure and will punish the government if the systems are successfully attacked or exploited in ways that do serious harm. The government knows this, and it will act.

We know a bit about what the government is doing in this respect already, and what we know permits reasonable inferences about what it might try to do in the future as the cyberthreat grows and becomes more public.

The Government in the Network: What Is Happening Now

Begin with the government's little-known sensor and software system, EINSTEIN 2. This system is installed in Internet connection points between government computer systems and the public Internet. It scans a copy of all Internet traffic to and from government computers (including traffic from private parties). It then examines both the content and metadata of these copied communications for known "signatures" of malicious computer code—viruses, spyware, Trojan horses, exploitation agents, and "phishing" exploits that seek usernames, passwords, and social security numbers—that might be used to gain access to or harm a government computer system. When EINSTEIN 2 identifies a communication with a malicious signature, it automatically acquires and stores the entire message, including, for example, the content of e-mails. (It also deletes copied messages that do not contain a malicious signature.) The identified and stored messages are then reviewed by government officials charged with computer network defense. All of this takes place without a warrant from a court or any other review by any party outside the executive branch.[3]

The government is planning to supplement EINSTEIN 2, an intrusion detection system, with EINSTEIN 3, an intrusion prevention system. A summary of the Comprehensive National Cybersecurity Initiative states that EINSTEIN 3 "will have the ability to automatically detect and respond appropriately to cyberthreats before harm is done, providing an intrusion-prevention system supporting dynamic defense."[4] Former homeland security secretary Michael Chertoff has said that if EINSTEIN 2 is "the cop who is on the side of a road with a radar gun who can say if someone is drunk or speeding and they can phone ahead and warn that that person is coming," then EINSTEIN 3 is the cop who "make[s] the arrest" and "stop[s] the attack."[5]

EINSTEIN 3 will reportedly use "active sensors" to detect malicious attack agents and take real-time steps—most of which will be computer automated—to prevent the attack from reaching the government system. In

Chertoff's words, it "would literally, like an anti-aircraft weapon, shoot down an attack before it hits its target."⁶ Many people believe EINSTEIN 3 will involve operations by the government, or by private backbone providers and Internet service providers (ISPs) acting at the behest of the government, in private telecommunication channels (or on copies of such communications) before the malicious communication reaches or adversely affects government computers.⁷

The National Security Agency plays an important role in the EINSTEIN projects. It is America's signals-intelligence and government information–assurance agency. It is technically a component of the Department of Defense (DoD), and it is typically headed by a lieutenant general or vice admiral. While its collection capabilities are mostly directed outside the United States, the NSA also has domestic responsibilities. It was the operator of the Terrorist Surveillance Program that involved warrantless wiretapping of certain terrorist communications with one end in the United States. And it has been heavily involved in the development of the EINSTEIN systems. The Department of Homeland Security has stated that EINSTEIN 3 capabilities are "based on technologies developed by the NSA."⁸ According to the government, the "threat signatures determined by NSA in the course of its foreign intelligence and DoD information assurance missions" will be used in the EINSTEIN system.⁹ And based on threats identified by EINSTEIN 3, "alerts that do not contain the content of communications" will be sent to the NSA, which will use the information to check cyber attacks in unknown ways that the government assures us are consistent with NSA's "lawfully authorized missions."¹⁰

The NSA also has the lead in the recently established Cyber Command, which is headed by NSA director General Keith Alexander. Cyber Command is charged with coordinating U.S. offensive cyber activities and U.S. defensive efforts in protecting the U.S. military network. Consistent with the above analysis, Cyber Command is also tasked with the responsibility of providing "support to civil authorities" in their cybersecurity efforts.¹¹ In addition, Deputy Secretary of Defense William Lynn recently stated that Cyber Command "works closely with private industry to share information about [cybersecurity] threats and to address shared vulnerabilities."¹²

The NSA is involved with domestic cybersecurity in these and doubtlessly other ways because it possesses extraordinary technical expertise and experience, unmatched in the government, in exploring and exploiting computer and telecommunication systems. The agency also has close relationships with private telecommunications firms and other companies central to national cybersecurity.¹³ These relationships are important because cybersecurity requires the government to work closely with the telecommunication firms whose hardware and software constitute the Internet's backbone and Internet connection points. These firms already have enormous experience and expertise identifying and eliminating certain types of bad actors and agents on their systems, which the government leverages in stopping threats that concern it.

The Government in the Network:
What Might Happen in the Future

The EINSTEIN intrusion detection and intrusion prevention systems are needed to protect government networks because optimal defense of these malicious attack and exploitation agents requires (among many other things) real-time traffic analysis, real-time detection, and real-time response. Many private firms (including telecommunication firms and ISPs) have intrusion detection and intrusion prevention systems akin to the government's EINSTEIN system. But many do not, and on the whole between the government and private systems there are huge gaps in the national network, leaving it swarming with malware that can be used to do serious harm.

One solution to this broader problem is to extend the government's intrusion prevention system to operate in the private communications system inside the United States.[14] Deputy Secretary of Defense Lynn has been pushing this view of late. "We need to think imaginatively about how [the EINSTEIN 3] technology can also help secure a space on the Internet for critical government and commercial applications," he recently said. Private firms that refuse to opt in to such a system would "stay in the wild wild west of the unprotected internet" in ways that "could lead to physical damage and economic disruption on a massive scale."[15] Lynn later argued that "policymakers need to consider, among other things, applying the National Security Agency's defense capabilities beyond the '.gov' domain, such as to domains that undergird the commercial defense industry," and added that the Pentagon is "working with the Department of Homeland Security and the private sector to look for innovative ways to use the military's cyberdefense capabilities to protect the defense industry."[16]

At least four considerations argue for a comprehensive government-mandated, government-coordinated intrusion prevention system throughout the U.S. network.[17] First, the government, and especially the NSA, can provide novel information about threat vectors based on its espionage and related technical capacities. Second, the government might be best positioned to coordinate different malicious signature lists generated by itself, backbone providers, ISPs, and security firms and thus best able to create a comprehensive picture of the threat. Third, a mandatory system would fill in the significant gaps created by the many computers throughout the network that lack intrusion detection systems. Fourth, the government has the responsibility and appropriate incentives to invest in levels of network defense appropriate for national security; private firms that control our information infrastructure have many technological advantages, but they lack this responsibility or these incentives. As Stewart Baker recently noted, alluding to British Petroleum's failure to invest in precautions or responses appropriate to the national interest in environmental protection, "If you like the BP spill, you'll love cyberwar."[18]

A mandatory nationwide intrusion prevention system might place sensors at the point of entry for all communications coming into the United States, as well as at each Internet exchange point among Internet backbone providers and between the backbone and major cloud service providers and the large private firms associated with critical infrastructure. The government itself would be involved in identifying or coordinating both the signatures that triggered intrusion in such systems and the responses to such intrusions. But it would likely work closely with the telecommunication firms whose hardware and software constitute the Internet's backbone, for these firms already have enormous experience and expertise identifying and eliminating certain types of bad actors and agents on their systems that the government will try to use in stopping threats that concern it.

If intrusion prevention systems extend into the private network in this way, the NSA will inevitably play an important role. As noted above, the agency already has a large role in the identification of threat signatures for EINSTEIN 3 and in the use of threat information generated by EINSTEIN 3. It is thus noteworthy that the NSA is building a $1.5 billion, 1 million square-foot cybersecurity data center at Camp Williams near Salt Lake City, Utah.[19] The Camp Williams facility will provide "critical support to national cybersecurity priorities" and "intelligence and warnings related to cybersecurity threats, cybersecurity support to defense and civilian agency networks, and technical assistance to the Department of Homeland Security."[20] Tasks at Camp Williams might include NSA data collection, storage, and analysis and identification of threat signatures (as with the EINSTEIN programs). Tasks may also involve government expansion of such programs into private critical infrastructure protection.

The NSA is also likely to play a role in supporting new authorities that Congress might give the president in the event of a cyber emergency. The draft Cybersecurity Act of 2009 is one example of what such an authority might look like.[21] The bill originally granted the president power to "declare a cybersecurity emergency and order the limitation or shutdown of Internet traffic to and from any compromised federal government or U.S. critical infrastructure information system or network."[22] This proposal was controversial, and a later, more carefully worded draft granted the president, in the "event of an immediate threat to strategic national interests involving compromised Federal Government or United States critical infrastructure information systems or networks," the power to "declare a cybersecurity emergency" and, if necessary, "direct the national response to the cyber threat and the timely restoration of the affected critical infrastructure information system or network."[23]

It is unclear what this authority would entail or why it might be needed. It might mean that the president would be empowered to use existing national security resources, such as some of the NSA capabilities discussed above, to block traffic at certain locations that is destined for critical infrastructure networks or to order backbone providers to shut down or apply certain filters at Internet connection points that happen to be "United States critical infrastructure information systems or networks" or that constitute threats to those systems or networks. One can also imagine, going even further and consonant with the speculations above, that the NSA or the U.S. Computer Emergency Readiness Team would monitor all communications traffic in the United States (and elsewhere) and be authorized to examine any packet in the network that satisfies statutory criteria of a possible threat and to order a shutdown of traffic to or from a particular IP address or provider deemed to be suspicious—all without a warrant.

Almost all of the governmental activities described above would require the significant, government-approved or government-mandated cooperation and information sharing with Internet backbone providers, ISPs, certain other communications firms, and firms related to critical infrastructure. As President Obama's *Cyberspace Policy Review* notes, "Network hardware and software providers, network operators, data owners, security service providers, and, in some cases, law enforcement or intelligence organizations may each have information that can contribute to the detection and understanding of sophisticated intrusions or attacks. A full understanding and effective response may only be possible by bringing information from those various sources together for the benefit of all."[24]

There is already a great deal of ad hoc information sharing and coordination between the government and various industries involved in critical infrastructure concerning malicious agents, cyber intrusions, digital espionage, and the like. EINSTEIN 3, for example, is being tested with help from AT&T. Google recently requested assistance from the NSA—technically under the rubric of a "cooperative research and development agreement"—in tracking down what happened in the alleged Chinese hack of its computers.[25] The Comprehensive National Cybersecurity Initiative and similar government programs contemplate coordination of government and private sector information sharing about cyberthreats to critical infrastructure on a broader and more systematic basis.[26] There have been many reports of the NSA's sharing classified threat information with defense contractors.[27] Extrapolating from these programs, one might expect the government to delegate many of the tasks for cybersecurity—including affirmative duties to identify, report, and eradicate malicious agents or anomalous activity on the network—to the private sector, and one might similarly expect the government and the private sector to have robust information-sharing arrangements.

Legal Changes

The above scenario is a nightmare for many civil libertarians: the dreaded all-powerful, privacy-destroying, DoD-affiliated, generals-run NSA cut loose to use its giant computing and analytical powers in the homeland, in conjunction with private firms, to suck up and monitor the content of private Internet communications; store those communications, temporarily; trace the source of malicious agents in these communications all over the globe, including inside the United States; and take active steps to thwart malicious communications, even when they originate in or use computers in the United States.

There is no way to know whether this scenario will come to pass. But the cyberthreat is much more serious and menacing than is generally realized. Malicious payloads are becoming ever more prevalent and ever more sophisticated and are harder and harder to stop; our vulnerabilities are endless, and our most precious national resources are in jeopardy. It might take the "digital Pearl Harbor" that Richard Clarke predicted in 2000 for something like the steps outlined above to be taken seriously, but significant losses short of a Pearl Harbor event might lead some of them to be implemented. It thus might be useful to assess, as these earlier chapters do, some of the legal hurdles the law might pose to these changes. It turns out that most of the hurdles are statutory and thus can be changed by Congress. The biggest constitutional hurdle is the Fourth Amendment, and, at the end of the day, the Fourth Amendment does not present as much of a hurdle to the program sketched above as one might expect.

Nonconstitutional Issues

The main change necessitated by the scenario I have described would be legislation to significantly alter the complex patchwork of mostly outdated restrictions on the government's ability to collect and analyze the content and metadata of communications in the homeland or involving Americans. "This patchwork exists," noted President Obama's *Cyberspace Policy Review,* "because, throughout the evolution of the information and communications infrastructure, the Federal government enacted laws and policies to govern aspects of what were very diverse industries and technologies."[28]

Most of these laws—including the Foreign Intelligence Surveillance Act (FISA), the Wiretap Act, and the Stored Communications Act—were written at a time when the idea of cyber attacks on critical infrastructure was inconceivable. And most would need to be revised, along three broad dimensions. First, Congress would need to clearly authorize the president, with some modicum of particularity, to take the affirmative steps outlined. Second, it would need to authorize the government to mandate the cooperation of private firms, as described above, to monitor the network, collect and analyze content and metadata in the network, and take proactive steps to meet cyberthreats. Third, it would need to implement various mechanisms of accountability and review, some of which I outline below.

One quasi-constitutional objection to the scheme I have outlined is that the military, under the guise of the NSA, would be active in the homeland. This certainly raises significant political concerns. But no fundamental legal barrier stands in the way of such an arrangement. Beyond the Third Amendment's prohibition on quartering of soldiers in private homes in peacetime without compensation, the Constitution places no bar on military activity in the homeland. The main source of constraint on homeland military activity is the Posse Comitatus Act, which prohibits, "except in cases and under circumstances expressly authorized by the Constitution or Act of Congress," the willful use of "any part of the Army or the Air Force as a posse comitatus or otherwise to execute the laws."[29] The Posse Comitatus law reflects the strong subconstitutional norms against military involvement in homeland security, but for several reasons it does not prohibit the NSA from assuming an aggressive domestic cybersecurity role.[30] First, Posse Comitatus is probably not implicated by the imagined NSA activity because such activity does not contemplate the execution of the laws. Second, its prohibitions by its own terms can be altered by statute. Congress has enacted many exceptions to its ban and can do so again.

A second quasi-constitutional objection concerns the involvement of private firms in domestic cybersecurity. In the scheme envisioned here, many frontline cybersecurity tasks—both in identifying threats and responding to them—are performed by private Internet backbone operators and ISPs. Again, there are many serious policy concerns here. One is ensuring that private firms are subject to carrots and sticks that induce them to have the proper incentives to perform U.S. national cybersecurity tasks. A second and related concern is that many of the most consequential private firms in this area (such as Verizon and AT&T) have a global presence (including in places like China) and are doubtless under analogous pressures from other countries to help with cybersecurity tasks. Delicate steps must be taken to ensure that these foreign entanglements do not jeopardize private cybersecurity cooperation with the U.S. government or that such cooperation does not, through private firms, end up serving the national security goals of our adversaries. There is also the related and very tricky problem that global consumers might not want to use the services of information technology firms that actively partic-ipate in cybersecurity efforts with the U.S. government, for fear the U.S. gov-ernment would be more likely to monitor their communications. These are all formidable policy concerns that are beyond the scope of this chapter. None of them, however, presents a fundamental legal bar to private involvement in national security. Indeed, for better or worse, the vast majority of U.S. defense and intelligence budgets are spent on private contractors.

The Fourth Amendment

The Fourth Amendment presents the most significant constitutional hurdle to this cybersecurity regime. The Fourth Amendment's fundamental prohi-bition is on "unreasonable searches and seizures." It also requires that all war-rants issued in support of a search or seizure be reasonable. But the Fourth Amendment does not require a warrant in impractical circumstances as long as the search or seizure is reasonable under those circumstances. The courts may not see the Fourth Amendment today as permitting the unfathomably massive copying, storage, and analysis of private communications described above—though, having not confronted a sufficiently similar question yet, they have never written anything that would preclude such actions, either. But if the national and economic security threat of cyber attacks comes to be viewed as sufficiently severe and sufficiently difficult to stop, then govern-ment steps like those outlined here, properly authorized and limited in ways proportionate to the task, could easily be deemed reasonable under the cir-cumstances, which is all the Fourth Amendment ultimately requires.

The doctrinal building blocks for this conclusion are already in place. Begin with the metadata that would be collected and analyzed. Metadata include the "to" and "from" addressing information for e-mails, IP addresses of visited Web sites, routing information that tracks a communication's path on the Internet, and possible traffic volume information. It is pretty well settled that there is no reasonable expectation of privacy in such information and thus that the government collection and analysis of such information do not implicate the Fourth Amendment.[31] Only statutes stand in the way, and these statutes can be amended.

The collection (or copying) and analysis of bulk communication content is constitutionally more controversial, but the doctrinal tools for permitting it are already in place as well. One such doctrinal tool can be found in what Christopher Slobogin, in his contribution to this book, describes as a "series of cases holding that people assume the risk that information disclosed to third parties will be handed over to the government and thus cannot reasonably expect it to be private." Another doctrinal tool, and the one I focus on here, is the Fourth Amendment's "special needs" doctrine.

The special needs doctrine establishes an exception to the Fourth Amendment warrant requirement for reasonable governmental actions with a purpose that goes "beyond routine law enforcement and [for which] insisting upon a warrant would materially interfere with the accomplishment of that purpose."[32] The doctrine requires courts to consider and weigh a number of public and private interest factors, discussed below. It has been used to uphold warrantless, non-law-enforcement searches without individualized suspicion in numerous contexts, including highway checkpoint stops, random drug testing, searches of government employees with dangerous jobs, and inspections of regulated businesses. It has also been used, more directly on point, to uphold various suspicionless, terrorism-related searches. Consider two examples.

The first involves a suspicionless vehicle and carry-on baggage search on ferries on Lake Champlain. In an opinion by Judge Sotomayor, the Second Circuit ruled that defendants' undiminished expectations of privacy in bags and cars were outweighed by the government's interest in searching these items, based on an analysis of the character and degree of the government intrusion, the nature and immediacy of its needs, and the efficacy of its policy in addressing those needs. On the first point, the court ruled that the brief duration of the search, advance notice of the search, and the responsible manner in which the search was conducted made the degree of intrusion on the privacy right minimal. On the second point, it ruled that "preventing or deterring large-scale terrorist attacks presents problems that are distinct from standard law enforcement needs and indeed go well beyond them."[33] Relying on *Von Raab*, a landmark drug-testing case, and airport search cases, the court noted that that the government "need not adduce a specific threat in order to demonstrate a 'special need'" and that "in its attempt to counteract the threat of terrorism, [it] need not show that every airport or every ferry terminal is threatened by terrorism in order to implement a nationwide security policy that includes suspicionless searches."[34] Finally, the court concluded that the searches in question were reasonably effective because they were reasonably calculated to deter potential terrorists.

The second example comes from *In re Directives*, a case from the United States Foreign Intelligence Surveillance Court of Review. The court was considering the legality of a government foreign intelligence surveillance order to a private communications service provider pursuant to the temporary (and now expired) 2007 Amendments to FISA. The 2007 statute authorized the director of national intelligence and the attorney general to authorize the acquisition of foreign intelligence information concerning persons "reasonably believed to be outside the United States" as long as five safeguards were employed.[35] Analogizing to the special needs cases, the court concluded that there was a "foreign intelligence exception" to the warrant requirement. The court first reasoned that no warrant was needed because the "programmatic purpose" of the surveillance was gathering foreign intelligence, not law enforcement, and because "requiring a warrant would hinder the government's ability to collect time-sensitive information and, thus, would impede the vital national security interests that are at stake." It then concluded (based on the totality of the circumstances) that the surveillance was reasonable and thus did not violate the Fourth Amendment, because the governmental interest (national security) was of "the highest order" and a "matrix of safeguards"— including techniques designed to be directed against foreign powers as well as minimization (privacy-protecting) procedures—adequately protected legitimate private interests.[36]

The cybersecurity efforts envisioned here are significantly broader than the searches in either of these two cases. But the logic of these cases applies pretty straightforwardly to the cybersecurity situation. As top government officials, including the president, have all made clear, the nation's most vital resources are "severely threatened" by cyberattacks and cyber exploitations.[37] The purpose behind the cybersecurity collection and analysis scheme would not be law enforcement but rather the protection of the critical infrastructure that undergirds our military and economic security. For a nationwide intrusion detection system to have a chance at legality, the government, backed by express congressional findings, would need to establish that networkwide coverage is necessary because deadly computer attack agents are tiny needles hidden inside giant haystacks consisting of billions of innocent communications that each day travel at the speed of light and are often designed to learn from computer defense systems—automatically and at computer speed—and morph to exploit their vulnerabilities; and that only comprehensive, speed-of-light collection and analysis will enable the government to find and thwart this threat and keep the network and the infrastructure connected to it safe.

A Model for Constitutional Cybersecurity Surveillance

The strong need for a nationwide intrusion detection system, the non-law-enforcement purpose of the system, and the impracticability of a warrant would help the government skirt the warrant requirement for domestic cyber-security activities only if they are reasonable under the totality of the circumstances. It is impossible to say what is reasonable without a concrete sense of the severity of the cybersecurity threat and the precise measures the government will take to meet it. One can speculate very generally that if the public perceives the threat to be severe enough to induce Congress and the president to take some of the steps I have outlined, and if these steps are implemented with adequate safeguards that ensure that the broad searches are conducted in ways proportionate to the task, it would likely survive a constitutional challenge. A useful model for such safeguards, and for a broader scheme of legitimating checks and balances, can be found in the innovative reforms in the FISA Amendments Act of 2008, which replaced the 2007 amendments at issue in the 2007 Foreign Intelligence Surveillance Court appellate case.[38]

The 2008 reforms reaffirmed the 2007 power of the director of national intelligence and the attorney general to authorize, without a warrant, "the targeting of persons reasonably believed to be located outside the United States to acquire foreign intelligence information."[39] But it included four fundamental checks (some of which were present in the 2007 law) that inform the reasonableness of searches under this authority. First is a requirement for an independent ex ante scrutiny by the Foreign Intelligence Surveillance Court that results in a certification that the government's general targeting procedures are reasonably designed to stay within statutory guidelines.[40] Second, and perhaps most important, are various privacy and Fourth Amendment–protecting requirements, most notably "minimization procedures" that are themselves subject to ex ante review and approval by the Foreign Intelligence Surveillance Court. Third are a variety of ex post oversight mechanisms: The attorney general and the director of national intelligence must assess legal compliance and report to Congress every six months, and inspectors general across the intelligence community and the Department of Justice must perform annual reviews for legal compliance and effectiveness.[41] Fourth, the 2008 law contains a 2012 sunset provision that requires Congress to revisit and reapprove (if it so chooses) the entire scheme after four years of operation.

These four programmatic mechanisms would inform the proportionality and reasonableness of the scheme and could form the foundation of any aggressive government cybersecurity activity in the domestic network.

Independent Ex Ante Scrutiny

The NSA (or, more likely, the NSA working in conjunction with another agency, like the Department of Homeland Security) might be required to seek prior independent approval for the basic procedures it uses both in collecting or copying masses of communications and in identifying the malicious signatures and other computer or telecommunication anomalies that its intrusion detection and intrusion prevention systems and related systems pick out and redress. This independent approval might come from the FISA court or a FISA-type court created just for this purpose. Such an ex ante check would ensure that the general collection criteria are proportionate and reasonable. It would provide general congressional sanction and executive implementation subject to an ex ante global judicial approval of the reasonableness of the system in achieving the congressional aim.

Privacy-Protecting Mechanisms

Concrete mechanisms to protect privacy and to ensure that the government's search is minimally intrusive and reasonably efficacious will be central to any Fourth Amendment special needs analysis. It is hard to be specific about what this might entail without knowing the specifics of the program in question or the details of particular searches. But the following factors would be relevant under the special needs cases.

First, if the logic of the EINSTEIN 3 program is applied to the private network, then private Internet communications will be copied and searched by machines for malicious signatures, and then copied communications that contain no malicious signatures—the vast bulk of copied communications—will be destroyed. If this works as planned, then the vast bulk of the intrusions on privacy are temporary, and no human being will ever see communications without known signatures. Moreover, communications that are identified as containing malicious signatures might have reduced expectations of privacy under the line of cases holding that a search technique that reveals only illegal activity does not infringe on legitimate expectations of privacy.[42] These cases are suggestive and not directly on point because many and maybe most communications that contain malicious agents will do so inadvertently or negligently and thus will not (at least under the law as it stands now) be illegal.

Second, the government could place significant use restrictions on the communications identified as containing malicious signatures. The government would not be precluded from using criminal information found in a special needs, non-law-enforcement search as part of a criminal investigation or trial. But to demonstrate the narrowness and reasonableness of the search and to minimize the chilling effect on communications, the government might limit what it can do with the filtered communications that are presumptively threatening to national security. It might, for example, create a tiered response—from least invasive (such as stripping off the malicious code) to most intrusive (destroying the communication)—to communications containing malicious signatures. And it might limit the criminal uses to which presumptively threatening communications can be put—for example, by limiting the use of such communications in a specified list of computer-related or national security crimes.

Third, the intrusion prevention system would require a variety of minimization procedures to ensure that (among other things) communications identified as false positives are immediately destroyed and communications that match threat signatures are examined in ways that do not reveal any more private information than is necessary to meet the threat. In this context, the government might develop what John Poindexter, during his Total Information Awareness days, called "privacy appliances"—software devices that automatically filter out or encrypt all nonessential private information in communications examined by human beings.[43] The government could also employ David Brin's strategy of snooping on itself to ensure that it does not go further than necessary in snooping on its citizens.[44] It could, for example, record all relevant, individual government official computer activities and establish credible, immutable log and auditing trails that permit ex post auditing and investigation of what government officials were doing with their access to citizen communications.

Extensive Ex Post Auditing

Broad government network operation would also have to be checked by a number of ex post auditing and reporting requirements. Senior leaders would have a duty to certify effectiveness and abuse to Congress. And inspectors general would have a duty to audit the program for effectiveness and abuse and report the results to the executive branch and Congress. These ex post requirements would influence official behavior ex ante.

Sunset Provision

A sunset provision is a useful and has been a frequently used tool in the context of novel national security challenges. We still have relatively little information about the aims and capacities and threats posed by cyber enemies, and we have little information on how any government network activity will work in practice or what effect it will have on liberty and security. Congress should thus force itself to revisit the design and operation of the system in a few years, after more information becomes available.

Conclusion

Without a warrant or particularized suspicion, U.S. citizens are forced through invasive screening procedures at U.S. airports, sports events, and courthouses. Citizens' laptops, mail, and luggage are also checked at the border and at the entrances to critical infrastructure components and other sites attractive to terrorists. We allow such warrantless searches because the government's order and security interests are high and the searches reasonable and proportionate to the task. Analogous searches for analogous reasons on masses of domestic communications seem untoward because of the number of communications involved and because we do not think bits of data or strings of code can do much harm. But bits and strings can do, and are doing, enormous harm, and there might be little the government can do to check this harm short of having a comprehensive picture of what is happening in the network. In such a world, massive government snooping in the network can be lawful if proper and credible safeguards are put in place.

Notes

1. See Richard Clarke and Robert Knake, *Cyberwar: The Next Threat to National Security and What to Do about It* (New York: Ecco, 2010); Franklin Kramer and others, eds., *Cyberpower and National Security* (National Defense University Press/Potomac Books, 2009).

2. President Barack Obama, "Remarks by the President on Securing Our Nation's Cyber Infrastructure," May 29, 2009 (www.whitehouse.gov/the_press_office/Remarks-by-the-President-on-Securing-Our-Nations-Cyber-Infrastructure/).

3. This description of EINSTEIN 2.0 is drawn from memorandum opinion from Steven G. Bradbury, principal deputy assistant attorney general, to the counsel to the president, January 9, 2009, 2009 WL 3029765.

4. National Security Council, *The Comprehensive National Cybersecurity Initiative* (www.whitehouse.gov/cybersecurity/comprehensive-national-cybersecurity-initiative).

5. Quoted in Brynn Koeppen, "Former DHS Secretary Michael Chertoff Says NSA's Einstein 3 Is 'Where We Have to Go' in Cyber Security; Calls for International Cyber Security Cooperation," ExecutiveBiz, August 7, 2009 (http://blog.executivebiz.com/former-dhs-secretary-michael-chertoff-says-nsa's-einstein-3-is-'where-we-have-to-go'-in-cyber-security-calls-for-international-cyber-security-cooperation/3882).

6. "Homeland Security Seeks Cyber Counterattack System," CNN.com, October 4, 2008 (www.cnn.com/2008/TECH/10/04/chertoff.cyber.security).

7. For accounts of EINSTEIN 3, see generally "Behind 'Project 12,'" *Newsweek*, March 7, 2008 (www.newsweek.com/id/119902/page/1); Ellen Nakashima, "Cybersecurity Plan to Involve NSA, Telecoms: DHS Officials Debating the Privacy Implications," *Washington Post*, July 3, 2009 (www.washingtonpost.com/wp-dyn/content/article/2009/07/02/AR2009070202771.html?wprss=rss_nation); Koeppen, "Chertoff Says NSA's Einstein 3 Is 'Where We Have to Go' in Cyber Security"; Siobhan Gorman, "Troubles Plague Cyberspy Defense," *Wall Street Journal*, July 3, 2009, A1 (http://online.wsj.com/article/SB124657680388089139.html); Chris Strohm, "Official Says Einstein Security System Won't Read E-mails," Nextgov.com, October 15, 2009 (www.nextgov.com/nextgov/ng_20091015_6734.php?oref=rss?zone=itsecurity); *Cybersecurity: Preventing Terrorist Attacks and Protecting Privacy in Cyberspace, Hearing Before the Subcommittee on Terrorism and Homeland Security of the Senate Committee on the Judiciary*, 111th Cong. (2009) (statement of Philip Reitinger, deputy under secretary, National Protection and Program Directorate, U.S. Department of Homeland Security) (http://kyl.senate.gov/legis_center/subdocs/Reitinger.pdf).

8. Department of Homeland Security, *Privacy Impact Assessment for the Initiative Three Exercise* (www.dhs.gov/xlibrary/assets/privacy/privacy_pia_nppd_initiative 3.pdf).

9. National Security Council, *Comprehensive National Cybersecurity Initiative*.

10. Ibid.

11. Robert M. Gates, U.S. secretary of defense, memorandum to secretaries of the military departments and others, June 23, 2009 (http://aviationweek.typepad.com/files/cyber-command-gates-memo1.pdf).

12. William J. Lynn III, "Defending a New Domain: The Pentagon's Cyberstrategy," *Foreign Affairs*, September–October 2010 (www.foreignaffairs.com/articles/66552/william-j-lynn-iii/defending-a-new-domain).

13. See Shane Harris, *The Watchers: The Rise of America's Surveillance State* (New York: Penguin Press, 2010); James Bamford, *The Shadow Factory: The NSA from 9/11 to the Eavesdropping on America* (New York: Doubleday, 2009).

14. Richard Clarke proposes such a system, though he would have it strictly run by private industry. See Clarke and Knake, *Cyberwar*.

15. Noah Shachtman, "Cyber Command: We Don't Wanna Defend the Internet (We Just Might Have To)," Wired.com, May 28, 2010 (www.wired.com/dangerroom/2010/05/cyber-command-we-dont-wanna-defend-the-internet-but-we-just-might-have-to/#more-25377#ixzz0pPBH0nKB) (emphasis added).

16. Lynn, "Defending a New Domain."

17. There are also many downsides, of course, some of which (such as privacy concerns) are discussed below and others of which (such as the problems that adhere in a monoculture of security) I do not address here. For an example of the latter category of problems, see, for example, "McAfee Anti-Virus Program Goes Berserk, Reboots

PCs," USAToday.com, April 21, 2010 (www.usatoday.com/tech/news/2010-04-21-mcafee-antivirus_N.htm).

18. Stewart Baker, "If You Like the BP Spill, You'll Love Cyberwar," *The Volokh Conspiracy* (blog), May 29, 2009 (http://volokh.com/2010/05/29/if-you-like-the-bp-spill-youll-love-cyberwar).

19. J. Nicholas Hoover, "NSA to Build $1.5 Billion Cybersecurity Center," InformationWeek.com, October 29, 2009 (www.informationweek.com/news/government/security/showArticle.jhtml?articleID=221100260).

20. Ibid.

21. *Cybersecurity Act of 2009,* draft, S. 773, 111th Cong. (2009) (www.opencongress.org/bill/111-s773/text).

22. Id. at § 18(2).

23. Id. at § 201(2).

24. White House, *Cyberspace Policy Review* (www.whitehouse.gov/assets/documents/Cyberspace_Policy_Review_final.pdf).

25. John Markoff, "Google Asks Spy Agency for Help with Inquiry into Cyberattacks," *New York Times,* February 4, 2010, A6 (www.nytimes.com/2010/02/05/science/05google.html).

26. "Behind 'Project 12.'"

27. Shane Harris, "The Cyber Defense Perimeter," *National Journal,* May 2, 2009 (www.nationaljournal.com/njmagazine/id_20090502_5834.php).

28. White House, *Cyberspace Policy Review.*

29. *Posse Comitatus Act of 1878,* 18 U.S.C. § 1385.

30. For an outstanding overview, see William O. Scharf, "Cybersecurity, Cybercommand, and the Posse Comitatus Statute," 2010, unpublished manuscript (on file with author).

31. *Smith* v. *Maryland,* 442 U.S. 735, 743–44 (1979); *Quon* v. *Arch Wireless Operating Co., Inc.,* 529 F.3d 892, 904–05 (9th Cir. 2008); *United States* v. *Forrester,* 512 F.3d 500, 510 (9th Cir. 2008).

32. *In re Directives [redacted text] Pursuant to Section 1058 of the Foreign Intelligence Surveillance Act,* 551 F.3d 1004, 1009 (FISA Ct. Rev. 2008) (quoting *Vernonia School District 47J* v. *Acton,* 515 U.S. 646, 653 [1995]); *O'Connor* v. *Ortega,* 480 U.S. 710, 725 (1987) (plurality opinion); id. at 732 (Scalia, J., concurring); *National Treasury Employees Union* v. *Von Raab,* 489 U.S. 656, 665–66 (1989); *Griffin* v. *Wisconsin,* 483 U.S. 868, 872 (1987).

33. *Cassidy* v. *Chertoff,* 471 F.3d 67 (2d Cir. 2006).

34. *Cassidy,* 471 F.3d at 83; *Von Raab,* 489 U.S. 656.

35. *Foreign Intelligence Surveillance Act,* 50 U.S.C. § 1801, 1805b (2007).

36. *In re Directives,* 551 F.3d at 1013.

37. Obama, "Remarks."

38. *FISA Amendments Act of 2008,* Pub. L. No. 110-261, 122 Stat. 2436.

39. *Foreign Intelligence Surveillance Act,* 50 U.S.C. § 1881a(a).

40. Id. at (i)(3).

41. Id. at (l)(3).

42. See, for example, *United States* v. *Jacobsen,* 466 U.S. 109 (1984) (chemical field test that reveals only whether white powder is cocaine infringes on no legitimate expectation of privacy); *United States* v. *Place,* 462 U.S. 696, 706–07 (1983) (sniff by a police dog trained to detect narcotics was not a search under the Fourth Amendment).

43. See Harris, *The Watchers*; see also K. A. Taipale, "Technology, Security, and Privacy: The Fear of Frankenstein, the Mythology of Privacy, and the Lessons of King Ludd," 7 *Yale Journal of Law and Technology* (2004): 123, 179–97.

44. David Brin, *The Transparent Society* (Reading, Mass.: Addison-Wesley, 1998).

PART II

The Future of
Free Expression and Privacy

JEFFREY ROSEN

5

The Deciders:
Facebook, Google, and the Future
of Privacy and Free Speech

It was 2025 when Facebook decided to post live feeds from public and private surveillance cameras, so they could be searched online. The decision hardly came as a surprise. Ever since Facebook passed the 500 million–member mark in 2010, it found increasing consumer demand for applications that allowed users to access surveillance cameras with publicly accessible IP addresses. (Initially, live feeds to cameras on Mexican beaches were especially popular.) But in the mid-2020s, popular demand for live surveillance camera feeds was joined by arguments from the U.S. government that an open-circuit television network would be invaluable in tracking potential terrorists. As a result, Facebook decided to link the public and private camera networks, post them live online, and store the video feeds without restrictions on distributed servers in the digital cloud.

Once the new open-circuit system went live, anyone in the world could log onto the Internet, select a particular street view on Facebook's maps site, and zoom in on a particular individual. The user could then back-click on that individual to retrace her steps since she left the house in the morning or forward-click on her to see where she was headed. Using Facebook's integrated face recognition application, users could click on a stranger walking down any street in the world, plug his image into the Facebook database to identify him by name, and then follow his movements from door to door. Since cameras were virtually ubiquitous in public and commercial spaces, the result was the possibility of identification and surveillance of all citizens virtually anywhere in the world—and by anyone. In an enthusiastic launch, Mark Zuckerberg dubbed the new round-the-clock surveillance system Open Planet.

Open Planet is not a technological fantasy. Most of the architecture for implementing it already exists, and it would be a simple enough task for Facebook or Google, if either chose, to get the system up and running: face recognition is already plausible, and storage capacity is increasing exponentially; the only limitations are the coverage and scope of the existing cameras, which are broadening by the day. Indeed, at a Legal Futures Conference at Stanford Law School in 2007, Andrew McLaughlin, then the head of public policy at Google, said he expected Google to get requests to put linked surveillance networks live and online within the decade. How, he asked the audience of scholars and technologists, should Google respond?

One way of deciding how to respond would be to ask whether Open Planet, if it went live, would violate the Constitution. Under Supreme Court doctrine as it now exists, it might not—at least not if it were a purely private affair, run by private companies alone and without government involvement. Both the First Amendment, which protects free speech, and the Fourth Amendment, which prohibits unreasonable searches and seizures, restrict only government actions. On the other hand, if the government directed the construction of Open Planet, or used the system to track citizens on government-owned, as well as private sector, cameras, perhaps Facebook might be viewed as the equivalent of a state actor and therefore restricted by the Constitution.

At the time of the framing of the Constitution, a far less intrusive invasion of privacy—namely, the warrantless search of private homes and desk drawers for seditious papers—was considered the paradigmatic case of an unreasonable and unconstitutional invasion of privacy. The fact that round-the-clock surveillance might not violate the Constitution today suggests the challenge of translating the framers' values into a world in which Google and Facebook now have far more power over the privacy and free speech of most citizens than any king, president, or Supreme Court justice could hope for. In this chapter I examine four different areas where new technologies will challenge our existing ideas about constitutional protections for free speech and privacy: ubiquitous surveillance with global positioning systems (GPS) devices and online surveillance cameras; airport body scanners; embarrassing Facebook photos and the problem of digital forgetting; and controversial YouTube videos. In each area, I suggest, preserving constitutional values requires a different balance of legal and technological solutions, combined with political mobilization that leads to changes in social norms.

Let's begin with Open Planet. I can imagine sufficient government involvement to make the courts plausibly consider the Facebook program the equivalent of state action. I can also imagine that the Supreme Court in 2025 would be unsettled by Open Planet and inclined to strike it down. But a series of other doctrines might bar judicial intervention. The Court has come close to saying that citizens have no legitimate expectations of privacy in public places, at least when the surveillance technologies in question are in general public use by ordinary members of the public.[1] As mobile camera technology becomes ubiquitous, the Court might hold that the government is entitled to have access to the same linked camera system that ordinary members of the public have become accustomed to browsing. Moreover, the Court has said that we have no expectation of privacy in data that we voluntarily surrender to third parties.[2] In cases in which digital images are captured on cameras owned by third parties and stored in the digital cloud—that is, on distributed third-party servers—we have less privacy than citizens took for granted at the time of the American founding. And although the founders expected a degree of anonymity in public, that expectation would be defeated by the possibility of round-the-clock surveillance on Facebook.

The doctrinal seeds of a judicial response to Open Planet, however, do exist. A Supreme Court inclined to strike down ubiquitous surveillance might draw on recent cases involving decisions by the police to place a GPS tracking device on the car of a suspect without a warrant. The Supreme Court has not yet decided whether prolonged surveillance, in the form of "dragnet-type law enforcement practices," violates the Constitution.[3] Two federal circuits have held that the use of a GPS tracking device to monitor someone's movements in a car over a prolonged period is not a search because we have no expectations of privacy in our public movements.[4] But in a visionary opinion in 2010, Judge Douglas Ginsburg of the U.S. Court of Appeals disagreed. Prolonged surveillance is a search, he recognized, because no reasonable person expects that his movements will be continuously monitored from door to door; all of us have a reasonable expectation of privacy in the "whole" of our movements in public.[5] Ginsburg and his colleagues struck down the warrantless GPS surveillance of a suspect that lasted twenty-four hours a day for nearly a month on the grounds that prolonged, ubiquitous tracking of citizens' movements in public is constitutionally unreasonable. "Unlike one's movements during a single journey, the whole of one's movements over the course of a month is not actually exposed to the public because the likelihood anyone will observe all those movements is effectively nil," Ginsburg wrote. Moreover, "That whole reveals more—sometimes a great deal more—than does the sum of its parts."[6] Like the "mosaic theory," a method invoked by the government in national security cases that tries to learn about suspects by connecting the dots between fragmented pieces of personal data, "prolonged surveillance reveals types of information not revealed by short-term surveillance, such as what a person does repeatedly, what he does not do, and what he does ensemble. These types of information can each reveal more about a person than does any individual trip viewed in isolation."[7] Ginsburg understood that round-the-clock surveillance differs from more limited tracking not just in degree but in kind—it looks more like virtual stalking than a legitimate investigation—and therefore is an unreasonable search of the person.

Because prolonged surveillance on Open Planet potentially reveals far more about each of us than round-the-clock GPS tracking does, providing real-time images of all our actions rather than simply tracking the movements of our cars, it could also be struck down as an unreasonable search of our persons. And if the Supreme Court struck down Open Planet on Fourth Amendment grounds, it might be influenced by the state regulations of GPS surveillance that Ginsburg found persuasive or by congressional attempts to regulate Facebook or other forms of round-the-clock surveillance, such as the Geolocational Privacy and Surveillance Act proposed by Senator Ron Wyden (D-OR) and Representative Jason Chaffetz (R-UT) that would require officers to get a warrant before electronically tracking cell phones or cars and would prohibit commercial service providers from sharing customers' geolocational information without their consent.[8]

The Supreme Court in 2025 might also conceivably choose to strike down Open Planet on more expansive grounds, relying not just on the Fourth Amendment but also on the right to autonomy recognized in cases like *Roe* v. *Wade, Planned Parenthood of Southeastern Pennsylvania* v. *Casey,* and *Lawrence* v. *Texas.* The right-to-privacy cases, beginning with *Griswold* v. *Connecticut,* are often viewed as cases about sexual privacy, but in *Planned Parenthood* and *Lawrence,* Justice Anthony Kennedy recognized a far more sweeping principle of personal autonomy that might well protect individuals from totalizing forms of ubiquitous surveillance. Imagine an opinion written in 2025 by an eighty-nine-year-old Justice Kennedy: "In our tradition the State is not omnipresent in the home. And there are other spheres of our lives and existence, outside the home, where the State should not be a dominant presence," Kennedy wrote in *Lawrence.* "Freedom extends beyond spatial bounds. Liberty presumes an autonomy of self that includes freedom of thought, belief, expression, and certain intimate conduct."[9]

Kennedy's vision of an "autonomy of self" that depends on preventing the state from becoming a "dominant presence" in public as well as private places might well be invoked to prevent the state from participating in a ubiquitous surveillance system that prevents citizens from defining themselves and expressing their individual identities. Just as citizens in the Soviet Union were inhibited by ubiquitous KGB surveillance from expressing and defining themselves, Kennedy might hold, the possibility of ubiquitous surveillance on Open Planet also violates the right to autonomy, even if the cameras in question are owned by the private sector, as well as the state, and a private corporation provides the platform for their monitoring. Nevertheless, the fact that the system is administered by Facebook, rather than the government, might be an obstacle to a constitutional ruling along these lines. And if Kennedy (or his successor) struck down Open Planet with a sweeping vision of personal autonomy that did not coincide with the actual values of a majority of citizens in 2025, the decision could be the *Roe v. Wade* of virtual surveillance, provoking backlashes from those who do not want the Supreme Court imposing its values on a divided nation.

Would the Supreme Court, in fact, strike down Open Planet in 2025? If the past is any guide, the answer may depend on whether citizens, in 2025, view round-the-clock surveillance as invasive and unreasonable or, instead, have become so used to it, on and off the web, in virtual space and real space, that they demand Open Planet rather than protesting against it. In the age of Google and Facebook, technologies that thoughtfully balance privacy with free expression and other values have tended to be adopted only when companies see their markets as demanding some kind of privacy protection or when engaged constituencies have mobilized in protest against poorly designed architectures and demanded better ones, helping to create a social consensus that the invasive designs are unreasonable.

The paradigmatic case of the kind of political mobilization on behalf of constitutional values that I have in mind is presented by my second case, involving body scanners at airports. In 2002 officials at Orlando International Airport first began testing the millimeter wave body scanners that are currently at the center of a national uproar. The designers of the scanners at Pacific Northwest Laboratories offered U.S. officials a choice: "naked" machines or "blob" machines. The same researchers had developed both technologies, and both were equally effective at identifying contraband. But, as their nicknames suggest, the former displays graphic images of the human body, while the latter scrambles the images into a humiliation-avoiding blob.[10]

Since both versions of the scanners promise the same degree of security, any sane attempt to balance privacy and safety would seem to favor the blob machines over the naked machines. And that is what European governments chose. Most European airport authorities have declined to adopt body scanners at all, because of persuasive evidence that they are not effective at detecting low-density contraband such as the chemical powder PETN that the trouser bomber concealed in his underwear on Christmas Day 2009. But the handful of European airports that have adopted body scanners, such as Schiphol airport in Amsterdam, have opted for a version of the blob machine. This is in part owing to the efforts of European privacy commissioners, such as Germany's Peter Schaar, who have emphasized the importance of designing body scanners in ways that protect privacy.

The U.S. Department of Homeland Security made a very different choice. It deployed the naked body scanners without any opportunity for public comment—then appeared surprised by the backlash. Remarkably, however, the backlash was effective. After a nationwide protest inspired by the Patrick Henry of the anti–naked machines movement, a traveler who memorably exclaimed "Don't touch my junk," President Obama called on the Transportation Security Administration (TSA) to go back to the drawing board. A few months after authorizing the intrusive pat downs, in February 2011, the TSA announced that it would begin testing, on a pilot basis, versions of the very same blob machines that the agency had rejected nearly a decade earlier. For the latest version, tested in Las Vegas and Washington, D.C, the TSA installed software filters on its body scanner machines that detect potential threat items and indicate their location on a generic, bloblike outline of each passenger that appears on a monitor attached to the machine. According to news reports, the TSA began testing the filtering software in the fall of 2010—precisely when the protests against the naked machines went viral—and declared in July 2010 that it would be adopted throughout the country. Thus, after nearly a decade, in the wake of political pressure, the blob machine prevailed over the naked machine. Better late than never.

Of course, it is possible that courts might have struck down the naked machines as unreasonable and unconstitutional, even without the political protests. In a 1983 opinion upholding searches by drug-sniffing dogs, Justice Sandra Day O'Connor recognized that a search is most likely to be considered constitutionally reasonable if it is very effective at discovering contraband without revealing innocent but embarrassing information.[11] The backscatter machines seem, under O'Connor's view, to be the antithesis of a reasonable search: They reveal a great deal of innocent but embarrassing information and are remarkably ineffective at revealing low-density contraband.

It is true that the government gets great deference in airports and at the borders, where routine border searches do not require heightened suspicion. But the Court has held that nonroutine border searches, such as body cavity or strip searches, do require a degree of individual suspicion. And although the Supreme Court has not evaluated airport screening technology, lower courts have emphasized, as the U.S. Court of Appeals for the Ninth Circuit ruled in 2007, that "a particular airport security screening search is constitutionally reasonable provided that it 'is no more extensive nor intensive than necessary, in the light of current technology, to detect the presence of weapons or explosives.'"[12]

It is arguable that since the naked machines are neither effective nor minimally intrusive—that is, because they might be redesigned with blob machine–like filters that promise just as much security while also protecting privacy—courts might strike them down. As a practical matter, however, both lower courts and the Supreme Court seem far more likely to strike down strip searches that have inspired widespread public opposition—such as the strip search of a high school girl wrongly accused of carrying drugs, which the Supreme Court invalidated by a vote of 8-1—than they are of searches that, despite the protests of a mobilized minority, the majority of the public appears to accept.[13]

The tentative victory of the blob machines over the naked machines provides a model for successful attempts to balance privacy and security: government can be pressured into striking a reasonable balance between privacy and security by a mobilized minority of the public when the privacy costs of a particular technology are dramatic, visible, and widely distributed and when people experience the invasions personally as a kind of loss of control over the conditions of their own exposure.

But can we be mobilized to demand a similarly reasonable balance when the threats to privacy come not from the government but from private corporations and when those responsible for exposing too much personal information about us are none other than ourselves? When it comes to invasions of privacy by fellow citizens, rather than by the government, we are in the realm not of autonomy but of dignity and decency. (Autonomy preserves a sphere of immunity from government intrusion in our lives; dignity protects the norms of social respect that we accord to one another.) And since dignity is a socially constructed value, it is unlikely to be preserved by judges—or by private corporations—in the face of the expressed preferences of citizens who are less concerned about dignity than exposure.

This is the subject of my third case, which involves a challenge that, in big and small ways, is confronting millions of people around the globe: how best to live our lives in a world where the Internet records everything and forgets nothing—where every online photo, status update, Twitter post, and blog entry by and about us can be stored forever.[14] Consider the case of Stacy Snyder. Four years ago, Snyder, a twenty-five-year-old teacher in training at Conestoga Valley High School in Lancaster, Pennsylvania, posted a photo on her MySpace page that showed her at a party wearing a pirate hat and drinking from a plastic cup, with the caption "Drunken Pirate." After discovering the page, her supervisor at the high school told her the photo was "unprofessional," and the dean of Millersville University School of Education, where Snyder was enrolled, said she was promoting drinking in virtual view of her under-age students. As a result, days before Snyder's scheduled graduation, the university denied her a teaching degree. Snyder sued, arguing that the university had violated her First Amendment rights by penalizing her for her (perfectly legal) after-hours behavior. But in 2008 a federal district judge rejected the claim, saying that because Snyder was a public employee whose photo did not relate to matters of public concern, her "Drunken Pirate" post was not protected speech.[15]

When historians of the future look back on the perils of the early digital age, Stacy Snyder may well be an icon. With websites like LOL Facebook Moments, which collects and shares embarrassing personal revelations from Facebook users, ill-advised photos and online chatter are coming back to haunt people months or years after the fact.

Technological advances, of course, have often presented new threats to privacy. In 1890, in perhaps the most famous article on privacy ever written, Samuel Warren and Louis Brandeis complained that because of new technology—like the Kodak camera and the tabloid press—"gossip is no longer the resource of the idle and of the vicious but has become a trade."[16] But the mild society gossip of the Gilded Age pales before the volume of revelations contained in the photos, videos, and chatter on social media sites and elsewhere across the Internet. Facebook, which surpassed MySpace in 2008 as the largest social networking site, now has more than 500 million members, or 22 percent of all Internet users, who spend more than 500 billion minutes a month on the site. Facebook users share more than 25 billion pieces of content each month (including news stories, blog posts, and photos), and the average user creates seventy pieces of content a month.

Today, as in Brandeis's day, the value threatened by gossip on the Internet—whether posted by us or by others—is dignity. (Brandeis called it an offense against honor.) But American law has never been good at regulating offenses against dignity—especially when regulations would clash with other values, such as protections for free speech. And indeed, the most ambitious proposals in Europe to create new legal rights to escape one's past on the Internet are hard to reconcile with the American free speech tradition.

The cautionary tale here is Argentina, which has dramatically expanded the liability of search engines like Google and Yahoo for offensive photographs that harm a person's reputation. Recently, an Argentinean judge held Google and Yahoo liable for causing "moral harm" and violating the privacy of Virginia Da Cunha, a pop star, by indexing pictures of her that were linked to erotic content. The ruling against Google and Yahoo was overturned on appeal in August, but there are at least 130 similar cases pending in Argentina to force search engines to remove or block offensive content. In the United States, search engines are protected by the Communications Decency Act, which immunizes Internet service providers from hosting content posted by third parties. But as liability against search engines expands abroad, it will seriously curtail free speech: Yahoo says that the only way to comply with injunctions is to block all sites that refer to a particular plaintiff.[17]

In Europe, recent proposals to create a legally enforceable right to escape one's past have come from the French. The French data commissioner, Alex Turc, has proposed a right to oblivion—namely, a right to escape one's past on the Internet. The details are fuzzy, but it appears that the proposal would rely on an international body—say, a commission of forgetfulness—to evaluate particular take-down requests and order Google and Facebook to remove content that, in the view of commissioners, violated an individual's dignitary rights.

From an American perspective, the very intrusiveness of this proposal is enough to make it implausible: how could we rely on bureaucrats to protect our dignity in cases where we have failed to protect it on our own? Europeans, who have less of a free speech tradition and have been far more inclined to allow people to remove photographs taken and posted against their will, will be more sympathetic to the proposal. But from the perspective of most American courts and companies, giving people the right selectively to delete their pasts would pose unacceptably great threats to free speech and public discourse, since other people would be prohibited from sharing or discussing these deleted items that had once been in the public domain.

A more promising solution to the problem of forgetting on the Internet is technological. And there are already small-scale privacy applications that offer to disappear data. An app called TigerText allows text-message senders to set a time limit from one minute to thirty days, after which the text disappears from the company's servers on which it is stored, and therefore from the senders' and recipients' phones. (The founder of TigerText, Jeffrey Evans, has said he chose the name before the scandal involving Tiger Woods's alleged texts to a mistress.)[18]

Expiration dates could be implemented more broadly in various ways. Researchers at the University of Washington, for example, are developing a technology called Vanish that makes electronic data "self-destruct" after a specified period of time. Instead of relying on Google, Facebook, or Hotmail to delete the data that are stored "in the cloud"—in other words, on their distributed servers—Vanish encrypts the data and then "shatters" the encryption key. To read the data, your computer has to put the pieces of the key back together, but they "erode" or "rust" as time passes, and after a certain point the document can no longer be read. The technology does not promise perfect control—you cannot stop someone from copying your photos or Facebook chats during the period in which they are not encrypted. But as Vanish improves, it could bring us much closer to a world where our data do not linger forever.

Facebook, if it wanted to, could implement expiration dates on its own platform, making data disappear after, say, three days or three months unless a user specified otherwise. It might be a more welcome option for Facebook to encourage the development of Vanish-style apps that would allow individual users who are concerned about privacy to make their own data disappear without imposing the default on all Facebook users.

So far, however, Mark Zuckerberg, the Facebook chief executive officer, has been moving in the opposite direction—toward transparency, rather than privacy. In defending Facebook's recent decision to make the default for profile information about friends and relationship status public, Zuckerberg told the founder of the blog *TechCrunch* that Facebook had an obligation to reflect "current social norms" that favored exposure over privacy. "People have really gotten comfortable not only sharing more information and different kinds but more openly and with more people, and that social norm is just something that has evolved over time," he said.[19]

Will a market emerge for technologies of virtual deletion? It is true that a German company, X-Pire, recently announced the launch of a Facebook app that will allow users automatically to erase designated photos. Using electronic keys that expire after short periods of time, and obtained by solving a Captcha, or graphic that requires users to type in a fixed number combination, the application ensures that once the time stamp on the photo has expired, the key disappears.[20] X-Pire is a model for a sensible, blob machine–like solution to the problem of digital forgetting. But unless Facebook builds similar apps into its platform—an unlikely outcome, given its commercial interests—a majority of Facebook users are unlikely to seek out disappearing-data options until it is too late. X-Pire, therefore, may remain for the foreseeable future a technological solution to a grave privacy problem—but a solution that does not have an obvious market.

The courts, in my view, are better equipped to regulate offenses against autonomy, such as round-the-clock surveillance on Facebook, than offenses against dignity, such as drunken Facebook pictures that never go away. But that regulation in both cases will likely turn on evolving social norms whose contours in twenty years are hard to predict.

Finally, let us consider one last example of the challenge of preserving constitutional values in the age of Facebook and Google, an example that concerns not privacy but free speech.[21] Until recently, the person who arguably had more power than any other to determine who may speak and who may be heard around the globe is not a king, a president, or a Supreme Court justice. She was Nicole Wong, the deputy general counsel of Google. Her colleagues called her "The Decider." Until her resignation, it was Wong who decided what controversial user-generated content went down or stayed up on YouTube and other applications owned by Google, including Blogger, the blog site; Picasa, the photo-sharing site; and Orkut, the social networking site. Wong and her colleagues also oversee Google's search engine: they decide what controversial material does and does not appear on the local search engines that Google maintains in many countries in the world, as well as on Google.com. As a result, Wong arguably had more influence over the contours of online expression than anyone else on the planet.

Wong seemed to exercise that responsibility with sensitivity to the values of free speech. Google and Yahoo can be held liable outside the United States for indexing or directing users to content after having been notified that it was illegal in a foreign country. In the United States, by contrast, Internet service providers are protected from most lawsuits involving having hosted or linked to illegal user-generated content. As a consequence of these differing standards, Google has considerably less flexibility overseas than it does in the United States about content on its sites, and its "information must be free" ethos is being tested abroad.

For example, on the German and French default Google search engines, Google.de and Google.fr, you cannot find Holocaust denial sites that can be found on Google.com, because Holocaust denial is illegal in Germany and France. Broadly, Google has decided to comply with governmental requests to take down links on its national search engines to material that clearly violates national laws. But not every overseas case presents a clear violation of national law. In 2006, for example, protesters at a Google office in India demanded the removal of content on Orkut, the social networking site, that criticized Shiv Sena, a hard-line Hindu political party popular in Mumbai. Wong eventually decided to take down an Orkut group dedicated to attacking Shivaji, revered as a deity by the Shiv Sena Party, because it violated Orkut terms of service by criticizing a religion, but not to take down another group because it merely criticized a political party.

Over the past couple of years, Google and its various applications have been blocked, to different degrees, by twenty-four countries. Blogger is blocked in Pakistan, for example, and Orkut in Saudi Arabia. Meanwhile, governments are increasingly pressuring telecommunications companies like Comcast and Verizon to block controversial speech at the network level. Europe and the United States recently agreed to require Internet service providers to identify and block child pornography, and in Europe there are growing demands for network-wide blocking of terrorist incitement videos.

As a result, Wong worried that Google's ability to make case-by-case decisions about what links and videos are accessible through Google's sites may be slowly circumvented, as countries are requiring the companies that provide Internet access to build top-down censorship into the network pipes.

It is not only foreign countries that are eager to restrict speech on Google and YouTube. In May 2006, Senator Joseph Lieberman, who has become the A. Mitchell Palmer of the digital age, had his staff contact Google and demand that the company remove from YouTube dozens of what he described as jihadist videos. After viewing the videos one by one, Wong and her colleagues removed some of the videos but refused to remove those that they decided did not violate YouTube guidelines. Lieberman was not satisfied. In an angry follow-up letter to Eric Schmidt, the chief executive officer of Google, Lieberman demanded that all content he characterized as being "produced by Islamist terrorist organizations" be immediately removed from YouTube as a matter of corporate judgment—even videos that did not feature hate speech or violent content or violate U.S. law. Wong and her colleagues responded by saying, "YouTube encourages free speech and defends everyone's right to express unpopular points of view." Recently, Google and YouTube announced new guidelines prohibiting videos "intended to incite violence."

That category scrupulously tracks the Supreme Court's rigorous First Amendment doctrine, which says that speech can be banned only when it poses an imminent threat of producing serious lawless action. Unfortunately, Wong and her colleagues recently retreated from that bright line under further pressure from Lieberman. In November 2010, YouTube added a new category that viewers can click to flag videos for removal: "promotes terrorism." Twenty-four hours of video are uploaded on YouTube every minute; viewers can request removal for a series of categories, including "violent or repulsive content" or inappropriate sexual content. Although hailed by Senator Lieberman, the new "promotes terrorism" category is potentially troubling because it goes beyond the narrow test of incitement to violence that YouTube had previously used to flag terrorism-related videos for removal. YouTube's capitulation to Lieberman shows that a user-generated system for enforcing community standards will never protect speech as scrupulously as unelected judges enforcing strict rules about when speech can be viewed as a form of dangerous conduct.

Google remains a better guardian of free speech than Internet companies like Facebook and Twitter, which have refused to join the Global Network Initiative, an industry-wide coalition committed to upholding free speech and privacy. But the recent capitulation of YouTube shows that Google's "trust us" model may not be a stable way of protecting free speech in the twenty-first century, even though the alternatives to trusting Google—such as authorizing national regulatory bodies around the globe to request the removal of controversial videos—might protect less speech than Google's "Decider" model currently does.

I would like to conclude by stressing the complexity of protecting constitutional values like privacy and free speech in the age of Google and Facebook, which are not formally constrained by the Constitution. In each of my examples—round-the-clock Facebook surveillance, blob machines, escaping our past on the Internet, and promoting free speech on YouTube and Google—it is possible to imagine a rule or technology that would protect free speech and privacy while also preserving security—a blob machine–like solution. But in practice, those solutions are more likely to be adopted in some areas than in others. Engaged minorities may demand blob machines when they personally experience their own privacy being violated; but they may be less likely to rise up against the slow expansion of surveillance cameras, which transform expectations of privacy in public. Judges in the American system may be more likely to resist ubiquitous surveillance in the name of *Roe* v. *Wade*–style autonomy than to create a legal right to allow people to edit their Internet pasts, which relies on ideas of dignity that in turn require a social consensus that in America, at least, does not exist. As for free speech, it is being anxiously guarded for the moment by Google, but the tremendous pressures from consumers and government are already making it hard to hold the line on removing only speech that threatens imminent lawless action.

In translating constitutional values in light of new technologies, it is always useful to ask: What would Brandeis do? Brandeis would never have tolerated unpragmatic abstractions, which have the effect of giving citizens less privacy in the age of cloud computing than they had during the founding era. In translating the Constitution into the challenges of our time, Brandeis would have considered it a duty actively to engage in the project of constitutional translation in order to preserve the framers' values in a startlingly different technological world. But the task of translating constitutional values cannot be left to judges alone: it also falls to regulators, legislators, technologists, and, ultimately, to politically engaged citizens. As Brandeis put it, "If we would guide by the light of reason, we must let our minds be bold."[22]

Notes

1. See *Florida* v. *Riley*, 488 U.S. 445 (1989) (O'Connor, J., concurring).
2. See *United States* v. *Miller*, 425 U.S. 435 (1976).
3. See *United States* v. *Knotts*, 460 U.S. 276, 283–84 (1983).

4. See *United States* v. *Pineda-Morena*, 591 F.3d 1212 (9th Cir. 2010); *United States* v. *Garcia*, 474 F.3d 994 (7th Cir. 2007); *United States* v. *Marquez*, 605 F.3d 604 (8th Cir. 2010).

5. See *United States* v. *Maynard*, 615 F.3d 544 (D.C. Cir. 2010).

6. Id. at 558.

7. Id. at 562.

8. See Declan McCullagh, "Senator Pushes for Mobile Privacy Reform," CNet News, March 22, 2011 (http://news.cnet.com/8301-31921_3-20045723-281.html).

9. *Lawrence* v. *Texas*, 539 U.S. 558, 562 (2003).

10. The discussion of the blob machines is adapted from "Nude Breach," *New Republic*, December 13, 2010, 2–10.

11. *United States* v. *Place*, 462 U.S. 696 (1983).

12. *United States* v. *Davis*, 482 F.2d 893, 913 (9th Cir. 1973).

13. *Safford Unified School District* v. *Redding*, 557 U.S. ___ (2009).

14. The discussion of digital forgetting is adapted from "The End of Forgetting," *New York Times Magazine*, July 25, 2010.

15. *Snyder* v. *Millersville University*, No. 07-1660 (E.D. Pa. Dec. 3, 2008).

16. Samuel D. Warren and Louis D. Brandeis, "The Right to Privacy," 4 *Harvard Law Review* (1890): 193.

17. Vinod Sreeharsha, "Google and Yahoo Win Appeal in Argentine Case," *New York Times*, August 20, 2010, B4.

18. See Belinda Luscombe, "Tiger Text: An iPhone App for Cheating Spouses?" Time.com, February 26, 2010 (www.time.com/time/business/article/0,8599,1968 233,00.html).

19. Marshall Kirkpatrick, "Facebook's Zuckerberg Says the Age of Privacy Is Over," ReadWriteWeb.com, January 9, 2010 (www.readwriteweb.com/archives/facebooks_ zuckerberg_says_the_age_of_privacy_is_ov.php).

20. Aemon Malone, "X-Pire Aims to Cut Down on Photo D-Tagging on Facebook," Digital Trends, January 17, 2011 (www.digitaltrends.com/social-media/x-pire-adds-expiration-date-to-digital-photos/).

21. The discussion of free speech that follows is adapted from Jeffrey Rosen, "Google's Gatekeepers," *New York Times Magazine*, November 30, 2008.

22. *New State Ice Co.* v. *Liebmann*, 285 U.S. 262, 311 (1932) (Brandeis, J., dissenting).

TIM WU

6

Is Filtering Censorship?
The Second Free Speech Tradition

When Google merged with telecommunications giant AT&T there was, of course, some opposition. Some said, rather heatedly, that an information monopolist of a kind never seen before was in the works. But given the state of the industry after the crash, and the shocking bankruptcy of Apple, there were few who would deny that some kind of merger was necessary. Necessary, that is, not just to save jobs but to save the communications infrastructure that millions of Americans had come to depend on. After it went through, contrary to some of the dire warnings, everything was much the same. Google was still Google, the telephone company was still AT&T, and after a while, much of the hubbub died down.

It was a few years later that the rumors began, mostly leaks from former employees, suggesting that the post-merger GT&T was up to something. Some said the firm was fixing its search results and taking other steps to ensure that Google itself would never be displaced from its throne. Of course, while it made for some good headlines, no one paid much attention. The fact is that there are always conspiracy theorists and disgruntled employees out there, no matter what the company. When GT&T went ahead and acquired the New York Times *as part of its public campaign to save the media, most people cheered. Yes, there was some of the typical outcry from the usual sources, but then again, Comcast had been running NBC for years without incident.*

Looking back, I suppose it was really only after the presidential election that things came to a head. In a way, it might have been obvious that Governor Tilden, who had pledged to aggressively enforce the antitrust laws, was not going to be GT&T's favorite candidate. That was fine, and of course corporations have the right, just like anybody else, to support a politician they like or oppose one they do not like. But what came out only much later was the full extent of the company's campaign against Tilden. It turned out that every part of the information empire—from the news site to the media properties to the search engines, the mobile video, and the access to e-mails—all of it was mobilized to ensure Tilden's defeat. In retrospect, it was foolish for Tilden's campaign to rely on GT&T phones, Gmail, and Google apps so heavily. Then again, doesn't everyone?

We all know the effect that the press can have on elections. We have come to expect that newspapers will take one side or another. But no one quite understood or realized the importance of controlling the very information channels themselves—from mobile phones all the way through search and video.

Well, Hayes is now president, and nothing is going to change that. But the whole incident has begun to make people wonder. Should we be worried about the influence of the information channel over politics? Are Google or AT&T possibly subject to the First Amendment? Are they common carriers, and if so, what does that mean for speech?

Mention "speech" in America, and most people with legal training or an interest in the Constitution think immediately of the First Amendment and its champion, the U.S. Supreme Court. The great story of free speech in America is the pamphleteer peddling an unpopular cause, defended by courts against arrest and the burning of his materials. That is the central narrative taught in law schools, based loosely on Justice Holmes's dissenting opinions[1] and Harvard law professor Zechariah Chafee's 1919 seminal paper, "Freedom of Speech in Wartime." Chafee wrote:

> The true meaning of freedom of speech seems to be this. One of the most important purposes of society and government is the discovery and spread of truth on subjects of general concern. This is possible only through absolutely unlimited discussion. . . . Nevertheless, there are other purposes of government. . . . Unlimited discussion sometimes interferes with these purposes, which must then be balanced against freedom of speech. . . . The First Amendment gives binding force to this principle of political wisdom.[2]

This is what has become known as the first free speech tradition, the centerpiece of how free speech has been understood in America.[3] Yet while not irrelevant, it has become of secondary importance for many of the free speech questions of our times. Instead, a second free speech tradition, dating from the 1940s, much less well known and barely taught in school, has slowly grown in importance.

The second tradition is different. It cares about the decisions made by concentrated, private intermediaries who control or carry speech. It is a tradition in which the main governmental agent is not the Supreme Court but the Interstate Commerce Commission (once) or Federal Communications Commission (FCC). And in the second tradition the censors, as it were, are not government officials but private intermediaries, who often lack a censorial instinct of their own but are nonetheless vulnerable to censorial pressures from others. Above all, it is a speech tradition linked to the technology of mass communications.

In its heyday from the 1930s through the 1960s, the second tradition was anchored in the common carriage rules applied to the telephone company and also, at times, to radio and, later on, in the cajoling of and the public interest duties imposed on broadcasters. In its midcentury incarnation, the regime was a reaction to the concentration at every layer of the communications industry. But today the industry is different, and in our times the concerns have changed. As Jeffrey Rosen notes in the preceding chapter,

> At the moment, the person who arguably has more power than any other to determine who may speak and who may be heard around the globe is not a king, a president, or a Supreme Court justice. She is Nicole Wong, the deputy general counsel of Google. . . . Wong and her colleagues decide what controversial user-generated content goes down or stays up on [Google-owned] applications . . . [and] . . . what controversial material does and does not appear on the . . . search engines that Google maintains. . . . As a result, Wong and her colleagues arguably have more influence over the contours of online expression than anyone else on the planet.[4]

Captured in this paragraph is an essential feature of the speech architecture of our times and the way it affects the speech environment. We live in an age when an enormous number of speakers, a "long tail" in popular lingo, are layered on top of a small number of very large speech intermediaries.[5] Consequently, understanding free speech in America has become a matter of understanding the behavior of intermediaries, whether motivated by their own scruples, by law, or in response to public pressure.

Anyone who wants to understand free speech in America in the twenty-first century needs to understand the second tradition as deeply as, if not more than, the first. The doctrines of common carriage and network neutrality are perhaps the most important speech-related laws of our times. It is a messier tradition and much less familiar, but no less important.

First Principles

For some readers, what I am calling a second speech tradition may not seem to be about free speech as they understand it, because it is not about government censorship. But the underlying principles of the first and second traditions really are not that different. I want to suggest that the First Amendment and the common carriage doctrine are premised, basically, on the same concept: nondiscrimination. It is crucial to understand this point if we are to understand how common carriage and its recent manifestation, "net neutrality," are becoming so important as speech doctrines.[6] The underlying similarity between the First Amendment and common carriage was less clear in earlier times, when common carriage referred to the transport of goods and people and applied mainly to sea ferries, ports, and such.

At its most fundamental, both the First Amendment and common carriage are centered on the problem of wrongful discrimination in communications. The idea animating First Amendment jurisprudence is that government should use its power to prevent wrongful discrimination toward different forms of content or speakers. Common carriage, when applied to information carriers, is premised on the same idea. The government is again insisting that speech be carried regardless of either its content or its source. The setting and government actors are different, but the central norm is the same.

Dating from somewhere in the fifteenth century or earlier, English courts began to require certain businesses, known as "public callings," to operate in a nondiscriminatory fashion. A public calling, for example, such as an inn or a ferry, was required to serve all customers, typically at posted rates. As explained by an anonymous English judge in 1450, "When a smith declines to shoe my horse, or an innkeeper refuses to give me entertainment at his inn, I shall have an action on the case [that is, be entitled to sue.]"[7]

The concept made its way to the United States and was at first applied, as in Britain, to innkeepers, ferries, and the like. Eventually, however, the law of common carriage was applied to information carriers, namely, telegraph companies, telephone companies, and firms offering radio transmission. All existing telecommunications firms were made subject to the Interstate Commerce Act by the Mann-Elkins Act in 1910.[8] That law specified that whatever the telephone company did, it would treat its like customers alike—and thereby not favor some speech over others. As the law stated, "It shall be unlawful . . . [for any carrier] to make or give any undue or unreasonable preference or advantage to any particular person . . . or any particular description of traffic, in any respect whatsoever."[9]

At the time of its passage, the primary interest of the Mann-Elkins Act was commercial or economic; the Interstate Commerce Commission was originally designed to regulate railroads and was motivated mainly by the perceived abuses of the Standard Oil Company. However, when applied to an industry that moves information, the common carriage rule automatically became a law affecting speech.

Consider, for example, Bell Telephone (which evolved into AT&T, the phone monopolist), federally a common carrier from 1910 onward. Under common carriage law, Bell was not allowed to act as a censor. Customers, for instance, were free to speak of immoral, obscene, or illegal topics on the telephone, and Bell, even if it had the technological capacity to monitor conversations and block bad content, was not permitted to act as a filter, even if that is what the state might have liked. Compare this with the First Amendment's ban on governmental interference with speech. If it is fair to summarize the First Amendment this way, the Supreme Court has insisted, since the 1950s or so, that the government refrain from blocking speech or discriminating in favor of one speaker over another unless it has a good reason. This is not a full description of what the First Amendment prohibits, but it is at the amendment's core. In this sense, the First Amendment is, like common carriage, an antidiscrimination rule.

We can see this fact reflected in the First Amendment jurisprudence, where it appears in concepts like "content neutrality," today a cornerstone of First Amendment law. That concept creates an important distinction between laws considered content specific or viewpoint specific and those considered content (or viewpoint) neutral. A law considered "specific" is subject to a higher level of judicial scrutiny and is therefore likely to be struck down, absent a truly compelling interest. In the famous case *R. A. V. v. City of St. Paul,* for example, the Supreme Court struck down a city ordinance that banned hateful displays (like a burning cross or a Nazi swastika) because it sought to punish speakers based on the content of their message.[10] On the other hand, content-neutral regulations are subject to less intense scrutiny. Based on this rationale, the Supreme Court once upheld as neutral a New York City rule requiring that concerts use equipment limiting their total sound volume.[11] In this doctrinal rule the First Amendment is not telling the government that it cannot regulate speech at all but that it must do so in a nondiscriminatory way. The content of the speech was not relevant to the ruling.

Of course, First Amendment jurisprudence is far more complex than described here, for it also contains a concern for matters like vagueness and the "tailoring" of regulations that do not have a counterpart in common carriage regulation. Nonetheless, a basic aim of the law is clear: to require neutrality from the government in its treatment of speech. As such, it shares a basic similarity with the common carriage rule requiring neutral treatment of carried information.

Thinking of the First Amendment as a free speech law is familiar. In contrast, thinking of common carriage rules as speech rules (when applied to information carriers) is novel. But taking a few steps back, one cannot help but notice that both laws enforce an antidiscrimination norm and that both are, in their nature, efforts to control enormous concentrations of power. One happens to be a concentration of public power, the other private.

I suspect that many readers have noticed that the comparison focuses on the similarities between the First Amendment and common carriage doctrine, not the differences. Before proceeding, it is worth considering whether the differences render the comparison inapt.

First, and most important, the First Amendment restrains governments (state actors), and common carriage is a constraint on private companies. But they seek to contain the same evil, as it were.[12] It is common to have laws that ban the private and public version of the same misfeasance. We are comfortable saying that both Title VII (the federal law against employment discrimination) and the equal protection clause of the Fourteenth Amendment are, most of all, meant as a remedy for racism and other forms of harmful discrimination. Similarly, wiretapping is a restricted act when performed by either private parties or government. One version of the restraint binds states, the other private parties, but the point is basically the same. It should not be hard to see, similarly, the common points of the First Amendment and common carriage (as applied to communications) or net neutrality in the sense that both are means of dealing with the problem of discrimination and between speakers.

Second, calling common carriage a speech rule arguably misses the fact that what I am calling discrimination is, in fact, also a form of speech.[13] Consider briefly the more difficult objection that discrimination is a form of editing, and hence speech itself, not a form of speech control. When a newspaper or magazine includes some stories and rejects others, that act can be described as an act of discrimination. But it can also be described as an act of speech: the act of selecting itself is an act of self-expression. So when an information carrier decides to carry some speech and not others, perhaps the discrimination is simply editorial judgment and the common carriage law itself a device of censorship.[14] The answer is that an act of discrimination can be both a form of speech and censorship at the same time. If a carrier like Western Union in the nineteenth-century telegraph industry were to decide (as it did) to use its telegraph network to favor the Republican Party over the Democratic Party, it is in a sense expressing itself politically. Yet the decision also holds a danger of warping the political process. Hence the possibility, at least, that some channels of communication are essential enough that the problem of private censorship is more important than the use of that channel for expression. This analysis opens up a new question: namely, how far should government go in the regulation of private intermediaries for speech-related reasons? It is one thing, and a less controversial proposition, to demand that AT&T or Western Union not favor some speakers over others. But what about the printed press or news broadcasters, entities that, by their very nature, need to make selections as to what they will carry, selections that are inherently driven by their viewpoint? More broadly, is it possible to distinguish regulations like the Mann-Elkins Act of 1910 that applied common carriage rules to telephone and radio companies from the more general issue of regulating the media and the press?

This is a challenging question. I have said that common carriage (or net neutrality), when applied to information firms, is a speech law. But to whom, exactly, does common carriage apply? About whom are we talking when we say "common carriers"? That is a hard question to answer in general terms, beyond the rather circular point that firms that offer information carriage— moving information from one place to another, without modification, editing, and the rest—attract nondiscrimination duties.[15] Surely it excludes the press, bookstores, and other information-relevant firms who exercise discretion in what they carry. This is what distinguishes common carriage from the more general idea of media regulation.

History offers some guidance on what it might mean to regulate speech intermediaries—not just carriers but also broadcast networks and everything once called the "mass media." We can get some insight into this issue by looking back to the 1930s and 1940s as the FCC came to life and began to exercise its powers over both the telephone companies and broadcast, or mass, media.

The Second Tradition in the Midcentury

In 1961, in one of his less remembered speeches, John Kennedy said to a group of TV broadcasters, "You are the guardians of the most powerful and effective means of communications ever designed."[16] Kennedy was correct about the power of American broadcasting at the time. A broadcast of the musical *Cinderella* in 1955 attracted 107 million viewers, nearly 60 percent of the entire U.S. population.[17] Shows like *I Love Lucy* or the *Ed Sullivan Show* regularly attracted more than half of American TV households, reaching more than 80 percent of the public for such popular broadcasts as the first appearance of Elvis Presley on *Ed Sullivan*. Since the final *M*A*S*H* episode, in 1983, U.S. television viewership has never equaled these numbers. The period from the 1930s until the early 1990s was the era of the true national mass media—a thing that did not exist before, and a thing that has been unraveling since. Lasting, by coincidence, roughly the same length of time as the communist state, it was a time, to a degree unparalleled in history, when people in the same nation mostly watched and listened to the same information.

It was in the middle part of the twentieth century, this age of the true mass media, that the second speech tradition in the United States took its furthest reach and faced the hardest questions. During that time, in scholarship that has been long forgotten, scholars observed that to control broadcasting or the telephone lines was to control a huge part of speech in the United States. They pushed the government and other entities to take an active role in shaping the behavior of both common carriers and more selective speech intermediaries—namely, broadcasters.

In the view of some, including many free speech scholars, the federal government went too far in this era, and in that sense the origins of the tradition can serve as a lesson. The FCC blurred the line between the regulation of pure information carriers and regulation of firms that made editorial choices, most clearly and controversially in the use of the fairness doctrine. The tradition, in this respect, remains controversial to this day. But instead of engaging in the lengthy debate over the fairness doctrine and related policies, I want instead to understand what it was and how it operated.

In 1960 Newt Minow was an obscure Chicago lawyer and a friend of the Kennedy family. That year, at the age of thirty-four, Minow became the youngest FCC chair in the history of the organization. Minow was an outsider: no expert on telecom law or media policy and a complete unknown to the broadcasting industry. But he did have his opinions about TV, and he had been influenced by writers like Walter Lippmann, the founder of the *New Republic* and the author of a famous tract on media policy, *The Phantom Public*. Minow, in any event, was determined to put some teeth in the FCC's role in overseeing what broadcasters did with their trusteeship of the nation's communications spectrum—their right to reach the masses.

After a few months on the job, Minow gave his first speech at the National Association of Broadcasters. He said some nice things. However, it is not for that that his speech is remembered but for this:

I invite each of you to sit down in front of your own television set when your station goes on the air and stay there, for a day, without a book, without a magazine, without a newspaper, without a profit and loss sheet or a rating book to distract you. Keep your eyes glued to that set until the station signs off. I can assure you that what you will observe is a vast wasteland. You will see a procession of game shows, formula comedies about totally unbelievable families, blood and thunder, mayhem, violence, sadism, murder, western bad men, western good men, private eyes, gangsters, more violence, and cartoons. And endlessly commercials—many screaming, cajoling, and offending. And, most of all, boredom. True, you'll see a few things you will enjoy. But they will be very, very few. And if you think I exaggerate, I only ask you to try it.[18]

Decades later, what is so interesting about Minow's speech is not just that he had the guts to attack the broadcast lobby at the very beginning of his FCC career. What is interesting is what he presumed: the networks—three of them only—were the source of television content. Period. And it was the job of government to cajole, pressure, and tell them how to do their job better. Today, it is hard to imagine an FCC chair's telling bloggers to improve their work, or telling the hosts of cable news to quit fighting. The reason for the difference is industry structure.

Minow's comments, while bold, reflected FCC policy. In 1946 the FCC published what was informally known as the Blue Book, a detailed criticism of the quality of radio broadcasting at the time.[19] The commission asserted that it "not only has the authority to concern itself with program service, but that it is under an affirmative duty, in its public interest determinations, to give full consideration to program service."[20] Minow's comments and the Blue Book reflected a particular conception of government's role in the speech environment. Broadcasters and the television networks were highly concentrated industries and owed their existence to the spectrum licenses issued by the FCC. As such, they were subject to certain duties of good behavior, enforced not so much by legal orders as by official nagging.

At all times, any broadcaster had, and still has, under the law a duty to use the airwaves—the property of the people—in the public's interest. The nagging involved an implicit threat of loss of licensure.

Early on, that meant a duty to produce what was called "sustaining" content in network jargon, paid for by the networks themselves: what we might call "public service" programming. A long-standing example was *America's Town Meeting of the Air*. This NBC show invited experts to face a town hall meeting on the issues of the day. Its motto was "dedicated to the advancement of an honestly formed public opinion." Its ambitions were summed up by its host, George Denny, who said in 1936, "If Democrats go only to hear Democrats, and Republicans go out only to hear Republicans, and Isolationists to hear Isolationists, can we possibly call this an honest or intelligent system of political education?"[21]

But perhaps the most important expression of this role was the news department, a money loser, but a department that ideally took seriously its duty to educate the public and restrain government and private powers. Oddly enough, then, it was the government that pushed the networks to push back on the government.

Regulating the conduct of news departments were complex rules of fairness, most famously the fairness doctrine—a federal rule, enforced mainly through pressure backed by threats of enforcement, that required the presentation of both points of view on an issue and required broadcasters to allow response time when they attacked a public or private figure. It all fit the tenor of balance, fairness, or generality that the networks and government wanted.

The importance of these means of regulating the mass media was the subject of the constitutional scholar Zechariah Chafee's less famous book on free speech written in 1947, *Government and Mass Communications.*[22] We have already seen that Chafee was the anchor and perhaps the creator of the free speech theories that prevented government censorship under the First Amendment. But here is Chafee's lost commentary on what we call the second tradition. As the coauthored preamble to that work (technically, a commission report) says, "in matters of speech, governmental action is only part of the main problem . . . perhaps a small part. As one wise informant told us, it is not governmental restraint which either creates nor can completely solve the problem of free communication. Not even ten percent of the problems of a free press arise from governmental action."[23]

The book goes on to say that though government may be unable to solve many of these problems, it should do what it can to help. "If we think of the flow of news and opinions as the flow of intellectual traffic," wrote Chafee, "government can also try to widen the channels and keep traffic moving smoothly."[24]

Chafee advanced the idea that it was the FCC's role to push broadcasting to do its best; he discussed, but stopped short of, more radical ideas, such as a common carriage policy for newspapers. Nonetheless, what is evident from his treatment is that the control of intermediaries was essential to the question of free speech in America.

I describe the midcentury role of the FCC to give one version—in American history, the strongest version—of what the second free speech tradition can mean. As discussed earlier, a central challenge for the second tradition has been, and will always be, the challenge of boundaries. Who are the critical private intermediaries whose influence over speech is so great that their actions and their regulation make such a difference?

From the 1930s through the 1960s, the FCC and scholars like Chafee took the view that all of the "new media," the telephone and the radio, operating on a mass level, held enough power over speech that their behavior needed to be carefully overseen, and at times directly controlled. They did not think that the same types of regulation suited all private intermediaries but rather adopted different approaches for different actors.

Implicit in this approach was a rough categorization of private speech intermediaries into three groups. One was the common carrier, to whom the most rigorous rules applied: a strict nondiscrimination standard. A second group, made up, in practice, of broadcasters, was subject to government oversight and the fairness doctrine, mostly owing to the sheer power these entities had over American speech, along with the fact that their power came from a federal license to operate on scarce, publicly owned radio airwaves. Unlike the common carriers, by their nature these entities chose what to broadcast. But as we have seen, the FCC attempted to pressure them into carrying a broad variety of content and to present all views on controversial subjects. The third group, comprising small carriers and everything related to the printed movement of information, was subject to no direct regulation whatsoever.

There is much about the second tradition in the 1940s that may seem hard to swallow today. In particular, in its regulation of broadcasters, it is easy to argue that there was just too much government meddling with private speech. The FCC, for its part, insisted (and the Supreme Court agreed) that the scarcity of the power of broadcasting—very few people got to be broadcasters—justified rules like the fairness doctrine.[25] In this sense, the second tradition began to run afoul of the first.

My point here is not to endorse the regulation of mass media as it was in its earlier days, for we do not have the problems or the industry of the 1940s. I do not think that we want the media regulations of the 1940s for the twenty-first century. Rather, I am trying to suggest that some of the underlying concerns that animated regulators in the midcentury period remain today, and we may see them take on a primary importance during the next decades.

The Present

The second free speech tradition may be assuming (or retaking) a primary place in the early twenty-first century. A reasonable reader may ask why. Don't we live in an era of unprecedented speech pluralism? Yes, but matters are not

Figure 6-1. Television Broadcasting, Mid-Twentieth Century

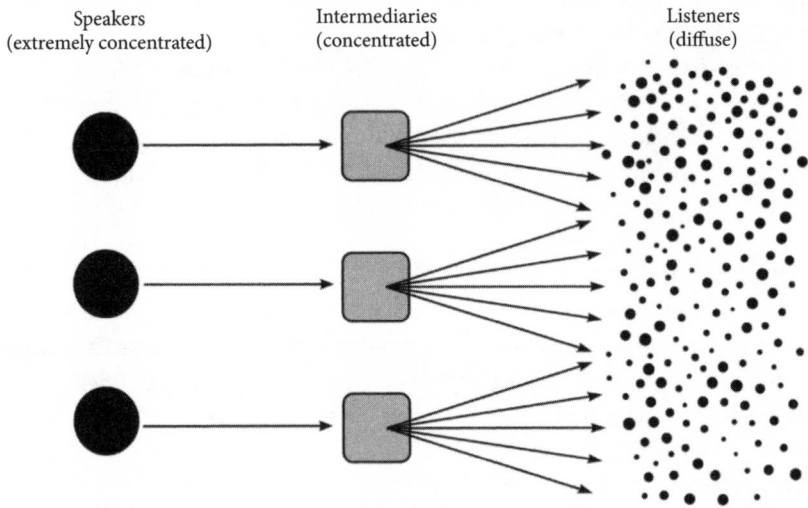

that simple. The American speech industry today is less concentrated in some ways than in the past, but it is more concentrated in others. In short, the speech architecture has changed.

We need to focus on the architecture of speech during different periods and how that affects the perceived need for regulation.[26] Consider, first, television broadcasting at midcentury. The effective "speaker" industry was heavily concentrated in the three networks, though there were also independent producers. The intermediary or distribution industry (stations) was somewhat less concentrated; yet still, it was hardly a competitive industry, as it was based on the grant of an FCC license.

Meanwhile, the telephone industry, as a speech carrier, was as concentrated as possible—as a monopoly, under AT&T. Yet it carried speech from any speaker to any listener.

That was then. Now, the architecture of speech features an enormous number of speakers, layered on top of a small number of intermediaries. That is why the behavior of large intermediaries has become so important.

This means that we live in an age of concentrated distribution and switching (that is, connecting one party to another, better known as "searching") but extremely diffuse speech. It is easy to publish or to find nearly any viewpoint relevant to a given issue. That is why there is only limited demand for something like a fairness doctrine for the Internet.

Figure 6-2. *Telephone Industry, Mid-Twentieth Century*

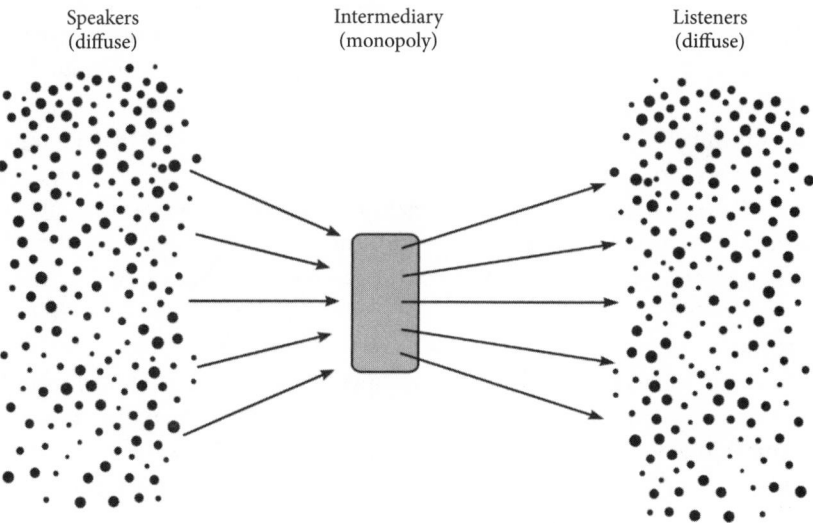

Speakers
(diffuse)

Intermediary
(monopoly)

Listeners
(diffuse)

Figure 6-3. *Telecommunications, Twenty-First Century*

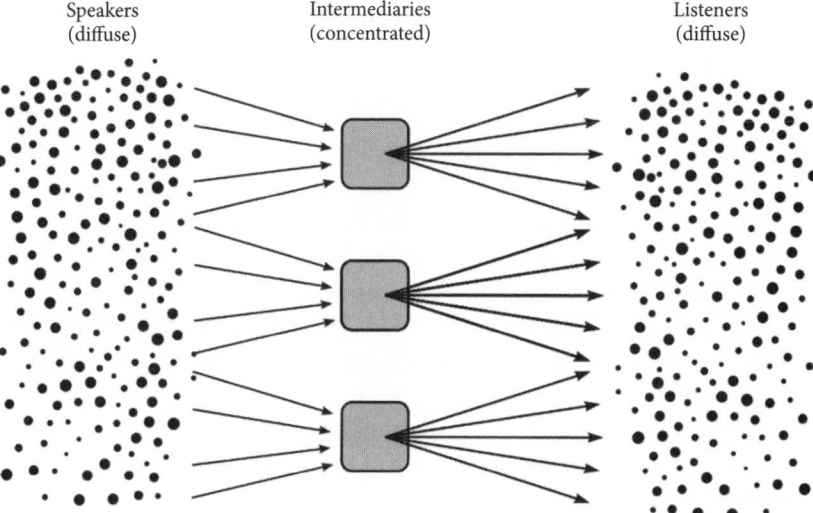

Speakers
(diffuse)

Intermediaries
(concentrated)

Listeners
(diffuse)

In contrast, carriage is relatively concentrated. Here in the early years of the twenty-first century, there are merely a handful of companies that deliver or switch most of the information in the United States. They are the two main telephone companies, Verizon and AT&T, the cable industry, and a handful of crucial switches, Google most obviously.[27] An astonishing volume of content runs through or is switched by these firms, and consequently they are in a unique position to control speech in America.

This explains why the focus of speech questions has come to center on net neutrality, the contemporary version of common carriage. The concentrated Internet speech intermediaries of our time look and act like carriers. Consequently, the perceived demands for their regulation are similar to those applied, historically, to the carrier industry, the telephone and telegraph firms. The general concern is with the potential misbehavior of the great carriers and switches, the firms already named, because that is where the industrial concentration is found. The discussion of the influence of powerful entities in American speech is a discussion of common carriage or network neutrality rather than Newt Minow–style efforts to tell powerful speakers what they should be doing.

In 2011 the FCC adopted a new set of net neutrality rules, albeit on somewhat shaky jurisdictional grounds. This chapter is not the place for a lengthy discussion of the limits of the FCC's jurisdiction. The more important fact is that questions of private discrimination will always have a central place in the regulation of communications.[28] That is true whether the issue is common carriage, net neutrality, cable regulation, spectrum regulation, or whatever else the future may bring. That, in turn, suggests that the second speech tradition is certain to have a lasting significance in the next several decades.

Conclusion

This chapter began with an Ishiguro-esque portrayal of the potential political consequences that can come from abuse of the most powerful speech infrastructures in the nation. The story may strike some as far-fetched—science fiction, perhaps. And yet the example is based not on fiction but on fact: the events surrounding the election of 1876.

In the early 1870s, Western Union, not AT&T, was the uncontested monopolist of the telegraph, the only instantaneous long-distance communications technology at the time. It made an agreement with the Associated Press making the latter the exclusive source of wire news in the United States. As historians have documented, Western Union and the Associated Press used their combined power to promote or suppress wire news and the device of spying on private telegraphs in an effort to destroy the candidacy of the Democratic candidate, Ohio governor Samuel Tilden, and make Rutherford Hayes president.[29] An election is a complex thing, and it is impossible to measure exactly the effects of the Western Union–AP campaign on the election, but that it had an effect, and a potentially decisive one, also cannot be doubted.

The broader point is simply that private sector power over speech can be nearly as terrifying as public power. And why not? Power is power, wherever it is found. We already know that the more tyrannical the government, the more important the First Amendment becomes. But it is important to understand the same idea in a private setting: the greater the concentration of the speech industry grows, the more important the second free speech tradition will become.

Notes

1. For example, *Abrams v. United States*, 250 U.S. 616 (1919) (Holmes, J., dissenting).

2. Zechariah Chafee, "Freedom of Speech in Wartime," 32 *Harvard Law Review* (1919): 932, 956–57.

3. Scholars will know that describing Chafee's "Free Speech in Wartime" as representative of the first free speech tradition is controversial, for Chafee is considered by some to have abrogated an older First Amendment tradition and constructed his own twentieth-century "tradition." See Mark Graber, *Transforming Free Speech: The Ambiguous Legacy of Civil Libertarianism* (University of California Press, 1991). It would probably be more accurate to speak of three, or four, or five major free speech traditions in the United States, and a few minor ones thrown in as well.

4. See also Jeffrey Rosen, "Google's Gatekeepers," *New York Times Magazine*, November 30, 2008 (www.nytimes.com/2008/11/30/magazine/30google-t.html).

5. "For every diverse Long Tail there's a 'Big Dog': a boring standardized industry that isn't sexy like Apple . . . but that delivers all that niche content you're hungry for." Tim Wu, "The Wrong Tail," *Slate*, July 21, 2006 (www.slate.com/id/2146225/).

6. See Tim Wu, "Network Neutrality, Broadband Discrimination," 2 *Journal on Telecommunications and High Technology Law* (2003): 141.

7. Anonymous note quoted in Bruce Wyman, "The Law of the Public Callings as a Solution to the Trust Problem," 17 *Harvard Law Review* (1903): 156, 158.

8. *Mann-Elkins Act*, 36 Stat. 539 (1910), chap. 309.

9. *Interstate Commerce Act*, 24 Stat. 379 (1887), chap. 104.

10. *R. A. V. v. City of St. Paul*, 505 U.S. 377 (1992).

11. See *Ward v. Rock Against Racism*, 491 U.S. 781 (1989).

12. The point is clearest when who we are calling the "private censor" is so entwined and supported by the state that it approaches what other countries call a crown corporation. In American history, the Bell telephone companies and parts of the broadcast

industry were nominally private firms, but they have been so close to government for so long, and owe so much of their livelihood to public spectrum and rights-of-way, that they can in many respects be better understood as what other nations term crown corporations.

13. What I mean by *free speech*, and particularly the word *free*, is the cost of speech. Free speech sets out an ideal—that the cost of speech might be zero. It is, of course, unattainable. So what I am talking about is really society's interest in cheap speech.

14. Similar arguments animated the First Amendment cases surrounding the cable industry, which claimed to be a speaker based on selective carriage. See, for example, *Turner Broadcasting System, Inc. v. F.C.C.*, 512 U.S. 622 (1994).

15. For a much deeper look at who, historically, is and is not classified as a common carrier, see Thomas B. Nachbar, "The Public Network," 17 *Journal of Communications Law and Policy* (2008): 67, 127.

16. President John F. Kennedy, address delivered at the 39th Annual Convention of the National Association of Broadcasters, May 8, 1961 (www.presidency.ucsb.edu/ws/index.php?pid=8120).

17. Irving Haberman, "The Theatre World Brings A Few Musicals and a Stage Success to Television This Week," *New York Times*, March 31, 1957.

18. Newton N. Minow, chairman, Federal Communications Commission, "Television and the Public Interest," address delivered at the 39th Annual Convention of the National Association of Broadcasters, May 9, 1961 (www.americanrhetoric.com/speeches/newtonminow.htm).

19. Federal Communications Commission, *Public Service Responsibility of Broadcast Licensees* (1946).

20. Ibid., 12.

21. George Denny, address delivered at the League for Political Education spring luncheon (April 3, 1936), cited in *NBC: America's Network*, edited by Michele Hilmes (University of California Press, 2007), 46–47.

22. Zechariah Chafee, *Government and Mass Communications: A Report from the Commission on Freedom of the Press* (University of Chicago Press, 1947).

23. Ibid., ix.

24. Ibid.

25. See *Red Lion Broadcasting Co. v. FCC*, 395 U.S. 367 (1969).

26. This basic point, that the architecture of the Internet itself was responsible for plural speech, and could be changed, was made memorably in 1998 by Lawrence Lessig, in a paper titled "What Things Regulate Speech." As he puts it, "Our tradition is to fear government's regulation, and turn a blind eye to private regulation. Our intuitions are trained against laws, not against code. But my argument in this essay has been that we understand the values implicit in the Internet's architecture as well as the values implicit in laws. And they would be as critical of the values within the architecture as we are of the values within the law." "What Things Regulate Speech," Social Science Research Network, September 1997 (http://ssrn.com/abstract=33067), 55.

27. While technically Google is a search engine, not a switch, it can be understood to perform the function of a switch in a network architecture—namely, it takes people to the party they are seeking, the classic function of the telephone switch.

28. See Tim Wu, "Why Have a Telecommunications Law? Anti-Discrimination Norms in Communications," 5 *Journal of Telecommunications and High Technology Law* (2006): 15.

29. See, for example, Menahem Blondheim, *News over the Wires: The Telegraph and the Flow of Public Information in America, 1844–1897* (Harvard University Press, 1994).

JONATHAN ZITTRAIN

7

A Mutual Aid Treaty
for the Internet

By 2030 all of humanity's books will be online. Google's ambitious book scanning project—or something like it—will by then have generated high-quality, searchable scans of nearly every book available in the world. These scans will be available online to library partners and individual users with certain constraints—what those will be, we do not know yet. It will be a library in the cloud, far larger than any real-world library could hope to be. It will make no sense for a library to store thousands of physical books in its basement. Rather, under a Google Books plan, there will be one master copy of the book in Google's possession.[1] The library partners will display it and access it according to particular privileges. A user will be able to access it from anywhere. One master book shared among many drastically lowers the costs of updates—or censorship. For example, if one book in the system contains copyright-infringing material, the rights holder can get a court order requiring the infringing pages of the book to be deleted from the Google server. Google will have no choice but to comply, at least as long as it continues to have tangible interests within the country demanding a change.

This vulnerability will affect every text distributed through the Google platform. Anyone who does not own a physical copy of the book—and a means to search it to verify its integrity—will lack access to that material. Add

The author wishes to acknowledge the contributions of Tim Berners-Lee in the development of this paper, in particular in originating the mirror-as-you-link idea. This paper grew out of a report the author prepared for the Global Agenda Council for the Future of the Internet at the World Economic Forum. Thanks also to Heather Casteel, Kendra Albert, and Molly Sauter for impeccable research assistance.

in orders arising from perceived defamation or any other cause of action, and holes begin to appear in the historical record in a way they could not before.

Some people—and I am in this camp—are alarmed by this prospect; others regard it as important but not urgent. Still others see this as a feature, not a bug. What, after all, is the constitutional problem? Court orders in the United States are subject to judicial review (indeed, they issue from judges), so would it not be possible to harmonize them with the First Amendment? Not so easily. Current constitutional doctrine has little to say about redactions or impoundment of material after it has had its day in court. What has protected such material from thorough and permanent erasure is the inherent leakiness of a distributed system where books are found everywhere: in libraries, bookstores, and people's homes. By centralizing (and, to be sure, making more efficient) the storage of content, we are creating a world in which all copies of once-censored books like *Candide, The Call of the Wild,* and *Ulysses* could have been permanently destroyed at the time of the censoring and could not be studied or enjoyed even after subsequent decisionmakers lifted the ban.[2] Worse, content that may be every bit as important—but not as famous—can be quietly redacted or removed without anyone's even noticing. Orders need only be served on a centralized provider, rather than on one bookstore or library at a time.

The systems to make this happen are being designed and implemented right now and can be fully dominant over the decades this volume asks us to chart. One helpful thought experiment flows from an incident that could not have been invented better than it actually happened. In 2009 a third-party seller offered, through Amazon, a Kindle version of *1984* by George Orwell.[3] People bought it. Later, Amazon had reason to think there was a copyright issue that was not cleared by the source who put it on Amazon. Amazon panicked and sent instructions that deleted *1984* from all the Kindles to which it had been downloaded. It was as if the user had never bought *1984*. It is current, not future, technology that makes this possible. The only reason this was more a curiosity than a major issue was that other copies of *1984* were so readily available—precisely because digital centralization has yet to fully take root. This is not literally cloud computing; for the period of time the user possessed it, *1984* technically resided physically on his or her Kindle. But because it was not the user's to copy or to otherwise manipulate, and it was solely Amazon's power to reach in and revise or delete, it was as good as a Google Books configuration—or, in this case, as bad.

By 2030 most global communications, commerce, and information storage will take place online. Much of this activity will be routed through a small set of corporate, governmental, and institutional actors. For much but not all of our online history, a limited number of corporate actors have framed the way people interact online. In the 1990s it was the proprietary online Internet service providers (ISPs) such as Prodigy and AOL that regulated our nascent digital interactions. Today, most people have direct access to the web, but now their online lives are conscribed by consolidating corporate search engines, content providers, and social networking sites.

With greater online centralization comes greater vulnerability, whether the centralization is public or private. Corporations are discrete entities, subject to pressures from repressive governments and criminal or terrorist threats. If Google's services were to go offline tomorrow, the lives of millions of people would be disrupted.

This risk grows more acute as both the importance and centralization of online services increase. The Internet already occupies a vital space in public and private life. By 2030 that place will only be more vital. Threats to cybersecurity will thus present threats to human rights and civil liberties. Disruptions in access to cloud-hosted services will cut off the primary and perhaps the only socially safe mode of communication for journalists, political activists, and ordinary citizens in countries around the world. Corrupt governments need not bother producing their own propaganda if selective Internet filtering can provide just as sure a technique of controlling citizens' perception of news and other information. This is the Fort Knox problem: putting all our valuables in one location. We allow a handful of bottlenecks to be placed in the path to our data or, worse, create a single logical trove of those data.

This scenario has implications for both free speech and cybersecurity. The Fort Knox mentality exposes vulnerable speech to unilateral and obliterating censorship: losing the inherent leakiness of the present model means we lose the benefits of the redundancies it creates. These redundancies protect our civil liberty and security in ways as important as any scheme of constitutional rights. Indeed, the Constitution is interpreted with such reality in mind. The ease with which an order can be upheld to impound copyright-infringing materials, or to destroy defamatory texts, can be understood only in the context of how difficult such actions were to undertake in the predigital world. Those difficulties make such actions rare and expensive. Should the difficulties in censorship diminish or evaporate, there is no guarantee that compensating protections would be enacted by Congress or fashioned by judges.

Moreover, threats to free speech online come not only from governments wishing to censor through the mechanisms of law but from anyone wishing to censor through the mechanisms of cyberattack, such as denial of service. A site that has unpopular or sensitive content can find itself brought down— forced to either abandon its message or seek shelter under the umbrella of a well-protected corporate information-hosting apparatus. Such companies may charge accordingly for their services—or, fearing that they will be swamped by a retargeted attack, refuse to host at all. This is why the more traditional government censorship configurations are best understood with a cybersecurity counterpart.

What appears safer in the short term for cybersecurity—putting all our bits in the hands of a few centralized corporations—makes traditional censorship easier.

The key to solving the Fort Knox problem is to make the current decentralized web a more robust one. This can be done by reforging the technological relationships among sites and services on the web, drawing conceptually from mutual aid treaties among states in the real world. Mutual aid lets us envision a new socially and technologically based system of redundancy and security.

The Problem

The threats that are creating market forces for this kind of consolidation are real, and their destructive potential has already been amply demonstrated. For example, a venerable form of cyberattack involves hitting a website with so many requests for information that it has, in essence, a nervous breakdown. One such coordinated "denial-of-service" attack in 2007 paralyzed a huge swath of Estonia's Internet infrastructure[4]—and there is no reason it could not happen again tomorrow. Denial of service attacks are only one threat among several. In 2008 a single ISP in Pakistan sought to prevent its subscribers from getting to YouTube, on orders from the Pakistani government. It misconfigured its Internet routers to make that happen, and within minutes YouTube was unavailable not just to the ISP's subscribers but to nearly everyone in the world.[5] The harm from such disruptions grows with our level of reliance on the Internet. And when natural disaster strikes—whether a hurricane in New Orleans or an earthquake in Haiti—the loss of vital communications lines can eliminate Internet access when it is needed most. The current vulnerabilities in the Internet's structure, combined with the increasing sophistication of would-be cyberterrorists and restrictive government censors, suggest a frightening image for the future of the World Wide Web: an unstable and constantly besieged space where only the biggest and baddest sites are able to stay online.[6] We have already seen a preview of this world in the fallout from the WikiLeaks diplomatic cable leak in November of 2010. After some large sites such as PayPal, Amazon, MasterCard, and Visa cut their commercial ties to Wikileaks, they found their own websites targeted as thousands of hacktivists engaged in organized, voluntary distributed denial-of-service attacks.[7] Large corporate entities were not the only targets. Smaller, less well defended sites were also targeted, with the hacktivists responding quickly to any perceived slight against the Wikileaks organization. Easy-to-use distributed denial-of-service tools, such as the LOIC ("low orbit ion cannon") program favored in the Operation Payback attacks, are freely available for download across the net, and LOIC was downloaded from SourceForge more than eighty-eight thousand times in a week's time.[8] It seems unlikely that the clock can be turned back. Rather, it seems more and more likely that hacktivist-like actions—whether launched by individuals, groups, or governments—will become a reality of the Internet, driving sites to obtain their own private security forces, something that is both inefficient and deeply unfair, as sites without resources would remain exposed—or compelled to take shelter in configurations that amount to corporate consolidation of web hosting. The latter configurations make censorship easier as hosts could be pressured to deny service to unpopular sites—as Amazon was with Wikileaks, even in the absence of formal legal action against either party.

A centralized deliberative solution to this problem is not likely. Attempts to gather major public and private stakeholders in one room—literally or metaphorically—are necessarily limited. Furthermore, it is far from clear that a centralized response is the most desirable. Responses implemented by governments are necessarily subject to government control. The tools to facilitate such regulation can, especially when used by regimes that do not embrace the rule of law, threaten free expression and even the safety of political dissidents. It was originally thought that the decentralized nature of the Internet would cause problems for restrictive governments—that they would face the attenuating problem of regulating their own people because of the difficulties of regulating the Internet.[9] However, any government can still lean on plenty of intermediaries to control its citizens' access to the Internet, and a centralized regulatory scheme intended for the salutary purpose of increasing security would tend to make such censorship easier.

Traditional corporate interventions are similarly unsatisfying in the cybersecurity context. On first glance, it may seem tempting to centralize web hosting in a few major, stable players; doing so would improve the overall robustness of smaller individual sites by sheltering them under a larger umbrella. However, concentrating control over vast amounts of web content in only a few hosting providers introduces a host of undesirable security and political control problems—starting with the Fort Knox problem.

A more promising approach to the cybersecurity problem would capture the essence of cooperation and concerted action that made the Internet possible to begin with and has roots in the physical world as well: mutual aid. By reframing the issues most commonly mentioned as problems for the fabric of the Internet to encourage mutually beneficial, reciprocal actions among many Internet participants, it becomes clear that a spirit of mutual aid, backed up by corresponding technologies and practices, can make a difference, while avoiding some of the gravest hurdles and unintended consequences that arise when governments alone, or formally chartered multistakeholder groups, attempt to regulate or intervene.

The Internet's structure is often conceived as a series of layers. In its most basic form, the network includes a physical layer, wired or wireless, by which signals representing data are transmitted and received; a logical layer, which comprises the protocols—then implemented in Internet-compatible hardware and software—that allow data to be routed and understood properly between sender and recipient; and an application layer, where services and software visible to the general public are placed. Modularization means that expertise in one layer need not implicate much about another, and the firms and other parties involved in providing connectivity for one layer need not exercise control over another.[10]

The vision for mutual aid can be implemented at each layer of the Internet. These implementations are meant to show the elasticity of the mutual aid principle as a means of dealing with very real problems. The particular details can always be refined and varied. Mutual aid can also identify those parties best positioned to take a lead in bringing such implementations to life, showing how the most helpful parties may vary from problem to problem and layer to layer. This is just another reason to emphasize an underappreciated, collaborative framework for problem solving rather than the process-oriented institutional framework that is effective in so many other areas of interest to the global agenda.

Mutual Aid for a More Robust Web

The World Wide Web is perhaps the most successful application to which the Internet has been put. Indeed, the web is now so fundamental to being online that it is itself rightly viewed as a form of infrastructure. Many applications, whether interacting with one's bank, buying and selling things, or browsing and conveying news, rely on functioning web servers and browsers.

Imagine someone sitting at a computer. He or she accesses a site and reads a web page there. The page generally has links, and links generally look the same, whether they point to another page on that site or to a different site entirely. By clicking on the link, the user asks the browser to visit a new destination. Too often, the link does not work: the user clicks and nothing happens. This can be because a server has crashed or eliminated the page in question; because it is experiencing a denial-of-service attack; or because there is some network interruption between the user and his or her desired destination.

Cybersecurity is a multifaceted problem, but the possibility that any site will become unavailable at any moment as a consequence of a sudden denial of service is a prominent threat. Currently, only those sites with significant financial resources can hope to weather such attacks, and then only through nontrivial tactics.

State-of-the-art thinking on cybersecurity relies on traditional defense notions honed during the Cold War, such as effective deterrence. To achieve effective deterrence one must have the capacity to reach (and usually to identify) an attacker to exact a price for the attack. This, in turn, has led to some calls for redesigning the architecture of the Internet to solve the attribution problem: that is, to enable effective identification of the source of any particular set of data sent over the Internet. Many implementations would require a fundamental rewriting and reimplementing of Internet protocol—a practical challenge—and, if successful, such attribution could carry dire consequences for civil liberties. Not only could a repressive government demand access to the identities of political enemies within its country, but the mere existence of data linking online activity with identity would deter the free and open discourse for which the Internet is currently uniquely suited.[11]

How might the philosophy of mutual aid help? Imagine a very small tweak to the way web servers work. At the choice of a site operator—and that of the external sites referenced on its web pages—a site could implement a practice that might be called Mirror as You Link. Here, the user visits a website and is shown a page there. As the page is displayed, the site follows (or has previously followed) the links shown and, if the destination server is amenable, makes a copy of the linked page for safekeeping. In the meantime, the user might click on a link on the page that points to the previous site, but this time, for any of the reasons noted above, he is unable to get there. He then has the option of asking the linking site to show him its best rendition of what he is missing at the linked site.[12]

Such an approach could have an impact on this particular dimension of the cybersecurity problem in a way that helps everyone, not just those with substantial money to spend on private defenses, and without the downsides of more traditional interventions on the table. The decentralized nature of the solution renders it more affordable at the same time as it reduces the problems associated with the centralization of Internet content and regulation. An inexpensive solution that can be adopted by individual users draws on the principles of self-help that marked the Internet's beginnings while perpetuating the values of free expression. The practical implementation details are not nearly as fundamental as reworking Internet protocol or establishing a broad-based identity scheme—an elusive if ongoing goal. Rather, because nearly 80 percent of web servers worldwide are accounted for by two vendors, Apache and Microsoft, the option to join such a mutual aid scheme could be added through updates to two pieces of software.[13]

In addition, as with most forms of mutual aid, many actors can be motivated to participate through self-interest rather than charity. Consider long-standing practices on the high seas, where private parties will respond to an SOS without any obligation to do so—indeed, even those of business competitors to the firm owning the ship in distress. They do so not only because they may consider it the right thing to do but also because they adhere to a larger scheme of reciprocity: if they should be the ones in trouble next time, they can expect that others will help. This is also the animating logic behind a standard military alliance: an attack on one is an attack on all. A state may see the downsides of joining—being called on to defend another state in an unasked-for fight—balanced against the benefit of knowing that others will come to its aid should it be attacked. So long as no one knows ahead of time who will be the next target, it can make sense to band together. Moreover, such a scheme creates a natural overall deterrent: cyberattacks on participating sites will be naturally less effective, since inbound-linking sites will have copies of the data the attacker is attempting to take offline.

Participation in a mutual aid scheme of this sort can be entirely voluntary, since incentives are a natural part of the scheme. Those sites that do not want their data mirrored for any reason can decline to participate, and their preference will be respected by inbound-linking sites. Those who fail to participate by actively mirroring other sites may find that they are not themselves mirrored—eliminating free riding as a reliable option.

Mirror as You Link is only one concrete example of the larger principle of distributed reciprocity aided by appropriate technologies. Of course, there are many further details and issues to be worked out for such a tangible proposal. For example, one might want to safeguard interactive database-stored content and transactional services where successful connection to a website is crucial for purposes other than simply viewing information on a page ideally accessible to all. One might also want to see a principle of mutual aid applied to link persistence, not just accessibility, leading to the ability to see what used to be at a link—even if something different is there now. (Currently such a service is provided by the private, nonprofit, but administratively centralized Internet Archive's Wayback Machine, started by an Internet user with a vision for preserving the contents of the web at large.)[14] The idea here is to sketch a proposal that demonstrates the power of looking at an Internet problem through the lens of mutual aid. Existing standards organizations such as the World Wide Web Consortium might be impelled to flesh out implementing protocols that in turn could be made available by the makers of web servers and implemented by website owners one server at a time.

Possibilities for mutual aid are evident at other layers of the Internet. For example, at the physical layer, should traditional Internet service be disrupted in times of natural disaster or unrest, so-called ad hoc mesh networking could allow each Internet user's device to also serve as a router, allowing data to hop from one device to another until they find their way out of the troubled zone—with no ISP needed in the middle. The key value is of reciprocity: participating Internet users would see their devices expending power and bandwidth carrying others' data—in exchange for having their own data carried similarly.

At the application layer, another problem of cybersecurity might be addressed: that of users' personal computers and other machines becoming compromised by malware. Often a website visited by a user will be able to detect that his or her machine is under attack but will fail to issue a warning lest the messenger be blamed. One could imagine a network of websites that agree to warn simultaneously: a compromised user will see persistent warnings from one site to the next and thus be alerted to a problem regardless of configuration of extra security software on the infected machine, and in a way that does not implicate any particular website.

Conclusion

By emphasizing and applying a particular principle—mutual aid—rather than a particular institutional structure in a domain containing many overlapping organizations and forums, it may be possible to generate solutions to cybersecurity problems that arise from the same collaborative principles that gave rise to the Internet itself. Cooperation can arise from a recognition of mutual interests and the implementation of technologies and practices designed to further those interests—technologies and practices that can come about in a variety of ways, from any number of existing stakeholders. Historically, the Internet domain has seen infrastructural advances not through carefully planned interventions, but rather through an open architecture that allows ideas to be floated for general adoption: applications that in turn can become infrastructure. On the communications level, it is this same pattern of evolution that renders the Internet such an effective forum for speech, discussion, and the percolation of new and potentially risky ideas. Society relies too heavily on the Internet to allow the cybersecurity problem to persist unaddressed. But the form of the solution must reflect a commitment to preserving online speech as an avenue for dissidents, activists, and the politically unpopular—and for ensuring that speech deemed contraband cannot be put down the memory hole.

The critical lesson is that multistakeholder cooperation can take many forms, and the Internet can be mediated minute-to-minute through technology and praxis as much as through formal hierarchy. Mirror as You Link is only one concrete example of this promising approach. The original structure of the Internet, which allows any node to join on equal terms as sender or receiver without gatekeeping or negotiation, itself suggests a realistic frame for taking on problems that, left unchecked, will call for much more costly and complex forms of intervention.

Notes

1. See generally Google Books Settlement Agreement (http://books.google.com/googlebooks/agreement).

2. See John M. Ockerbloom, "Books Banned Online," Online Books (http://online books.library.upenn.edu/banned-books.html); Jonathan Zittrain, *The Future of the Internet—And How to Stop It* (Yale University Press, 2008), 116.

3. See Brad Stone, "Amazon Erases Two Classics from Kindle (One Is '1984')," *New York Times,* July 18, 2009, B1.

4. See Steven Lee Myers, "Estonia Computers Blitzed, Possibly by the Russians," *New York Times,* May 19, 2007 (www.nytimes.com/2007/05/19/world/europe/19 russia.html).

5. See Bonnie Malkin, "Pakistan Ban to Blame for YouTube Blackout," *The (London) Telegraph,* February 25, 2008 (www.telegraph.co.uk/news/uknews/3356520/Pakistan-ban-to-blame-for-YouTube-blackout.html).

6. See, for example, Ellen Nakashima, "FBI Director Warns of 'Rapidly Expanding' Cyberterrorism Threat," *Washington Post,* March 4, 2010 (www.washingtonpost.com/wp-dyn/content/article/2010/03/04/AR2010030405066.html); posting by Kim Zetter, "Report: Critical Infrastructures under Constant Cyberattack Globally," *Wired Threat Level* (blog), January 28, 2010 (www.wired.com/threatlevel/2010/01/csis-report-on-cybersecurity).

7. See Christopher Walker, "A Brief History of Operation Payback," *Salon,* December 9, 2010 (www.salon.com/news/feature/2010/12/09/0).

8. See James Finke, "Wikileaks Hacktivists Look to Improve Attack Software," Reuters, December 15, 2010 (www.reuters.com/article/idUSTRE6BE5LB20101215).

9. See James Boyle, "Foucault in Cyberspace: Surveillance, Sovereignty, and Hard-wired Censors," 66 *University of Cincinnati Law Review* (1997): 177.

10. See generally David G. Post, *In Search of Jefferson's Moose: Notes on the State of Cyberspace* (Oxford University Press, 2009).

11. Anonymous speech has long been recognized as a fundamental right protected in America by the First Amendment. See, for example, *McIntyre* v. *Ohio Elections Comm'n,* 514 U.S. 334 (1995).

12. A similar system, called Globule, has been proposed by a group of academics in the Netherlands (www.globule.org/).

13. See Netcraft, Web Server Survey, February 2010 (http://news.netcraft.com/archives/2010/02/22/february_2010_web_server_survey.html).

14. Internet Archive: Wayback Machine (www.archive.org/web/web.php).

PART III

THE FUTURE OF NEUROLAW

STEPHEN J. MORSE

8

Neuroscience and the Future of Personhood and Responsibility

Collera, a twenty-eight-year-old man with a life-long history of aggressive behavior, including assault and verbal abuse, is driving his large SUV behind a slow-moving vehicle on a narrow road, with no room to pass. He honks and honks, but the driver in front neither speeds up nor pulls off the road to let Collera pass. Collera starts to curse vehemently and pulls dangerously close to the slower vehicle. Collera's passenger warns that he is taking a very serious risk. Collera finally announces in a fury that he is going to kill the [expletive deleted] in front of him. He allows his vehicle to drop back, then he floors the gas pedal, crashing into the slower vehicle at great speed. Neither he nor his passenger is hurt, but the driver of the slower vehicle is killed.

A functional brain image, which measures brain activation, conducted after the killing discloses that Collera has a type of neurophysiological activity in his frontal cortex that is associated with poor behavioral self-regulation.[1] Collera's life history includes a history of severe abuse. It is known that such abuse is strongly associated with later antisocial conduct if the person also has a genetic enzyme abnormality that affects particular neurotransmitter levels.[2] Collera indeed has the genetic abnormality and the associated neurotransmitter levels.

How should the law respond to people like Collera? Do we treat him, as we now do, as an acting agent who is properly subject to moral assessment and potential liability to just punishment? If so, how does the evaluation bear on his responsibility and future dangerousness? It appears from the limited facts that he has no specific doctrinal defense to murder. In deciding what the just punishment might be, however, how should the information from the evaluation be used? In the alternative, some would claim that Collera is simply a "victim of neuronal circumstances" and that no one is genuinely responsible.[3] Perhaps we might still think of him as an agent; but suppose that our prediction and control technology has immeasurably advanced. What should be the proper response?

Imagine that this takes place in the future, when we will have much better information about the biologically causal variables, especially neuroscientific and genetic factors, that in part produce all dangerous behavior and not just seemingly extreme cases like Collera's. The description of Collera's evaluation results makes no mention of disease or disorder. It simply reports a number of neuroscientific, genetic, and gene-by-environment interaction variables that played an apparently causal role in producing Collera's behavior and that might have helped us predict it. Will jurisprudence that respects agency, which enhances the dignity, liberty, and autonomy of all citizens, survive in a future in which neuroscience and genetics dominate our thinking about personhood and responsibility? Will we abandon the concepts of criminal, crime, responsibility, blame, and punishment and replace them with concepts such as "dangerous behavior" and "preventive control"? Will people in this brave new world be treated simply as biological mechanisms, and will doing harm be characterized simply as one mechanistic output of the system? As *The Economist* has warned, "Genetics may yet threaten privacy, kill autonomy, make society homogeneous, and gut the concept of human nature. But neuroscience could do all those things first."[4]

The law in our liberal democracy responds to the need to restrain dangerous people like Collera by what I have elsewhere termed "desert-disease" jurisprudence.[5] As a consequence of taking people seriously as people, as potential moral agents, we as a nation believe that it is crucial to cabin the potentially broad power of the state to deprive people of liberty. With rare exceptions, the state may restrain a citizen only if that citizen has been fairly convicted of crime and deserves the punishment imposed. If a citizen has not committed a crime but appears dangerous and not responsible for his or her dangerousness—usually as a result of mental disorder or other diseases that impair rationality—the citizen may be civilly committed. People who are simply dangerous but who have committed no crime and are responsible agents cannot be restrained. The normative basis of desert-disease jurisprudence is that it enhances liberty and autonomy by leaving people free to pursue their projects unless an agent responsibly commits a crime or unless through no fault of his or her own the agent is dangerous but not responsible for the dangerous proclivities. In the latter case, the agent's rationality is impaired, and the usual presumption in favor of liberty and autonomy yields to the need for societal protection. Preventive civil detention and involuntary treatment may thereby be warranted.

The law's concern with justifying and protecting liberty and autonomy is deeply rooted in the conception of rational personhood. Human beings are part of the physical universe and subject to the laws of that universe, but, as far as we know, we are the only creatures on earth capable of acting fully for reasons and self-consciously. Only human beings are genuinely responsive to reason and live in societies that are in part governed by behavior-guiding norms. Only human beings pursue projects that are essential to living a good life. Only human beings have expectations of one another and require justification for interference in one another's lives that will prevent the pursuit of projects and seeking the good. We are the only creatures to whom the questions Why did you do that? and How should we behave? are properly addressed, and only human beings hurt and kill one another in response to the answers to such questions. As a consequence of this view of ourselves, human beings typically have developed rich sets of interpersonal, social attitudes, practices, and institutions, including those that deal with the risk we present to one another. Among these are the practice of holding others morally and legally responsible, which depends on our attitudes and expectations about deserved praise and blame, and our practices and institutions that express those attitudes, such as reward and punishment.

There is little evidence at present that neuroscience, especially functional imaging, and genetic evidence are being introduced routinely in criminal cases outside of capital sentencing proceedings. That may well happen in the near future, however, especially as the technology becomes more broadly available and less expensive. So it is worth considering in detail neuroscience's radical challenge to responsibility, which sees people as victims of neuronal circumstances or the like. If this view of personhood is correct, it would indeed undermine all ordinary conceptions of responsibility and even the coherence of law itself.

Current Criminal Justice: Persons, Reasons, and Responsibility

Criminal law presupposes a "folk psychological" view of the person and behavior. This theory explains behavior in part by mental states such as desires, beliefs, intentions, willings, and plans. Biological, other psychological, and sociological variables also play a causal role, but folk psychology considers mental states fundamental to a full causal explanation and understanding of human action. Lawyers, philosophers, and scientists argue about the definitions of mental states and theories of action, but that does not undermine the general claim that mental states are fundamental. Indeed, the arguments and evidence disputants use to convince others presuppose the folk psychological view of the person. Brains do not convince; people do. Folk psychology presupposes only that human action will at least be rationalizable by mental-state explanations or that it will be responsive to reasons, including incentives, under the right conditions. For example, the folk psychological explanation for why you are reading this chapter is, roughly, that you desire to understand the relation of neuroscience to criminal responsibility, you believe that reading the chapter will help fulfill that desire, and thus you formed the intention to read it.

Brief reflection should indicate that the law's psychology must be a folk psychological theory, a view of the person as a conscious (and potentially self-conscious) creature who forms and acts on intentions that are the product of the person's other mental states. We are the sort of creatures that can act for and respond to reasons. The law treats persons generally as intentional creatures and not simply as mechanistic forces of nature.

Law is primarily action guiding and could not guide people directly and indirectly unless people were capable of understanding and then using rules as premises in their reasoning about how they should behave. Otherwise, law as an action-guiding system of rules would be useless, and perhaps incoherent. Legal rules are action guiding primarily because they provide an agent with good moral or prudential reasons for forbearance or action. Human behavior can be modified by means other than influencing deliberation, and human beings do not always deliberate before they act. Nonetheless, the law presupposes folk psychology, even when we most habitually follow the legal rules.

The legal view of the person does not hold that people must always reason or consistently behave rationally according to some preordained, normative notion of rationality. Rather, the law's view is that people are capable of acting for reasons and are capable of minimal rationality according to predominantly conventional, socially constructed standards. The type of rationality the law requires is the ordinary person's commonsense view of rationality, not the technical notion that might be acceptable within the disciplines of economics, philosophy, psychology, computer science, and the like.

Virtually everything for which agents deserve to be praised, blamed, rewarded, or punished is the product of mental causation and is, in principle, responsive to reason, including incentives. Machines may cause harm, but they cannot do wrong, and they cannot violate expectations about how people ought to live together. Machines do not deserve praise, blame, reward, punishment, concern, or respect because they exist or because of the results they cause. Only people, intentional agents with the potential to act, can violate expectations of what they owe one another, and only people can do wrong.

Many scientists and some philosophers of mind and action consider folk psychology to be a primitive or prescientific view of human behavior. For the foreseeable future, however, the law will be based on the folk psychological model of the person and behavior described. Until and unless scientific discoveries convince us that our view of ourselves is radically wrong, the basic explanatory apparatus of folk psychology will remain central. It is vital that we not lose sight of this model lest we fall into confusion when various claims based on neuroscience or genetics are made. If any science is to have appropriate influence on current law and legal decisionmaking, it must be relevant to and translated into the law's folk psychological framework.[6]

All of the law's doctrinal criteria for criminal responsibility are folk psychological, beginning with the definitional criteria, what the law terms the elements of crime. The first element of every crime, the "voluntary" act requirement is defined, roughly, as an intentional bodily movement (or omission in cases in which the person has a duty to act) done in a reasonably integrated state of consciousness. Other than crimes of strict liability, all crimes also require a culpable further mental state, such as purpose, knowledge, or recklessness. All affirmative defenses of justification and excuse involve an inquiry into the person's mental state, such as the belief that self-defensive force was necessary or the lack of knowledge of right from wrong.

Our concepts of criminal responsibility follow logically from the nature of law itself and its folk psychological concept of the person and action. The general capacity for rationality is the primary condition for responsibility, and the lack of that capacity is the primary condition for excusing a person. If human beings were not rational creatures who could understand the good reasons for action and were not capable of conforming to legal requirements through intentional action or forbearance, the law could not adequately guide action. Legally responsible agents are therefore people who have the general capacity to grasp and be guided by good reason in particular legal contexts.

In cases of excuse, the agent who has done something wrong acts for a reason but is either not capable of rationality generally or is incapable on the specific occasion in question. This explains, for example, why young children and some people with mental disorders are not held responsible. How much lack of capacity is necessary to find the agent not responsible is a moral, social, political, and ultimately legal issue. It is not a scientific, medical, psychological, or psychiatric issue.

Compulsion or coercion is also an excusing condition. Literal compulsion exists when the person's bodily movement is a pure mechanism that is not rationalizable by the agent's desires, beliefs, and intentions. These cases defeat the requirement of a "voluntary" act. For example, a tremor or spasm produced by a neurological disorder that causes harm is not an action because it is not intentional and it therefore defeats the ascription of a voluntary act. Metaphorical compulsion exists when the agent acts intentionally but in response to some hard choice imposed on the agent through no fault of his or her own. For example, if a miscreant holds a gun to an agent's head and threatens to kill her unless she kills another innocent person, it would be wrong to kill under these circumstances. Nonetheless, the law may decide as a normative matter to excuse the act because the agent was motivated by a threat so great that it would be supremely difficult for most citizens to resist. Cases involving internal compulsive states are more difficult to conceptualize because it is difficult to define "loss of control."[7] The cases that most fit this category are "disorders of desire," such as addictions and sexual disorders. The question is why these acting agents lack control but other people with strong desires do not. In any case, if an agent frequently yields to apparently very strong desires at great social, medical, occupational, or legal cost, the agent will often say that control was lost, that the behavior could not be helped, and that an excuse or mitigation was therefore warranted.

The criminal law's criteria for responsibility and excuse rest on acts and mental states. In contrast, the criteria of neuroscience are mechanistic: neural structure and function. Conceptually, the apparent chasm between those two types of discourse should be bridgeable, albeit with difficulty. The brain enables the mind. If your brain is dead, you are dead, you have no mind, and you do not behave at all. Therefore, facts we learn about brains in general or about a specific brain in principle could provide useful information about mental states and human capacities, both in general and in specific cases. While some people doubt this premise,[8] for present purposes let us assume that what we learn about the brain and nervous system can be potentially helpful in resolving questions of criminal responsibility.

The question is when the new neuroscience is legally relevant because it makes some given proposition about criminal responsibility more or less likely to be true. Any legal criterion must be established independently, and biological evidence must be translated into the criminal law's folk psychological criteria. That is, the expert must be able to explain precisely how the neuroevidence bears on whether the agent acted, formed a required mens rea, or met the criteria for an excusing condition. If the evidence is not directly relevant, the expert should be able to explain the chain of inference from the indirect evidence to the law's criteria.

At present, we lack the neuroscientific sophistication necessary to be genuinely legally relevant. The neuroscience of mental states and interpersonal behavior is largely in its infancy, and what we know now is quite coarse grained and correlational, rather than causal.[9] We lack the ability neurally to identify the content of a person's legally relevant mental states, such as whether the defendant acted intentionally or knowingly, but we are increasingly learning about the relationship between brain structure and function and behavioral capacities, such as executive functioning. And these are relevant to broader judgments about responsibility. Over time, these problems may ease, as imaging and other techniques become less expensive and more accurate and as the sophistication of the science increases.

Dangerous Distractions

It is important quickly to dispose of two dangerous distractions that neuroscience is thought to pose to ascriptions of criminal responsibility. The first is the threat of determinism. Many people think that neuroscience will prove once and for all that determinism (or something like it) is true and that we therefore lack free will and cannot be responsible. In this respect, however, neuroscience provides no new challenge to criminal responsibility. It cannot prove that determinism is true, and it is simply the determinism du jour, grabbing the attention previously given to psychological or genetic determinism. This challenge is not a problem for criminal law because free will plays no doctrinal role in criminal law and it is not genuinely foundational for criminal responsibility.[10] Nor is determinism inconsistent with the folk psychological view of the person. Moreover, there is a traditional, respectable philosophical reconciliation of responsibility and the truth of determinism called "compatibilism."[11]

Related confusions are the views that causes are per se excusing, whether they are biological, psychological, or sociological, or that causation is the equivalent of compulsion. If causation were per se an excusing condition or the equivalent of compulsion, then no one or everyone would be responsible because we live in a causal universe, which includes human action. Various causes can produce a genuine excusing condition, such as lack of rational or control capacity, but then it is the excusing condition, not causation, that is doing the legal work.

In contrast, the new neuroscientific challenge to personhood, exemplified by treating Collera as a victim of neuronal circumstances, is not saved by compatibilism or by the recognition that causation as an excuse cannot explain our practices, which hold most people responsible but excuse some. The radical challenge brain science allegedly poses threatens to undermine the very notions of agency that are presupposed by compatibilism and that are genuinely foundational for responsibility and for the coherence of law itself.

The Disappearing Person

At present, the law's official position—that conscious, intentional, rational, and uncompelled agents may properly be held responsible—is justified. But what if neuroscience or some other discipline demonstrates convincingly that humans are not the type of creatures we think we are? Asking a creature or a mechanistic force that does not act to answer to charges does not make sense. If humans are not intentional creatures who act for reasons and whose mental states play a causal role in their behavior, then the foundational facts for responsibility ascriptions are mistaken. If it is true that we are all automatons, then no one is an agent and no one can justifiably be held responsible. If the concept of mental causation that underlies folk psychology and current conceptions of responsibility is false, our responsibility practices, and many others, would appear unjustifiable.

This claim is not a strawperson, as the neuroscientists Joshua Greene and Jonathan Cohen illustrate:

> As more and more scientific facts come in, providing increasingly vivid illustrations of what the human mind is really like, more and more people will develop moral intuitions that are at odds with our current social practices. . . . Neuroscience has a special role to play in this process for the following reason. As long as the mind remains a black box, there will always be a donkey on which to pin dualist and libertarian positions. . . . What neuroscience does, and will continue to do at an accelerated pace, is elucidate the "when," "where" and "how" of the mechanical processes that cause behavior. It is one thing to deny that human behavior is purely mechanical when your opponent offers only a general philosophical argument. It is quite another to hold your ground when your opponent can make detailed predictions about how these mechanical processes work, complete with images of the brain structures involved and equations that describe their function. . . . At some further point . . . people may grow up completely used to the idea that every decision is a thoroughly mechanical process, the outcome of which is completely determined by the results of prior mechanical processes. What will such people think as they sit in their jury boxes?

Will jurors of the future wonder whether the defendant . . . *could have done otherwise*? Whether he really *deserves* to be punished. . . ? We submit that these questions, which seem so important today, will lose their grip in an age when the mechanical nature of human decision-making is fully appreciated. The law will continue to punish misdeeds, as it must for practical reasons, but the idea of distinguishing the truly, deeply guilty from those who are merely victims of neuronal circumstances will, we submit, seem pointless.[12]

Greene and Cohen are not alone among thoughtful people in making such claims. The seriousness of science's potential challenge to the traditional foundations of law and morality is best summed up in the title of an eminent psychologist's recent book, *The Illusion of Conscious Will*.[13] If Greene and Cohen are right, cases that involve alleged abnormalities are really indistinguishable from any other case and thus represent just the tip of the iceberg that will sink our current criminal justice system. In this view we are all "merely victims of neuronal circumstances."

But are we? Is the rich explanatory apparatus of intentionality simply a post hoc rationalization constructed by the brains of hapless homo sapiens to explain what their brains have already done? Will the criminal justice system as we know it wither away as an outmoded relic of a prescientific and cruel age? If so, not only criminal law is in peril. What will be the fate of contracts, for example, when a biological machine that was formerly called a person claims that it should not be bound because it did not make a contract? A contract is also simply the outcome of various neuronal circumstances.

This picture of human activity exerts a strong pull on the popular, educated imagination, too. In an ingenious recent study, investigators were able to predict accurately based on which part of the brain was physiologically active whether a shopper-subject would or would not make a purchase. This study was reported in the Science Times section of the *New York Times*. The story's spin began with its title, "The Voices in My Head Say 'Buy It!' Why Argue?"[14] It reflects once again the mechanistic view of human activity. What people do is simply a product of brain regions and neurotransmitters. The person disappears. There is no shopper. There is only a brain in a mall.

The law's fundamental presuppositions about personhood and action are indeed open to profound objection. Action and consciousness are scientific and conceptual mysteries. We do not know how the brain enables the mind, and we do not know how action is possible.[15] At most we have hypotheses or a priori arguments. Moreover, causation by mental states seems to depend on now largely discredited mind-brain dualism that treats minds and brains as separate entities that are somehow in communication with one another. How can such tenuously understood concepts be justifiable premises for legal practices such as blaming and punishing? And if our picture of ourselves is wrong, as many neuroscientists claim, then our responsibility practices are morally unjustified according to any moral theory we currently embrace.

Given how little we know about the brain-mind and brain-action connections, to claim based on neuroscience that we should radically change our picture of ourselves and our practices is a form of neuroarrogance. Although I predict that we will see far more numerous attempts to introduce neuroevidence in the future, the dystopia that Greene and Cohen predict is not likely to come to pass. There is little reason at present to believe that we are not agents.

Most scientists and philosophers of science are physicalists and monists. They believe, as I do, that all material and nonmaterial phenomena begin with matter subject to the universe's physical laws and that we do not have minds or souls independent of our bodies. But theorists such as Greene and Cohen go a step further. They appear to assume the validity of a complete reduction of mental states to brain states at the level of (apparently) neural networks. But the complete post-Enlightenment project of reducing all phenomena to the most basic physical building blocks is controversial even among physicalist monists, and most probably it is a chimera. Almost certainly, a complete explanation of human behavior will have to use multiple fields and multiple levels within each field.[16] The complete reductionists have to explain how molecules, which have no intentionality or temporal sense, produce intentional creatures with a sense of past, present, and future that guides our lives.

It is also possible that if we do ever discover how the brain enables the mind, this discovery will so profoundly alter our understanding of ourselves as biological creatures that all moral and political notions will change. Nevertheless, this argument is different from claiming that we are not agents, that our mental states do no explanatory work.

The Evidence for the "Victims of Neuronal Circumstances" Thesis

The real question behind the "victims of neuronal circumstances" thesis (VNC) is whether scientific and clinical investigations have shown that agency is rare or nonexistent, that conscious will is largely or entirely an illusion. Four kinds of indirect evidence are often adduced: first, demonstrations that a very large part of our activity is undeniably caused by variables we are not in the slightest aware of; second, studies indicating that more activity than we think takes place when our consciousness is divided or diminished; third, laboratory studies that show that people can be experimentally misled about their causal contribution to their apparent behavior; and, fourth, evidence that particular types of psychological processes are associated with heightened physiological activation in specific regions of the brain. None of these types of indirect evidence offers logical support to the VNC thesis. Although the science behind the claims for the thesis is often good, the claim itself is a non sequitur because these studies do not demonstrate that mental states play no causal role in most behavior we now consider intentional.[17]

There is also allegedly direct experimental evidence supportive of the VNC thesis from studies done by the neuroscientist Benjamin Libet and his followers, which have generated an immense amount of comment. Indeed, many claim that Libet's work is the first direct neurophysiological evidence of the validity of the VNC point of view. Libet's studies demonstrate that measurable electrical brain activity associated with the intentional actions of raising one's finger or flexing one's wrist at random occurs in the relevant motor area of the brain about 550 milliseconds before the subject actually acts and about 350–400 milliseconds before the subject is consciously aware of the intention to act. Let us assume, with cautious reservations, the basic scientific methodological validity of these studies. The crucial question is whether the interpretation of these findings as supporting the VNC thesis is valid. Do these findings mean that brain events are the entire causal explanation and that mental states played no causal role in explaining the subjects' finger raisings and wrist flexings?

This claim has been contested by numerous people, including the legal philosopher Michael Moore and the philosopher Alfred Mele, who have usefully shown that the Libetian conception of the role of brain events in causing behavior does not offer a coherent conceptual or empirical account of the relation between brain states and behavior.[18] My own work has contributed a more empirical and commonsense critique.[19] Indeed, it is at present an open question whether Libet's paradigm is representative of intentional actions in general because Libet investigated such trivial behavior. At least at present, this body of work does not remotely indicate that mental states play no causal role whatsoever in our intentional actions. I doubt that future science will change this conclusion.

Answers to the VNC thesis are rooted in common sense, a plausible theory of mind, our evolutionary history, and practical necessity. Virtually every neurologically intact person consistently has the experience of first-person agency, the experience that one's intentions flow from one's desires and beliefs and result in action. Indeed, this folk psychological experience is so central to human life and so apparently explanatory that it is difficult to imagine giving it up or a good reason to do so, even if it were possible to give it up. Folk psychology has much explanatory power, and we are capable of investigating its claims scientifically. There is compelling psychological evidence that intentions play a causal role in explaining behavior. Indeed, it is hard to imagine the nature of a scientific study that would prove conclusively that mental states have no influence on the creatures who have created that study and will assess it with mental states.

The plausible theory of mind that might support mental state explanations is thoroughly physical, but nonreductive and nondualist.[20] It hypothesizes that all mental and behavioral activity is the causal product of physical events in the brain, that mental states are real, that they are caused by lower-level biological processes in the brain, that they are realized in the brain—the mind-brain—but not at the level of neurons, and that mental states can be causally efficacious. It accepts that a fully causal story about behavior will be multifield and multilevel.

There is a plausible evolutionary story about why folk psychology is causally explanatory and why human beings need rules such as those provided by law. We have evolved to be self-conscious creatures that act for reasons and are responsive to reasons. Acting for reasons is inescapable for creatures like ourselves, who inevitably care about the ends we pursue. Because we are social, language-using creatures whose interactions are not governed primarily by innate repertoires, it is inevitable that rules will be necessary to help order our interactions in any minimally complex social group. Our ancestors would have been much less successful, and therefore much less likely to be our ancestors, if they had been unable to understand the intentions of others and to predict their behavior accordingly. Psychologists call this having a theory of mind, and people who do not adequately develop one experience profound difficulties in their interpersonal lives.

None of these considerations is an incontrovertible analytic argument against the VNC thesis, but surely the burden of persuasion is on those who argue to the contrary. At the very least, we remain entitled to presume that intentions are causal until the burden is met.

But let us suppose that we were convinced by the mechanistic view that we are not intentional, rational agents after all. (Of course, the notion of being "convinced" would be an illusion, too. Being convinced means that we are persuaded by evidence or argument, but a mechanism is not persuaded by anything. It is simply neurophysically transformed.) What should we do now? We know that it is an illusion to think that our deliberations and intentions have any causal efficacy in the world. We also know, however, that we experience sensations such as pleasure and pain and that we care about what happens to us and to the world. We cannot just sit quietly and wait for our brains to activate, for determinism to happen. We must, and will, of course, deliberate and act.

If we still thought that the VNC theory were correct and that standard notions of genuine moral responsibility and desert were therefore impossible, we might nevertheless continue to believe that the law would not necessarily have to give up the concept of incentives. Indeed, Greene and Cohen concede that we would have to keep punishing people for practical purposes. Such an account would be consistent with "black box" accounts of economic incentives that simply depend on the relation between inputs and outputs without considering the mind as a mediator between the two. For those who believe that a thoroughly naturalized account of human behavior entails complete consequentialism, such a conclusion might not be unwelcome.

On the other hand, this view seems to entail the same internal contradiction just explored. What is the nature of the "agent" that is discovering the laws governing how incentives shape behavior? Could understanding and providing incentives via social norms and legal rules simply be epiphenomenal interpretations of what the brain has already done? How do "we" "decide" which behaviors to reward or punish? What role does "reason"—a property of thoughts and agents, not a property of brains—play in this "decision"?

If the truth of pure mechanism is a premise in deciding what to do, this premise yields no particular moral, legal, or political conclusions. It will provide no guide as to how one should live or how one should respond to the idea that we are victims of neurological circumstances. Normativity depends on reason, and thus the VNC thesis is normatively inert. If reasons do not matter, then we have no reason to adopt any morals or politics, or any legal rule, or to do anything at all.

Given what we know and have reason to do, the allegedly disappearing person remains fully visible and necessarily continues to act for good reasons, including the reasons not yet to accept the VNC thesis. We are not Pinocchios, and our brains are not Gepettos pulling the strings.

In a world that accepts humans as victims of neurological circumstances, who knows what would happen to Collera? We would have no good, potentially action-guiding reason even to care. On the other hand, suppose it is true that we are incapable of not deliberating, no matter what we come to believe in theory. Perhaps the system will look not so different from the system we have today.

Do Liberty and Autonomy Hang by a Technological Thread?

The more plausible scenario is a world in which we continue to accept that agency is genuine, but in which the science of prediction and control has markedly advanced. This might realistically lead to alternative regimes based on prevention.

Our present scientific understanding of the causation of behavior and the ability to predict and control behavior are still quite limited, despite the vast increase in knowledge in recent decades. There are still good consequential reasons to limit a purely consequential response to potentially dangerous people: we will make many errors in prediction; we will intervene unnecessarily in many cases; and we often will not be able to fix the problems involved anyway.

If the power of science to predict and control human behavior becomes vastly more advanced than it currently is, however, that could change. Perfectly conscious, intentional, and rational behaviors, for which people can be held responsible, may nonetheless prove controllable and predictable. There is no inconsistency between predictability and control and responsibility. Consequently, we might well decide to move to a pure system of prediction and prevention for social control on consequential grounds. The lure of a safe, harmonious society might irresistibly cause us to abandon notions of guilt and innocence and instead simply to employ concepts like dangerousness and preventive intervention. Responsibility would not be rejected on conceptual grounds; it would simply be treated as normatively irrelevant because the attractions of social engineering were so great.

This system would differ vastly from current practices. Actually causing harm would not be necessary; it would simply be evidence of dangerousness, which we might be able to establish by other means. We would not require any showing that dangerousness resulted from lack of rational capacity. A therapeutic model of intervention would not be necessary, either. Predicted dangerousness from any cause would be a sufficient justification for the necessary intervention of any kind. Casting the whole scheme in the language of disorder and therapy might make it all seem more justifiable and less of an intrusion on liberty, but this would simply be a sleight of hand. Widespread screening to identify potentially dangerous people and involuntary intervention would be consistent with such a regime.

We might all be safer in such a world, but would we want to live in it? Would there be any limits on the state's power to predict and control for the good of us all? This is impossible to predict at present, but perhaps traditional notions of liberty and autonomy do hang by a technological thread.

There is a less dystopian version of this scenario, in which the concepts of responsibility and desert-disease jurisprudence are maintained, but dangerous persons in either the civil or criminal justice systems would not be punished but could become non-dangerous through therapeutic interventions. The term of incarceration would be only as long as necessary to change the agent to make him or her a safe member of a free society again. This sounds humane, and it would be vastly more protective of liberty and autonomy than the scheme just presented. Such a system would have problems of its own, however. It would undermine the deterrent value of the criminal law, especially if the interventions were effective, speedy, and not terribly painful or otherwise intrusive. The only reason not to offend would be the stigma of conviction and the inconvenience of the intervention, but these costs might be acceptable to many potential criminals. Moreover, what types of interventions would be acceptable, and should they be imposed against the will of the criminal? Over a half-century ago, C. S. Lewis warned against the "humanitarian theory of punishment" because it threatened dignity and respect for persons and could become the instrument of vast oppression.[21] Those concerns are no less valid today.

In our first hypothesized, prediction-prevention regime, we must assume that Collera's volatile aggressiveness would have been identified very early, perhaps even prenatally, and therapeutically transformed. In the second rehabilitative regime, the questions would be whether we could change him without his consent or how long could and would we incapacitate him for social safety. It is possible, however, that he would have been treated after he had committed his first assaultive crime and the subsequent homicide would never have occurred.

Conclusion

It is fun, I suppose, to speculate that neuroscience threatens a radical revision in our moral and legal doctrines and practices and, indeed, in our lives as a whole. Neuroscience poses no such threat at present, however, and it is unlikely ever to pose that threat unless it decisively resolves the mind-body problem. Until that happens, neuroscience might contribute to the reform of doctrines that do not accurately reflect truths about human behavior, to the resolution of individual cases, and to the efficient operation of various legal practices. If the power to predict and prevent dangerous behavior becomes sufficiently advanced, however, traditional notions of responsibility and guilt might simply become irrelevant.

Notes

1. Tiffany W. Chow and Jeffrey L. Cummings, "Frontal-Subcortical Circuits," in *The Human Frontal Lobes: Functions and Disorders,* edited by Bruce L. Miller and Jeffrey L. Cummings, 2d ed. (New York: Guilford Press, 2007), 25–43, 27–31. Damage to this region

is also associated with antisocial behavior. Steven W. Anderson and others, "Impairment of Social and Moral Behavior Related to Early Damage in Human Prefrontal Cortex," 2 *Nature Neuroscience* (1999): 1032; R. James Blair and Lisa Cipolotti, "Impaired Social Response Reversal: A Case of Acquired Sociopathy," 123 *Brain* (2000): 1122; Jeffrey L. Saver and Antonio R. Damasio, "Preserved Access and Processing of Social Knowledge in a Patient with Acquired Sociopathy Due to Ventromedial Frontal Damage," 29 *Neuropsychologia* (1991): 1241. I assume, however, that Collera is not obviously damaged.

2. Avshalom Caspi and others, "Role of Genotype in the Cycle of Violence in Maltreated Children," 297 *Science* (2002): 851–54.

3. Joshua Greene and Jonathan Cohen, "For the Law, the New Neuroscience Changes Nothing and Everything," in *Law and the Brain,* edited by Samir Zeki and Oliver Goodenough (Oxford University Press, 2006), 207–226, 217–18.

4. "The Ethics of Brain Science: Open Your Mind," *The Economist,* May 25, 2002, 77.

5. Stephen J. Morse, "Neither Desert Nor Disease," 5 *Legal Theory* (1999): 265, 267–70.

6. Stephen J. Morse, "Lost in Translation? An Essay on Law and Neuroscience," in *Law and Neuroscience,* edited by Michael Freeman (Oxford University Press, 2011), 529–62.

7. Stephen J. Morse, "Uncontrollable Urges and Irrational People," 88 *Virginia Law Review* (2002): 1025.

8. M. R. Bennett and P. M. S. Hacker, *Philosophical Foundations of Neuroscience* (Malden, Mass.: Blackwell, 2003); Michael Pardo and Dennis Patterson, "Philosophical Foundations of Neuroscience," *University of Illinois Law Review* (2010): 1211.

9. Gregory A. Miller, "Mistreating Psychology in the Decades of the Brain," 5 *Perspectives on Psychological Science* (2010): 716.

10. Stephen J. Morse, "The Non-Problem of Free Will in Forensic Psychiatry and Psychology," 25 *Behavioral Science and Law* (2007): 203.

11. Robert Kane, *A Contemporary Introduction to Free Will* (Oxford University Press, 2005), 12–22.

12. Greene and Cohen, "For the Law, the New Neuroscience Changes Nothing and Everything," 217–18 (emphasis in original).

13. Daniel Wegner, *The Illusion of Conscious Will* (MIT Press, 2002).

14. John Tierney, "The Voices in My Head Say 'Buy It!' Why Argue?" *New York Times,* January 16, 2007, F1.

15. Paul R. McHugh and Philip R. Slavney, *The Perspectives of Psychiatry,* 2d. ed. (Johns Hopkins University Press, 1998), 11–12.

16. Carl Craver, *Explaining the Brain: Mechanisms and the Mosaic Unity of Neuroscience* (Oxford: Clarendon Press; New York: Oxford University Press, 2007); Alva Noe, *Out of Our Heads: Why You Are Not Your Brain and Other Lessons from the Biology of Consciousness* (New York: Hill and Wang, 2009).

17. Stephen J. Morse, "Determinism and the Death of Folk Psychology: Two Challenges to Responsibility from Neuroscience," 9 *Minnesota Journal of Law, Science, and Technology* (2008): 1.

18. Michael S. Moore, "Libet's Challenges to Responsible Human Agency," in *Conscious Will and Responsibility: A Tribute to Benjamin Libet,* edited by Walter Sinnott-Armstrong and Lynn Nadel (Oxford University Press, 2011), chap. 18; Alfred Mele, *Effective Intentions: The Power of the Conscious Will* (Oxford University Press, 2009).

19. Morse, "Lost in Translation? An Essay on Law and Neuroscience."

20. For example, John R. Searle, *Mind: A Brief Introduction* (Oxford University Press, 2004), 113–14.

21. C. S. Lewis, "The Humanitarian Theory of Punishment," 6 *Res Judicatae* (1953): 224.

O. CARTER SNEAD

9

Cognitive Neuroscience
and the Future of Punishment

The jurors filed into the courtroom and took their seats in the jury box. It had been a long and emotionally draining couple of weeks. The guilt phase of the trial was relatively short—there was no real question of fact as to whether the defendant had murdered the two victims. The main contested questions—the defendant's legal competence, sanity, and capacity to formulate the requisite mens rea for first-degree murder—were also not terribly difficult to decide. Though clearly emotionally troubled and probably even mentally ill, the defendant easily met the (surprisingly low) cognitive and volitional standards for guilt. He knew what he was doing and appreciated that it was wrongful. He acted with malice aforethought. He could understand the charges against him and assist in his own defense. These were not hard questions.

The sentencing phase of the trial, by contrast, had proved far more difficult. The prosecutor had described in excruciating detail the murders themselves in an effort to show that they were especially "heinous, atrocious, and cruel, manifesting exceptional depravity." The prosecutor and counsel for the defense each recounted the details of the defendant's life and character. His broken childhood, marked by unspeakable abuse and neglect. His years of drug and alcohol use. His spotty and unstable employment history. His history of using violence to impose his will and pursue his interests. They even discussed the structure and function of his brain—with reference to an array of colorful poster board–sized images—showing diminished activity in the prefrontal cortex (the seat of reasoning, self-restraint, long-term planning) and above-average activity in his limbic system (the more primitive part of his brain, associated with fear and aggression). Relying on a raft of neuroimaging studies, the prosecutor argued that the pattern of activation and structural abnormalities in the defendant's brain were consistent with "low arousal, poor fear conditioning, lack of conscience, and decision-making deficits that have been found to characterize antisocial, psychopathic behavior." He further argued that this was not a temporary condition—it was permanent and unlikely to be correctable by any known therapeutic intervention. The prosecutor argued that, taken together, this was the profile of an incorrigible criminal who would certainly kill again if given the chance. The defense argued, to the contrary, that the evidence did not point to any tangible future risk of violence.

The judge then explained to the jurors that they must decide unanimously what punishment was fitting for the crime of conviction: life without parole or a sentence of death. Among other things, the judge explained that "before the death penalty can be considered, the state must prove at least one statutorily defined aggravating circumstance beyond a reasonable doubt" and that the aggravating factors outweigh all of the mitigating factors. He described mitigating factors as "any fact or circumstance, relating to the crime or to the defendant's state of mind or condition at the time of the crime, or to his character, background or record, that tends to suggest that a sentence other than death should be imposed."

The judge looked up from his jury instructions and turned toward the jury box.

Ladies and gentlemen, let me add a word of caution regarding your judgment about mitigating factors. Some of you may be tempted to ask yourselves, "Was it really the defendant that did this? Or was it his background? Or his brain?" You might be tempted to ask yourselves, "What does this defendant deserve in light of his character, biology, and circumstances?" Some of you might even be tempted to argue to your fellow jurors that "this man does not deserve the ultimate punishment in light of his diminished, though non-excusing, capacity to act responsibly borne from a bad past and a bad brain"; in other words, you might conclude that capital punishment in this case is disproportionate to the defendant's moral culpability.

The judge's eyes narrowed and he leaned even farther forward.

But, ladies and gentlemen of the jury, you must not ask such questions or entertain such ideas. The sole question before you, as a matter of law, is much narrower. The only question you are to answer is this: is this defendant likely to present a future danger to others or society? You should treat every fact that suggests that he does present such a danger as an aggravating factor; every fact suggesting the contrary is a mitigating factor. Matters of desert, retributive justice, or proportionality in light of moral culpability are immaterial to your decision. Ladies and gentlemen, this is the year 2040. Cognitive neuroscientists have long ago shown that moral responsibility, blameworthiness, and the like are unintelligible concepts that depend on an intuitive, libertarian notion of free will that is undermined by science. Such notions are, in the words of two of the most influential early proponents of this new approach to punishment, illusions generated by our cognitive architecture. We have integrated this insight into our criminal law. Punishment is not for meting out just deserts based on the fiction of moral responsibility. It is simply an instrument for promoting future social welfare. We impose punishment solely to prevent future crime. And this change has been for the better. As another pioneer of the revolution in punishment—himself an eminent cognitive neuroscientist—wisely wrote at the beginning of the twenty-first century, "Although it may seem dehumanizing to medicalize people into being broken cars, it can still be vastly more humane than moralizing them into being sinners."[1] So, please, ladies and gentlemen of the jury. Keep your eye on the ball, and do not indulge any of the old and discredited notions about retributive justice.

With that, the judge adjourned and dismissed the jury so that it could begin its deliberations.

The above hypothetical is obviously fanciful. But it borrows concepts and arguments directly from a current debate that has been unfolding alongside the advent of extraordinary advances in cognitive neuroscience (particularly as augmented by revolutionary imaging technology that affords novel ways to examine the structure and function of the brain). Such advances have breathed new life into very old arguments about human agency, moral responsibility, and the proper ends of criminal punishment. A prominent group of cognitive neuroscientists, joined by sympathetic philosophers, lawyers, and social scientists, have drawn on the tools of their discipline in an effort to embarrass, discredit, and ultimately overthrow retribution as a distributive justification for punishment. The architects of this cognitive neuroscience project regard retribution as the root cause of the brutality and inhumanity of the American criminal justice system, generally, and the institution of capital punishment, in particular. To replace retribution, they argue for the adoption of a criminal law regime animated solely by the forward-looking (consequentialist) aim of avoiding social harms. This new framework, they hope, will usher in a new era of what some have referred to as "therapeutic justice" for criminal defendants, which is meant to be both more humane and more compassionate.[2]

To be sure, not all cognitive neuroscientists subscribe to this program. Indeed, there are many thoughtful voices who raise opposition to this project on various grounds—some prudential and some principled. Whatever one thinks about the cognitive neuroscience project for criminal punishment, however, it deserves to be taken seriously, and its arguments should be followed to their ultimate conclusions. This is my aim in the present chapter. In it, I discuss the contours of the project and explore the radical conceptual challenge that it poses for criminal punishment in America. I also offer a critique of the project, arguing that jettisoning the notion of retributive justice in criminal punishment will not lead to a more humane legal regime as supporters of the project hope. Rather, by untethering punishment from moral culpability and focusing entirely on the prediction and prevention of socially harmful behavior, the cognitive neuroscience project eliminates the last refuge of defendants who are legally and factually guilty but are deemed to have diminished culpability owing to some aspect of their character, background, or biology. Indeed, viewed through the lens urged by the cognitive neuroscience project, the only relevance of a nonexcusing disposition to criminal behavior is as a justification for incapacitation. The logic of the cognitive neuroscience project could even lead to the embrace of more aggressive use of preventive detention as a solution for categories of criminals that inspire special fears in the polity—including sexual predators and terrorists.

The techniques of cognitive neuroscience are not yet sufficiently developed to support its aspirations. They may never be. But it is always wise to examine the consequences of a nascent moral-technological program before it is upon us and in widespread use. My purpose in this chapter is to take seriously the claims of the cognitive neuroscience project so that we may be clear eyed about its consequences before we consider embracing it.

Cognitive Neuroscience: Premises and Methods

Cognitive neuroscience seeks to understand how human sensory systems, motor systems, attention, memory, language, higher cognitive functions, emotions, and even consciousness arise from the structure and function of the brain. According to Francis Crick, "The overwhelming question in neurobiology" is "the relation between the mind and the brain."[3] Cognitive neuroscience has been described as a "bridging discipline"[4]—between biology and neuroscience, on the one hand, and cognitive science and psychology, on the other.

The focus of cognitive neuroscience has expanded from an inquiry into basic sensorimotor and cognitive processes to the exploration of more highly complex behaviors. Over the past decade, with the aid of neuroimaging, scientists have increasingly turned their attention to the neurobiological correlates of behavior and to the links between their science and vexing matters of public policy. Their efforts are motivated largely by the view, shared by many in the field, that "as we understand more about the details of the regulatory systems in the brain and how decisions emerge in neural networks, it is increasingly evident that moral standards, practices, and policies reside in our neurobiology."[5] Neuroscientists have explored matters relevant to the criminal justice context, including the detection of deception and the roots of both impulsive and premeditated criminal violence.

The foundational premise of cognitive neuroscience is that all aspects of the mind are ultimately reducible to the structure and function of the brain. As Joshua Greene and Jonathan Cohen have described it, cognitive neuroscience is the "understanding of the mind *as* brain."[6] Thus cognitive neuroscience seeks to provide "comprehensive explanations of human behavior in purely material terms."[7] Like other disciplines within the modern life and physical sciences, cognitive neuroscience is committed to the premise of physicalism, which the philosopher of science Alex Rosenberg defines as "the assumption that there is only one kind of stuff, substance, or thing in the universe, from matter, material substance, and physical objects all the way down to quarks."[8] Also like other disciplines within modern science, cognitive neuroscience operates by way of reduction. That is, its chief explanatory aspiration is to explicate complex matters in the most simple and elemental terms. It seeks to explain the macrophenomena of thought and action solely in terms of the microphenomena of the physical brain.[9] Combining the axioms of physicalism and reductionism in this way compels a methodological commitment to mechanism, namely, the evaluation and explanation of natural phenomena in terms of the structure, actions, and interactions of their most basic physical parts. Thus cognitive neuroscience follows the dominant approach of modern science, namely reductive mechanism. It proceeds according to the postulate that human thought and behavior are caused solely by physical processes taking place inside the brain—a three-pound bodily organ of staggering complexity, but a bodily organ nonetheless. It seeks explanations within this framework.[10]

Neuroimaging: The Indispensible Tool of Cognitive Neuroscience

Developments in neuroimaging have affected the law both directly and indirectly. The indirect developments are visible in the great deal of discussion that has occurred about speculative applications of nascent technological innovations. The direct impact has occurred where neuroimaging evidence has been introduced in courtrooms and has led to the creation of a body of decisional law that has shaped the legal landscape in this domain.

Henry Greely has provided an excellent account of the speculative uses of neuroimaging in the legal context. He suggests that such technology might eventually be used in the courtroom to detect lies or to compel truth, to determine bias on the part of jurors, witnesses, or parties, to elicit or evaluate memory, to determine competency (to stand trial, to be executed, or to make medical decisions), to prove the presence of intractable pain, to prove addiction or susceptibility thereto, to show a disposition to sexual deviance or predatory impulses (for purposes of involuntary civil commitment), or to show future dangerousness.[11]

As for actual applications, neuroimaging evidence has been proffered and admitted in a variety of jurisdictions, in both civil and criminal cases and for a variety of purposes. In the civil context, neuroimaging has been proffered and admitted to prove actual harm (and, to a lesser extent, causation) in personal injury cases involving toxic exposure, claims under the National Vaccine Act, head injuries, and medical malpractice. In contract disputes, neuroimaging has been admitted—and has been found persuasive by fact finders—to show that one of the parties lacked sufficient cognitive capacity to form a valid contract.

In the criminal context, defendants have proffered neuroimaging evidence at various stages of the process for a variety of purposes. For instance, courts have admitted neuroimaging evidence (or have held that a defendant was entitled to undergo neuroimaging tests) in connection with claims of mental incompetence. Defendants have had mixed success in seeking to admit neuroimaging evidence to show diminished capacity (the inability to formulate requisite mens rea) at the guilt phase of criminal trials or as an adjunct to their insanity defenses. The most famous example of the use of neuroimaging in an insanity defense is the case of John Hinckley Jr., who attempted to assassinate President Ronald Reagan in 1981. There, the court admitted a computed tomography (CT) scan to show that Hinckley's brain had atrophied, which the defense argued—over the vigorous argument of the government's expert—was evidence of organic brain disease.

Defendants have enjoyed the greatest success with neuroimaging evidence at the sentencing phase of capital trials in connection with mitigation claims. In support of these claims, experts have invoked cutting-edge neuroimaging research on the biological correlates of criminal violence.

The Cognitive Neuroscience of Criminal Violence

The foundation for many uses of neuroimaging evidence in criminal trials lies in a massive and growing body of scientific literature on both the neuroanatomical and neurochemical bases for the various types of violence. In 1998 and 1999, an interdisciplinary group of experts was convened under the auspices of the Aspen Neurobehavioral Conference to create a consensus statement on the relationship between the mind, the brain, and violence. To this end, they conducted an exhaustive literature survey of the role of the brain in violent behavior and issued a statement in 2001 noting that the limbic system and the frontal lobes "are thought to play preeminent roles in [violent] behavior." The statement asserts that

> aggressive behavior has been thought to arise from the operations of the limbic system under certain circumstances, and the amygdala is the structure most often implicated. . . . Prefrontal functions may . . . provide an individual with the capacity to exercise judgment in the setting of complex social situations in which actions have significant consequences. In many cases, this capacity for judgment may serve the important function of inhibiting limbic impulses, which, if acted on, could be socially inappropriate or destructive. . . . Therefore, there exists a balance between the potential for impulsive aggression mediated by temporolimbic structures and the control of this drive by the influence of the orbitofrontal regions.[12]

This theory of violence was informed, and has been reinforced, by neuroimaging studies. In addition to the iconic case of Phineas Gage, the nineteenth-century railroad worker whose personality was altered after an accident drove an iron rod into his head, there are striking modern examples of the relationship between frontal lobe injuries (or dysfunction) and a disposition to criminal violence. For example, following a concussive injury to his prefrontal cortex, Louis Culpepper was no longer able to restrain his impulses to molest his five-year-old stepdaughter. In a similar case, following the development of an egg-sized tumor in his prefrontal lobe, a school teacher with no criminal record and a stable marriage found himself unable to restrain his impulses to view child pornography, solicit sex, and make sexual overtures to his stepdaughter. Once the tumor was removed, his inhibitions and capacity for self-restraint were restored. A more recent example is Andrew Laing, who lost all sexual inhibitions and sense of propriety following a concussive injury to his prefrontal lobe in a skiing accident.

Many other prominent neuroscientists have similarly undertaken inquiries using neuroimaging tools to explore the potential connection between brain abnormalities and violence. By linking brain abnormalities to specific behaviors—and, specifically, to violent behavior—these studies provide a foundation for the use of neuroimaging evidence in criminal trials.

The Cognitive Neuroscience Project for Punishment

Over the past decade, certain eminent cognitive neuroscientists (along with sympathetic philosophers, social scientists, and lawyers) have argued for a radical conceptual revision of criminal punishment. More specifically, by using the premises and tools of neuroscience—and neuroimaging, in particular—they aim to embarrass, undermine, and ultimately overthrow retributive justice as a principle of punishment. Once retribution is discredited, they contend, criminal law will be animated solely by its proper end: namely, the purely forward-looking, consequentialist goal of avoiding socially harmful behavior. This new approach, it is hoped, will usher in a regime of therapeutic justice wherein criminal defendants will be treated more humanely.

The most comprehensive articulation and defense of this long-term aspiration for criminal punishment reform was advanced in two papers published in 2004—one by Joshua Greene, a Harvard philosopher, and Jonathan Cohen, a Princeton neuroscientist, and the other by Robert Sapolsky, a Stanford neuroscientist. As Green and Cohen write,

> Our penal system is highly counterproductive from a consequentialist perspective . . . and yet it remains in place because retributivist principles have a powerful moral and political appeal. It is possible, however, that neuroscience will change these moral intuitions by undermining the intuitive, libertarian conceptions of free will upon which retributivism depends. . . . At this time, the law deals firmly but mercifully with individuals whose behavior is obviously the product of forces beyond their control. Some day, the law may treat all convicted criminals this way. That is, humanely.[13]

Greene and Cohen argue that advances in cognitive neuroscience—enabled by neuroimaging—will ultimately demonstrate that "ordinary conceptions of human action and responsibility" are false. "As a result, the legal principles we have devised to reflect these conceptions may be flawed" and must be radically overhauled and replaced with principles that are grounded in a neuroscientific view of the truth about free will and human agency (1775). The primary focus of their critique is the principle of retributive justice—which, they assert, "depends on an intuitive, libertarian notion of free will that is undermined by science" (1776).

In defense of this thesis, the authors first reprise the familiar dichotomy of consequentialism ("which emerges from the classical utilitarian tradition" [1776]) and retribution as both the general and distributive justifications for criminal punishment. They define *consequentialism* as a doctrine that regards punishment as "merely an instrument for promoting future social welfare" (1775) and that seeks to prevent "future crime through the deterrent effect of the law and the containment of dangerous individuals" (1776). By contrast, they define *retribution* as the principle that "in the absence of mitigating circumstances, people who engage in criminal behaviour *deserve* to be punished" (1776, emphasis added).

They then turn to the ancient debate over the nature and intelligibility of free will. They articulate a tripartite typology of positions on the issue: hard determinism, libertarianism, and compatibilism. *Hard determinism,* as the name implies, rejects the concept of free will. It holds that the notion of free will is fundamentally incompatible with the premise that all human action can be sufficiently explained by material causes that are necessarily bound by the laws of physics and previous events. *Libertarianism,* as characterized by Greene and Cohen, accepts the claim that free will and determinism are incompatible but nevertheless concludes that the world is not, in fact, completely determined by the laws governing the motion and rest of matter. In contrast, *compatibilism* holds that material determinism and free will are reconcilable, though compatibilism's conception of free will is more metaphysically modest than that of libertarianism.

Insofar as advances in neuroscience have begun to reveal the purely material causes of human thought and choice, Greene and Cohen suggest, they have also begun to undermine the fundamental tenets of libertarianism and thus retributive punishment. Libertarianism supplies the strong conception of free will, and thus moral responsibility, on which the doctrine of retribution relies. The authors argue, however, that the strength of the concept of free will posited by libertarianism arises from its claim to operate through a nonmaterial mechanism—a proposition increasingly at odds with modern science. Ultimately, they contend, neuroimaging will entirely undermine the antimaterialist foundations of the libertarian position on free will, thus removing the grounding necessary for just deserts. Moreover, it is evident that retributive justice is conceptually irreconcilable with hard determinism: if all actions are sufficiently determined by material causes to be beyond anyone's control, the notions of culpability and just deserts on which retribution depends are unintelligible.

Greene and Cohen additionally assert that compatibilism's modest account of free will is not sufficiently robust to support the exacting demands of retribution, either as a general aim or as a distributive principle. They describe a compatibilist vision of free will, one that defines free will as the minimal capacity for rational action—namely, the ability to produce "behaviour that serves [one's] desires in light of [one's] beliefs" (1778). Stephen Morse has eloquently argued that the law is constructed with this minimalist conception of free will in mind. Law, Morse maintains, is compatibilist and thus is not threatened by any proof of determinism that neuroimaging may eventually offer. In support of his claim, Morse points to the criminal law, which refuses to excuse from guilt those defendants who are laboring under a defect of mind, so long as they satisfy a minimal cognitive and volitional threshold. Greene and Cohen respond that while the law may formally focus on the question of minimal rationality, what people in society really care about is whether the defendant is responsible in a richer sense—one rooted in libertarian conceptions of free will. That is, even if the defendant is shown to be minimally rational in a legal sense, citizens will still ask whether it was "really him" who committed the crime, or whether it was "his upbringing," "his genes," "his circumstances," or "his brain" that were truly responsible. These questions, Greene and Cohen argue, arise from a libertarian vision of free will that does not accept the materialist determinism of Morse's compatibilism but rather is animated by a dualist premise that the brain and the mind are distinct (though interacting) entities. Thus while the law as written may be (as Morse contends) formally compatibilist, it is actually driven by the libertarian moral intuitions of the citizens who implement it.

Greene and Cohen characterize this tension between the law's formal requirements and society's richer conception of free will as an unstable marriage of convenience. They predict that neuroimaging will force a crisis in this union: cognitive neuroscience (aided by neuroimaging) will ultimately show that there is no difference between "him" and "his brain," thus proving that the foundations of the libertarian dualist intuitions about human agency are untenable. This forms the basis for their belief that Morse underestimates the transformative power of neuroimaging on the law and especially on criminal punishment.

It is far beyond the scope of this chapter to try to resolve this rich and vexed dispute about the future impact of neuroimaging on the law as a whole. Nevertheless, it is necessary to briefly reflect on how this debate plays out in the context of capital sentencing. Morse is certainly correct that the legal standard for diminished capacity for the purpose of determining legal guilt is modest; defendants rightly can be characterized as needing only "minimal rationality" to be held fully accountable for their actions. This is borne out by the small percentage of cases in which defendants raise the defense of legal insanity and the even smaller portion of cases in which such a defense succeeds. But in the context of capital sentencing, which is animated by a particularly rich and textured conception of moral responsibility, Greene and Cohen's analysis is especially accurate. The Supreme Court has construed the Constitution to require the consideration of all mitigating factors relevant to a criminal defendant's culpability in meting out capital punishment. The very doctrine of mitigation is driven by questions like those that Greene and Cohen argue society "really" cares about, such as was it "him," or his brain, or his upbringing, or his circumstances? Morse is right that these questions do not currently bear on legal guilt, but they do bear significantly on the kind of punishment imposed on the legally guilty. So it would seem that capital sentencing is largely driven by a metaphysically ambitious conception of human agency—one that is at odds with the conception that animates our determinations of guilt and innocence.

According to Greene and Cohen, only libertarian incompatibilism can provide adequate support to the principle of retributive justice. And they predict—indeed, they hope—that cognitive neuroscience will shatter this foundation. They note that while philosophical arguments against free will have not proved persuasive to the general population, science supported by neuroimaging will succeed where philosophy has failed:

> Arguments are nice, but physical demonstrations are far more compelling. What neuroscience does, and will continue to do at an accelerated pace, is elucidate the "when," "where" and "how" of the mechanical processes that cause behavior. It is one thing to deny that human decision-making is purely mechanical when your opponent offers only a general, philosophical argument. It is quite another to hold your ground when your opponent can make detailed predictions about how these mechanical processes work, complete with images of the brain structures involved and equations that describe their function.[14]

Greene and Cohen argue that when and if the notion of human agency is shown to be illusory, societal attitudes may well change. Eventually, the law of punishment will have to follow suit and reflect the newly revealed truths about free will. In other words, once society internalizes the lessons of cognitive neuroscience as they bear on moral (and thus criminal) responsibility, retribution—relying as it does on a false understanding of human agency—will be eliminated as a legitimate general or distributive justification for punishment.

The authors consider this salutary and desirable. They assert that retributivism is largely responsible for the counterproductive state of the American penal system and advance consequentialism as the sole legitimate justification for punishment. Without free will—and hence, without retribution—punishment can be fashioned solely with the future benefits to society in mind. Criminal offenders can still be held responsible for their actions, but without the moral stigma and judgment that retributive justice implies. Sentencing can promote beneficial effects for society by deterring future harms and incapacitating only those who would visit such harms on the polity. Greene and Cohen's aspirational framework preserves excuse defenses (such as insanity and duress) for those cases in which it can be shown that the deterrence of such offenders would not be effective. But retribution would be laid to rest forever as a pernicious fiction.

They are not alone. Robert Sapolsky notes that "at a logical extreme, a neurobiological framework may indeed eliminate blame" but adds that the institution of criminal punishment is still necessary for the purpose of protecting society from future harms. Sapolsky echoes (in a fashion) Greene and Cohen: "To understand is not to forgive or to do nothing; whereas you do not ponder whether to forgive a car that, because of problems with its brakes, has injured someone, you nevertheless protect society from it."[15] Sapolsky shares Greene and Cohen's desire to shed a framework that implicitly regards criminal defendants as morally blameworthy, preferring a consequentialist system even though it adopts an arguably diminished understanding of human personhood.

The long-term goal of many practitioners of neuroimaging is very much in the spirit of late-eighteenth-century thinkers such as Jeremy Bentham and Cesare, Marquis of Beccaria, who regarded punishment of the guilty as justified only insofar as it was instrumental to the protection of society and promoting human happiness. As George Fletcher has observed, under their utilitarian approach, "No form of punishment could be justified unless it was the cheapest available means for serving these social ends."[16]

The long-term aim also mirrors, in many respects, the work of Barbara Wootton, Baroness of Abinger. Lady Wootton, a twentieth-century criminologist, rejected the notion of criminal punishment altogether, arguing instead that the only intelligible goal for the criminal law is to be a "system of purely forward-looking social hygiene in which our only concern when we have an offender to deal with is with the future and the rational aim of prevention of further crime."[17] This view led Wootton to argue for a complete abandonment

of mens rea as an element of guilt in favor of a system of strict criminal liability. She believed that a person's intentions at the time of a crime are not
knowable and, indeed, not relevant to the question of guilt. A defendant's
mental state, to Wootton, would only be relevant as a predictive instrument
to be used in preventing the same defendant from offending in the future.
Under her approach, the state would take custody of an offender upon his
conviction for a criminal act and give him medical treatment or incarcerate
him. Wootton's approach blurs the distinction between prisons and hospitals:
Both are "places of safety" where "offenders will receive the treatment which
experience suggest[s] is most likely to evoke the desired response" of preventing future crime. Wootton's framework thus explicitly and intentionally
conflates punishment with therapy.

It is worth noting that while Greene and Cohen fundamentally share with
Wootton the same view of the aims of criminal law, they have opposite views
on whether the reasons for antisocial choices can be known. Wootton regards
such reasons as unknowable, whereas Greene and Cohen are confident that
someday they will become discernible through neuroimaging.

The Consequences: The End of Mitigation and Punishment as Prevention

The first consequence of the cognitive neuroscience project is the elimination
of the doctrine of mitigation as traditionally understood. Mitigation involves
the presentation of evidence regarding the character, background, or other
pertinent features of an already convicted defendant that might convince the
jury that the defendant's degree of culpability merits life imprisonment rather
than death. However, defendants who reach the sentencing phase have, by
necessity, already satisfied the prerequisite legal thresholds for sanity, competence, and the capacity to formulate the relevant mens rea. At this stage of the
criminal process, therefore, "it is impossible to offer an 'excuse' for the defendant's acts. The jury already knows that no justifiable excuse exists for what
the defendant did."[18] Mitigation evidence is presented in order to "[inspire]
compassion . . . offer[ing] neither justification, nor excuse for the capital
crime."[19] A mitigation claim is thus a plea for leniency in spite of a prior finding of legal guilt.

There are many ways in which capital defendants and the experts working
on their behalf seek to move jurors toward leniency. One of the most frequent
strategies is to introduce evidence that the defendant was laboring under a
mental disturbance or incapacity that, while not an excuse for purposes of
guilt, should nevertheless reduce his culpability.

This strategy, however, is squarely rooted in a distributive theory of punishment that proponents of the cognitive neuroscience project explicitly repudiate as a principal source of the irrationality and brutality that plague the current system. Paul Robinson has called this theory "punishment according to desert," as it is an approach that distributes punishment "according to the offender's personal blameworthiness for the past offense, which takes account not only of the seriousness of the offense, but also the full range of culpability, capacity, and situational factors that we understand to affect an offender's blameworthiness."[20] The Supreme Court's death penalty jurisprudence confirms that the concept of mitigation grows directly out of the requirements of retributive justice:

> Underlying [the Supreme Court precedents bearing on the doctrine of mitigation] is the principle that punishment should be directly related to the personal culpability of the criminal defendant. If the sentencer is to make an individualized assessment of the appropriateness of the death penalty, "evidence about the defendant's background and character is relevant because of the belief, long held by this society, that defendants who commit criminal acts that are attributable to a disadvantaged background, or to emotional and mental problems, may be less culpable than defendants who have no such excuse."[21]

For purposes of capital mitigation, defendants increasingly invoke cognitive neuroscience evidence to advance the claim that the defendant "is a human being with redeeming value, and that he or she suffered . . . neurological . . . damage . . . that make[s] him or her less than 100 percent morally culpable for his or her behavior."[22] But this approach trades on the very dichotomy of "him" versus "his brain" that notions of just deserts invite—one that proponents of the long-term aspiration deplore as unintelligible. This claim indulges precisely the same principle of punishment that the cognitive neuroscience project rules out of bounds.

The cognitive neuroscience project would thus preclude the introduction of mitigation evidence that bears on diminished culpability. It would leave in place only those mechanisms that promote the avoidance of crime. The mechanisms of capital sentencing best suited to this end are those that are calibrated to predict the social harms to be contained or avoided. As John Monahan has observed, "Assessing the likelihood of future crime . . . is a central task of sentencing under the forward-looking principle of crime control."[23] By contrast, such considerations are "jurisprudentially irrelevant to sentencing under the backward-looking principle of punishment [according to] just deserts."[24] Nothing in capital sentencing embodies the purely consequentialist spirit of the long-term cognitive neuroscience project as much as the aggravating factor of future dangerousness. To fully appreciate the impact that the long-term plan would like to have on capital sentencing, it is thus necessary to explore briefly the nature and contours of this element of death penalty jurisprudence.

Future dangerousness is a commonly invoked aggravating factor in capital sentencing. Prosecutors seeking the death penalty bear the burden of persuading jurors beyond a reasonable doubt that at least one aggravating factor exists to make the defendant eligible for the death penalty. As one capital defense expert puts it, this is the stage of the trial where the government "suggest[s] to the jury that the defendant is a living hazard to civilization and a menacing threat to society."[25] To this end, prosecutors often submit the testimony of experts or laypersons regarding a defendant's future dangerousness or simply argue it themselves based on a variety of evidence. In those jurisdictions that prohibit the state from submitting an expert prediction of violence, prosecutors often try to establish future dangerousness through cross-examination of the defense's mitigation experts. Sometimes, prosecutors will try to turn the defendant's own mitigation claims against him, arguing that evidence of a violent disposition borne of abuse or a personality disorder is, in fact, demonstrative of future dangerousness.

Because the rules of evidence that govern criminal trials often do not apply to capital sentencing hearings, courts have wide latitude in deciding whether to admit evidence of future dangerousness at such proceedings. Thus actuarial and clinical evidence of future dangerousness has been admitted in jurisdictions following both the *Daubert* and *Frye* standards, and clinicians have been permitted to testify even where they have not examined the defendant.[26] David Faigman, an expert on the use and admissibility of scientific evidence in court, has observed that "most courts either entirely ignore evidentiary standards for expert testimony concerning future violence, or give it scant attention."[27]

Prosecutors regularly invoke diagnoses of psychopathy or antisocial personality disorder in capital sentencing, likely because both are highly correlated with recidivist violence. Courts have specifically permitted both diagnoses to be introduced as evidence of future dangerousness at the sentencing phase of capital trials. This has proved to be a highly effective strategy for prosecutors given that the diagnostic criteria for each condition sound to the lay juror essentially like a straightforward description of "irreparable corruption" (to borrow Justice Kennedy's phrase from *Roper*). More important, courts do not regard either psychopathy or antisocial personality disorder as an excusing condition for guilt or incompetence; neither is thought to sufficiently diminish the defendant's cognitive or volitional capacity for those purposes. Thus either diagnosis can have a devastating effect on the defendant's mitigation claims and can also create an expectation in jurors' minds "that no rehabilitation is possible and that future criminal violence is inevitable."[28]

The diagnoses of antisocial personality disorder and psychopathy have played a prominent role as aggravating factors in the capital context. Dr. James Grigson, an iconic and notorious figure in the jurisprudence of future dangerousness, serves as an extreme but illustrative example of how government experts sometimes wield their power to make these diagnoses. In more than 140 cases, Dr. Grigson (often without ever having examined the defendant) testified to the effect that the defendant "has a severe antisocial personality disorder and is extremely dangerous and will commit future acts of violence."[29] In the seminal case of *Barefoot* v. *Estelle*, Grigson testified with *"reasonable psychiatric certainty"* that Barefoot fell in the "most severe category" of sociopaths and that Barefoot would, with *"one hundred percent and absolute"* certainty, commit future criminal acts, constituting a continuing threat to society.[30] Prosecutors often reprise these arguments directly or raise them in response to mitigation claims of nondangerousness, in those few jurisdictions that prohibit the prediction of dangerousness in the prosecution's aggravation case in chief.

Studies have shown that capital juries often regard evidence of future dangerousness as the most important aggravating factor in their sentencing calculus. Indeed, two commentators have noted that "future dangerousness takes precedence in jury deliberations over any mitigating evidence, such as remorse, mental illness, intelligence, or drug/alcohol addiction, and any concern about the defendant's behavior in prison."[31] In fact, it has been observed that even in those jurisdictions that do not explicitly direct the capital jury to consider future dangerousness as an aggravating factor, jurors do so anyway.

As Paul Robinson has observed, within the context of sentencing, desert and dangerousness inevitably conflict as distributive criteria: "To advance one, the system must sacrifice the other. The irreconcilable differences reflect the fact that prevention and desert seek to achieve different goals. Incapacitation concerns itself with the future—avoiding future crimes. Desert concerns itself with the past—allocating punishment for past offenses."[32] The thrust-and-parry of this conflict is played out in dramatic fashion in the capital context. On one hand, capital defendants introduce mitigating evidence to diminish their moral culpability, thus seeking a final refuge in the concept of retribution. On the other, the prosecution tenders evidence of future dangerousness, trying to stoke the consequentialist fears of the jury about violent acts that the defendant might commit if he is not permanently incapacitated by execution. In capital sentencing, pure consequentialism is the gravest threat to the defendant's life, while appeals to retributive justice are often his last, and best, hope.

The cognitive neuroscience project decisively resolves this conflict between desert and crime control in favor of the latter by removing any consideration of diminished culpability. In so doing, the project eliminates the last safe haven for a capital defendant whose sanity, capacity for the requisite mens rea, competence, and guilt are no longer at issue. Thus in a final ironic twist, once retribution is replaced with a regime single-mindedly concerned with the prediction of crime and the incapacitation of criminals, the only possible use in capital sentencing of the neuroimaging research on the roots of criminal violence is to demonstrate the aggravating factor of future dangerousness.

Imagine for a moment how a jury concerned solely with avoiding future harms would regard a functional magnetic resonance imaging (fMRI) or positron emission tomography (PET) scan that purported to show the bio-logical causes of a nonexcusing disposition to criminal violence. Most likely, neuroimaging would radically amplify, in the minds of jurors, the aggravat-ing effect of a diagnosis of antisocial personality disorder or psychopathy. In a sentencing system that focused the jury's deliberation solely on the question of identifying and preventing crime, the work of the cognitive neuroscience project's architects would be transformed from a vehicle for seeking mercy into a tool that counsels the imposition of death.

It is only through the lens of just deserts that such evidence could possi-bly be regarded as mitigating. This conclusion is bolstered by capital defense experts who have observed that "evidence of neurological impairment . . . can be devastatingly damaging to the case for life. In presenting such evi-dence to a jury, counsel must be careful to avoid creating the impression that the defendant is 'damaged goods' and beyond repair."[33] In the regime con-templated by the cognitive neuroscience project—where claims of dimin-ished culpability are untenable—this is the only permissible inference that jurors can draw. Arguing for compassion or leniency in such a system would be as nonsensical as seeking mercy for a dangerously defective car on its way to the junkyard to be crushed into scrap metal. Reconciliation and forgive-ness are not useful concepts as applied to soulless cars; they are only intelli-gible as applied to sinners.

The grave implications of the cognitive neuroscience project for capital sentencing come into even sharper relief when one considers the role that retributive justice has played in modern death penalty jurisprudence. Con-trary to the intuitions of the project's architects, retribution has served as a crucial limiting principle on capital sentencing. The Supreme Court itself has referred to a "narrowing jurisprudence" of just deserts, which limits the ulti-mate punishment to "a narrow category of the most serious crimes" and defendants "whose extreme culpability makes them 'the most deserving of execution.'"[34] In the name of retributive justice, the Court has barred the execution of mentally retarded defendants, defendants who were under the age of eighteen when their offense was committed, rapists, and defendants convicted of felony murder who did not actually kill or attempt to kill the victim. In each instance, the Court ruled that such defendants were not eligible for the death penalty because such punishment would be categorically disproportionate to their personal culpability. These same results could not have been reached if deterrence were the sole animating principle guiding the Court. General deterrence may be a contested issue. However, specific deterrence is always advanced by the execution of a defendant, since execution guarantees that the same defendant will not cause future harm.

In fact, the widely shared intuition that seems to be motivating the long-term aspiration—namely, that retributive justice is the primary source of the brutality and harshness of the modern American criminal justice system—may generally be misguided. Many features of the criminal justice system that are frequently criticized as draconian and inhumane are, in fact, motivated by a purely consequentialist crime-control rationale. Such measures include laws that authorize life sentences for recidivists (for example, three-strikes laws), laws that reduce the age at which offenders can be tried as adults, laws that punish gang membership, laws that require the registration of sex offenders, laws that dramatically increase sentences by virtue of past history, and, most paradigmatically, laws that provide for the involuntary civil commitment of sexual offenders who show difficulty controlling their behavior. These laws are the progeny of the principle animating the long-term aspiration, and some are worrisome examples of its possible implications.

Paul Robinson has offered a provocative genealogy for such laws that provides further grounds for caution. He makes a powerful argument that abandoning retributive justice in favor of consequentialist values of rehabilitation laid the groundwork for the draconian measures described above. According to Robinson's account, once "the limited ability of social and medical science to rehabilitate offenders became clear," reformers tried to salvage what was left of the consequentialist project by turning to incapacitation as the principal means of avoiding future crimes. He concludes that "the harshness of the current system may be attributed in largest part to the move to rehabilitation, incapacitation, and deterrence, which *disconnected criminal punishment from the constraint of just desert*."[35] Robinson also points to the possibility that "if incapacitation of the dangerous were the only distributive principle, there would be little reason to wait until an offense were committed to impose criminal liability and sanctions; it would be more effective to screen the general population and 'convict' those found dangerous and in need of incapacitation."[36]

Questions of whether a given individual poses a continuing threat to society are central to the criminal justice system. In addition to capital sentencing, fact finders are charged with making such determinations in the context of noncapital sentencing, civil commitment hearings, parole and probation hearings, pretrial detention, and involuntary civil commitment of sexual offenders. Regardless of neuroimaging's capacity or incapacity to predict criminal behavior reliably, there is already a powerful demand for the use of such techniques in crime control. Moreover, far more controversial methods for predicting future social harms have already been accepted by the Supreme Court in the capital sentencing context. This problem would be dramatically aggravated by adopting a criminal framework that places an even higher premium on the prediction and prevention of violence than the present one does.

Indeed, as Stephen Morse has observed, the law already has mechanisms for the preventive detention of a restricted class of individuals based on predictions about their disposition to engage in criminal misconduct. At present, these mechanisms for preventive detention of this sort apply only to narrow circumstances, namely, where the individual in question is not morally responsible for his dangerousness because he is laboring under a cognitive impairment (like a mental disorder) or where he has committed a criminal act and deserves punishment, the imposition of which also involves incapacitation aimed at preventing future harms during the time of incarceration. Morse terms these constraints, respectively, "disease" and "desert." In the former case, preemptive involuntary civil commitment is deemed a fitting response to nonculpable dangerousness. In the latter case, judgments about future harms are integrated into the larger calculus of punishment.

The cognitive neuroscience project threatens to enlarge the "disease" justification to encompass all potential criminals. That is, the cognitive neuroscience project adopts the premise that no one is morally responsible for his or her actions, removing the threshold safeguard for involuntary civil commitment. This seemingly opens the door to treating all individuals for whom there is good predictive evidence of a criminal disposition as we currently treat dangerous mentally ill patients. Indefinite incapacitation without stigma appears to be the logical terminus of the cognitive neuroscience project.

We have already seen the seeds of such an approach in the sexual predator context. In the landmark cases of *Kansas* v. *Crane* and *Kansas* v. *Hendricks* the Supreme Court upheld the use of indefinite involuntary civil commitment for convicted sexual predators who had completed their prison terms, provided that the individual "suffers from a mental abnormality [defined as a 'congenital or acquired condition affecting the emotional or volitional capacity which predisposes the person to commit sexually violent offenses in a degree constituting such person a menace to the health and safety of others'] or personality disorder which makes the person likely to engage in the predatory acts of sexual violence."[37]

It is in some ways not surprising that the Court permitted this intervention, given the fear and loathing that sexual predators inspire. But there is no reason to think that this might be the only class of individuals subject to such deprivations of liberty in the name of diminished responsibility and a disposition to violence. One obvious category of especially grave perceived threats would be individuals deemed likely to engage in terrorism. Even the most committed advocates of civil liberties and human rights, such as David Cole and Doug Cassel, have begun to entertain the possibility of a narrowly circumscribed regime of administrative detention for those suspected of terrorism. The moral anthropology of the cognitive neuroscience project, if it is accepted, makes these argument all the more appealing.

Conclusion

If adopted, the cognitive neuroscience project will yield inhumane consequences for criminal defendants—defeating the chief aspirations of its architects. Thus, those committed to improving the lot of criminal defendants (especially those facing the death penalty) should be very wary of embracing the project. Is it possible or desirable to salvage the cognitive neuroscience project in a way that will preserve its humanitarian ends? Or is the reductive, mechanist account of human personhood and human agency posited by cognitive neuroscience—and, indeed, by modern science more generally—incommensurable with the account on which the criminal law is premised? Most fundamental, is the account of human behavior that undergirds the cognitive neuroscience project indeed an empirically demonstrated scientific conclusion, or rather simply the repackaging and extension of an undemonstrable axiom or metaphysical postulate of modern science, such as physicalism or reductive mechanism? Understanding where an argument leads in principle and practice is a necessary precursor to appraising its wisdom—an appraisal that is particularly essential when human lives hang in the balance.

Notes

1. Robert M. Sapolsky, "The Frontal Cortex and the Criminal Justice System," 359 *Philosophical Transactions of the Royal Society B* (2004): 1787, 1794.

2. See, for example, Jana L. Bufkin and Vickie R. Luttrell, "Neuroimaging Studies of Aggressive and Violent Behavior: Current Findings and Implications for Criminology and Criminal Justice," 6 *Trauma Violence and Abuse* (2005): 176, 186.

3. Francis Crick and Christof Koch, "The Problem of Consciousness," 267 *Scientific American* (September 1992): 153, 153.

4. Jamie Ward, *The Student's Guide to Cognitive Neuroscience* (New York: Psychology Press, 2006), 3.

5. Patricia Smith Churchland, "Moral Decision-making and the Brain in Neuroethics: Defining the Issues in Theory, Practice, and Policy," in *Neuroethics,* edited by Judy Illes (Oxford University Press, 2006), 3–16.

6. Joshua Greene and Jonathan Cohen, "For the Law, Neuroscience Changes Nothing and Everything," 359 *Philosophical Transactions of the Royal Society B* (2004): 1775, 1775 (emphasis added).

7. Martha J. Farah, "Neuroethics: The Practical and the Philosophical," 9 *Trends in Cognitive Science* (2005): 34.

8. Alex Rosenberg, *Darwinian Reductionism, or How To Stop Worrying and Love Molecular Biology* (University of Chicago Press, 2006), 2.

9. Patricia Smith Churchland, *Brain-wise: Studies in Neurophilosophy* (MIT Press, 2002), 20–21. ("A reduction has been achieved when the causal powers of the macrophenomenon are explained as a function of the physical structure and causal powers of the microphenomenon.")

10. For a discussion of such limitations and concerns, see O. Carter Snead, "Neuroimaging and the 'Complexity' of Capital Punishment," 82 *New York University Law Review* (2007): 1265.

11. Henry T. Greely, "Prediction, Litigation, Privacy, and Property: Some Possible Legal and Social Implications of Advances in Neuroscience," in *Neuroscience and the Law,* edited by Brent Garland (New York: Dana Press; Washington, D.C.: AAAS, 2004), 127–48.

12. Churchland, *Brain-wise.*

13. Greene and Cohen, "For the Law, Neuroscience Changes Nothing and Everything," 1783–84.

14. Ibid., 1781.

15. Sapolsky, "The Frontal Cortex and the Criminal Justice System."

16. George P. Fletcher, "The Metamorphosis of Larceny," 89 *Harvard Law Review* (1976): 469, 502.

17. H. L. A. Hart, "Review," 74 *Yale Law Journal* (1965): 1325, 1328 (reviewing Barbara Wootton, *Crime and the Criminal Law* [London: Stevens, 1963]).

18. Peter T. Hansen, "Mitigation: An Outline of Law, Method, and Strategy," 29 *Capital Defense Digest* (1992): 32.

19. John M. Fabian, "Death Penalty Mitigation and the Role of the Forensic Psychologist," 27 *Law and Psychology Review* (2003): 73, 78 (quoting Russell Stetler, "Mental Disabilities and Mitigation," 49 *The Champion* (April 1999): 49.

20. Paul H. Robinson, "The A.L.I.'s Proposed Distributive Principle of 'Limiting Retributivism': Does It Mean in Practice Anything Other than Pure Desert?" 7 *Buffalo Criminal Law Review* (2003): 3, 5.

21. *Penry* v. *Lynaugh*, 492 U.S. 302, 319 (1989) (quoting *California* v. *Brown*, 479 U.S. 538, 545 [1987] [O'Connor, J., concurring]), overruled in part by *Atkins* v. *Virginia*, 536 U.S. 304 (2002).

22. Michael N. Burt, "Forensics as Mitigation," Office of the Public Defender, San Francisco (www.goextranet.net/Seminars/Dallas/BurtForensics.htm).

23. John Monahan, "A Jurisprudence of Risk Assessment: Forecasting Harm among Prisoners, Predators, and Patients," 92 *Virginia Law Review* (2006): 391, 396.

24. Ibid.

25. Hansen, "Mitigation: An Outline of Law, Method, and Strategy," 32.

26. *Daubert* v. *Merrell Dow Pharmaceuticals, Inc.*, 509 U.S. 579 (1993); *Frye* v. *United States*, 293 F. 1013 (D.C. Cir. 1923).

27. David L. Faigman and others, *Science in the Law: Social and Behavioral Science Issues* (St. Paul, Minn.: West Group, 2002), 79–80 (including detailed discussion of why courts give little weight to evidentiary standards).

28. Mark D. Cunningham and Thomas J. Reidy, "Antisocial Personality Disorder and Psychopathy: Diagnostic Dilemmas in Classifying Patterns of Antisocial Behavior in Sentencing Evaluations," 16 *Behavioral Sciences and the Law* (1990): 333; see also John H. Blume and David P. Voisin, "Capital Cases," 24 *The Champion* (2000): 69 (calling antisocial personality disorder diagnosis "the kiss of death").

29. Quoted in Blume and Voisin, "Capital Cases," 69 (quoting *Satterwhite* v. *Texas*, 486 U.S. 249, 253 [1988]). For a provocative profile of Grigson, see Ron Rosenbaum, "Travels with Dr. Death," *Vanity Fair*, May 1990, as reprinted in Nina Rivkind and Steven F. Schatz, *Cases and Materials on the Death Penalty*, 2d ed. (St. Paul, Minn.: Thompson/West, 2005), 513.

30. *Barefoot* v. *Estelle*, 463 U.S. 880 (1983), 918–19 (emphases in the original).

31. Erica Beecher-Monas and Edgar Garcia-Rill, "Danger at the Edge of Chaos: Predicting Violent Behavior in a Post-*Daubert* World," 24 *Cardozo Law Review* (2003): 1845, 1897; see also Brief for the American Psychological Association and the Missouri Psychological Association as Amici Curiae Supporting Respondent, *Roper* v. *Simmons*, 543 U.S. 551 (2006) (No. 03-633), 18–19, 20.

32. Paul H. Robinson, "Punishing Dangerousness: Cloaking Preventive Detention as Criminal Justice," 114 *Harvard Law Review* (2001): 1429, 1441.

33. Burt, "Forensics as Mitigation."

34. *Roper* v. *Simmons*, 543 U.S. 551, 568 (2005) (quoting *Atkins*, 536 U.S. at 319).

35. Robinson, "Limiting Retributivism," 14 (emphasis in original).

36. Robinson, "Punishing Dangerousness," 1439–40.

37. *Kansas* v. *Crane*, 534 U.S. 407 (2002); *Kansas* v. *Hendricks*, 521 U.S. 346, 357 (1997).

PART IV

Genetic Engineering and the Future of Constitutional Personhood

JOHN A. ROBERTSON

10

Reproductive Rights and Reproductive Technology in 2030

Larry, a pediatrician, and David, a wills lawyer, meet in their late twenties, fall in love, and marry on June 15, 2025, in Indianapolis. Three years later they take in a foster child for eight months and find the experience rewarding. By 2030 they are well-enough established in their careers to think about having their own child. Larry's twenty-four-year-old sister, Marge, has agreed to donate her eggs, and David will provide the sperm, so that each partner will have a genetic connection with the child. They work with an agency that matches couples with gestational surrogates and settle on Janice, a thirty-four-year-old nurse and mother of two, who is willing to help them in exchange for a $75,000 fee.

In the process, Larry and David come to realize that they would prefer to have a male child that shares their sexual orientation. Reproductive cloning will not do—the Food and Drug Administration has not yet certified it as safe and effective. But gene studies show a strong correlation between five genes and sexual orientation in both males and females. Larry and David discuss with their doctors the feasibility of screening the embryos they create with Marge's eggs for male genes linked to a homosexual orientation. The clinic doctors are experts in embryo screening and alteration, but they cannot guarantee that the resulting children will, in fact, turn out to be homosexual. To increase the certainty, they will insert additional "gay gene" sequences in the embryos before they are placed in Janice. Embryos not used will be frozen for later use or for stem cell technology to create eggs from Larry's skin cells so that the resulting child would be the genetic offspring of both Larry and David.

The scenario painted here is futuristic, but only partially so. The techniques to be used—in vitro fertilization (IVF), egg donation, and gestational surrogacy—are now widely available, as is embryo screening for genetic disease and gender. Same-sex marriage is likely to be soon recognized as a federal constitutional right. No gay genes have yet been identified. But genomic knowledge is mushrooming. The genetic code for nonmedical traits such as sexual orientation may be unlocked in coming years. Altering a person's genes by inserting or deleting DNA sequences is still theoretical, but great progress has occurred with animals. Cloning is unlikely to be available by 2030, but producing gametes from somatic cells in a person's body might by then be feasible.

Technical prowess, however, should not be confused with ethical and social acceptability. The thirty years from 1980 to 2010, the period during which assisted reproduction, egg donation, surrogacy, and genetic screening of embryos became widely used, has been fraught with ethical, legal, and social controversy. These techniques pose major challenges for deeply held values of autonomy, family, the welfare of children, and the importance of reproduction to human flourishing. They call starkly into question the meaning of kinship and parenthood, and the degree of control that parents should have over their children's genes. Increased genetic screening, alteration of genes, and cloning or obtaining gametes from somatic cells will be even more contested.

In America, the law is often embroiled in public controversy, especially when sexual, family, and reproductive norms clash. Yet these techniques were launched and found a home with little legal scrutiny. Outside of abortion, the law has been largely absent from battles over reproductive and genetic technologies. As a result, there are few Supreme Court precedents directly on point. Legislation, for example, has not restrained the use of cutting-edge genetic technologies such as embryo screening and alteration. Reproductive cloning, though not yet feasible, is highly controversial, but most states have not banned it. When the law has inched forward with legal solutions to particular problems, such as disputes over lost or frozen embryos or how to share parentage among gamete donors and rearing parents, new techniques with new problems have sprung up. In Larry and David's case, it is the desire to choose their child's gender and shape its sexual orientation that is novel and challenging.

That situation might change as techniques evolve to expand choice over the genetic characteristics of children. Eventually, legal limits will be imposed, limits which will raise questions about the constitutionality of restrictions on reproductive and genetic choice. The Constitution, however, was written in an era when none of these techniques were practiced or even imagined. Indeed, it says nothing about reproduction at all. As a result, the Supreme Court has spoken often and most recently about abortion and contraception but seldom about engaging in reproduction as such, and not at all about parents' choosing the genes of their offspring.[1] When it did speak against forced sterilization of criminals, it assumed heterosexual and coital conception.[2] The principles underlying those decisions provide general guideposts for procreative rights in a technological age, but the specifics of those rights will have to be teased out from the logic of those precedents as new techniques challenge old values and new options for reproduction open. Larry and David and thousands of other couples will need answers so that they can have the families they wish.

Reproduction in the Laboratory: In Vitro Fertilization and Its Dilemmas

Larry and David's plan pushes all of the buttons of reproductive conflict. Most of the issues their case raises involve relatively well explored territory—or, at least, territory we can expect to be well explored by 2030. In some areas, however, their case involves radically new ground. I begin by briefly surveying the general state of the law as we can expect Larry and David to find it.

First, Larry and David make up a nontraditional family. In 1986 the Supreme Court found the claim for a right to homosexual sodomy to be "facetious."[3] Seventeen years later, it became part of the Constitution's fundamental liberties.[4] By 2010 same-sex marriage was legal in five states, with a federal court challenge looming that could lead to legal recognition nationwide.[5] Even if not constitutionally grounded, by 2030 same-sex marriage should have become routine and accepted in most states, including Indiana. The idea that gay individuals or couples will be having children, which they often did before legal recognition of same-sex marriage, is not especially surprising. Nor that they would want to choose their children's sexual orientation, as other couples might, once the technology for doing so is available. But we can expect that full acceptance of gays and lesbians—particularly when contriving to have gay and lesbian children—will not be universal.

Second, the technical innovation that has made Larry and David's reproduction and that of millions of infertile couples possible—in vitro fertilization of an egg outside of the body before placement of an embryo in the uterus—has been on the scene since 1978. By 2010 it represented 1 percent of U.S. births, a figure that is likely to grow as it becomes cheaper, safer, and more effective.[6] We are long past the original objections to IVF based on unnaturalness, wastage of embryos, and subjection of women, though these concerns still animate objections to particular procedures. Despite widespread ethical debate and the pleas of the Vatican, no legislature has banned IVF or even placed significant restrictions on it. Yet legal disputes remain about ownership and control of embryos and to a lesser extent about research and other uses of them.

The most important policy issue in IVF has been the need to reduce the high level of multiple births that plague the field. More than a third of IVF births every year produce two or more infants, well above the coital rate of 5 percent. Since success is measured by a live birth, this has led assisted reproduction technology programs and patients to implant several embryos at one time. Professional guidelines have brought down the number of triplets and higher-order multiples, but they have had less success in preventing twins. What is more, those guidelines have lacked teeth. They did not, for example, stop an assisted reproduction technology doctor from transferring six embryos to a thirty-two-year-old woman who already had six IVF children, leading to the birth of octuplets and a furor over the abuses of an unregulated fertility industry.[7]

Larry and David's efforts here will likely lead to the creation of more embryos than can be safely or permissibly implanted in Janice at one time, and by 2030 we can probably expect clear guidelines or laws to limit that number. Single-embryo transfer with a limit of two will probably be the norm in the most promising cases, as would be the case with eggs from a healthy, young donor like Marge. If Janice does not deliver after the first transfer or if Larry and David want to have additional children, they will probably have several frozen embryos to use in later attempts. Because limits on the number of embryos placed in the uterus at one time should not substantially affect success rates, such limits should not infringe the procreative liberty of infertile persons or gays and lesbians.

Right-to-life groups will continue efforts to limit the number of eggs fertilized to prevent the discarding of unused embryos. But they will have a hard time overcoming the strong deference accorded to parents and their doctors about how best to treat infertility. Constitutional rights to procreate may also limit state restrictions beyond the number of embryos transferred at one time. Laws, for example, that limit the number of embryos created will directly interfere with the ability to use IVF to reproduce and will be difficult to justify. Limits on the number of embryos transferred per IVF attempt, however, may pass muster because embryos not transferred when created can be frozen for later use.

Larry and David should also be aware of their ownership rights in their embryos and whose wishes take priority if they have a falling out. The law has long been clear that the couple is the "owner"—the unit with dispositional control—of the embryos.[8] The owner is not the clinic that has created them and now holds them in storage. Marge has given her eggs to Larry, and David has provided the sperm. Although Larry and David cannot totally control the number of embryos that will be placed in Janice at one time, they can decide how many eggs will be fertilized and whether they will be discarded, donated to others, or used in research or in therapy for themselves or their child. If the clinic loses the embryos, renders them unusable, or places them in the wrong uterus, it will have violated the couple's legal rights and will owe them compensation.[9]

The most active area of IVF litigation has involved disputes between divorcing couples over what to do with stored embryos. With heterosexual couples using their own gametes, the party who objects to the use of the embryos usually wins out, because that party will have been forced to reproduce against his or her wishes.[10] The same principle would partially hold if Larry and David were to divorce with one or more embryos in frozen storage. David, the sperm provider, could prevent Larry from using those embryos because their use would lead to unconsented reproduction by David. But the reverse is not true. Because Larry has not provided his own gametes—just those from his sister, who has relinquished her rights in them—he may not be able to stop David from using them if they had previously agreed to David's having that right.

Third, Larry and David's plans to have a child with the help of an egg donor and gestational surrogate touch another ethical and legal hotspot—the intentional blurring of family and kinship relations. Egg donation separates the genetic and the gestational mothers, and thus the child might never know his or her genetic mother. With sperm donation, the genetic father has usually been absent and unknown. Gestational surrogacy separates the woman bearing the child and the woman providing the egg, with sometimes a third woman doing the rearing. Surrogacy can also lead to conflicts over custody and rearing, conflicts that can also arise with respect to gamete donors. Sometimes, children of these arrangements feel cut off from or abandoned by their "true" (genetic) family. Because gamete donors and surrogates are invariably paid, there are charges of exploitation and commodification of gamete donors, surrogate mothers, and sought-for children.

By 2010 the use of egg donors and surrogates has been well-integrated into the practice of assisted reproduction technology. No records exist of the number of children born from donor sperm. Egg donors are used in 10 percent of IVF cycles.[11] Gestational surrogacy is used by many fewer persons, but it is accepted for a woman who has ovaries but lacks a uterus and for gay males. The main legal issue is whether the gestational surrogate mother can be held to her advance agreement to have no role in custody, visitation, or rearing. As of 2010, these questions have not been resolved in all states, but there is enough certainty for most persons needing surrogacy to go forward.[12] By 2030 a firm legal regime for surrogacy is likely to be in place, giving Larry, David, and Janice more certainty about what to expect if their plans go awry.

Larry and David present another variation on the gamete donation and surrogacy theme. Commonly, a couple or individual will need only one collaborator—a donor or a surrogate. Sometimes, however, both partners will lack gametes and will request egg and sperm donation, which can take the form of an embryo donation. Or the woman may lack both healthy eggs and the ability to carry a pregnancy.[13] In rare cases, the parents might need egg and sperm donation and surrogacy in order to produce a child. That situation, however, does not involve their own reproduction. Because they are contributing neither genes nor gestation, they are not exercising procreative liberty. Rather, they are making prebirth arrangements for conception and pregnancy so that they might then adopt the resulting child.

Larry and David are not going that far, but they are pushing the boundary a bit by involving both an egg donor and a surrogate. If the egg donor were unrelated, the child might have a nanny, perhaps a wet nurse, and babysitters but might spend no time with its genetic or gestational mother. The child may never be told who the donor or carrier was or have contact with either. In this case, Larry and David expect Marge to be more actively involved. They may tell their child that "Aunt Marge" is also his genetic mother, making Marge both an aunt and a mother at the same time. By 2030 related gamete donation or surrogacy will have become so common that a set of social norms or practices for how they are described and celebrated, including even a line of greeting cards tailored to them, will likely have emerged.

Larry and David's need to use technology to reproduce gives them protection against laws that limit them from doing so. While lesbians and single women can be inseminated with sperm from a donor, Larry and David will need the help of an egg donor and a gestational carrier to have a child. Their reproductive liberty—their interest in having and their need to have offspring—is at stake and should be recognized as a protected right to the same extent that heterosexuals have such rights. The U.S. Supreme Court has never had to rule on whether gays and lesbians have a right to use assisted reproduction technology to reproduce because it was never faced with a direct ban on individuals' doing so, just as it has never had to face that question with heterosexuals. Yet there is good reason to think that if government ever did try to stop IVF, egg donation, or gestational surrogacy for gays or straights, it would lead to constitutional recognition of a liberty right to reproduce in this way.

The basis for constitutional rights to reproduce derives from Court decisions dealing with compulsory sterilization and birth control and abortion.

The idea first pronounced in 1942 in *Skinner* v. *Oklahoma* that reproduction is a basic civil right of men and women has been reiterated frequently in dicta in cases about the importance of marrying, having a family, and raising one's children.[14] Indeed, in *Eisenstadt* v. *Baird*, a case involving access to contraceptives, Justice William Brennan stated that "if the right of privacy means anything, it is the right of the *individual*, married or single, to be free from unwarranted governmental intrusion into matters so fundamentally affecting a person as the decision whether to bear or beget a child."[15] These statements assume heterosexual marriage and coital conception, but the underlying values and interests at stake exist in noncoital, assisted reproduction, too. Infertile persons have the same interests in the primal human experience of having offspring—in having heirs, in nurturing children, and in enjoying their company—that fertile persons do. Because reproduction is as important to the infertile as it is to the fertile, they should not be denied that opportunity without a strong showing that their use of assisted reproductive techniques would cause substantial harm to others, a difficult standard to meet. Moral objection alone does not count as a compelling interest. Treating gays and lesbians equally would mean recognizing their reproductive rights as well.

While few states have tried to stop gay and lesbian reproduction directly, the family law structure has sometimes impeded it by not recognizing the prebirth or preconception agreements made for rearing rights and duties in the resulting child. This is less of a problem with gamete donation than it is with surrogacy. Most states have laws regulating parenting rights in sperm donation, whereby the donor agrees to relinquish all rearing rights and duties and the recipient couple or individual takes them on. The few states with egg donation statutes quite sensibly follow that model. Surprisingly, there have been few legal disputes arising from egg or embryo donation, and none that has drawn the Supreme Court's attention.

Thus we can expect that Marge's egg donation to Larry for use with David will pose fewer problems than Janice's role as a gestational surrogate. Quite wisely, Larry and David have chosen Janice, who, because she already has had children, knows what pregnancy is like and what the experience of birth might entail. She has chosen to be a surrogate to help a needy couple and also to earn money. In this case the $75,000 fee is half of what she would have earned if she continued as a nurse, but she likes the flexibility of surrogacy and has the support of her husband in doing so. She receives a payment every few months, with the bulk of it coming after the birth of the child.

Larry, David, and Janice have discussed her diet and activities during pregnancy. If medical problems develop, she is free to terminate the pregnancy. If as a consequence of spontaneous twinning she ends up with triplets or more, she has also agreed to selective reduction to one or two fetuses, as the three of them decide at the time. If prenatal testing shows that the fetus has a serious genetic defect, she has also agreed to terminate the pregnancy. Some of these provisions might not be legally enforceable, but they give the parties enough assurance to proceed.

The most likely source of conflict in surrogacy in 2010 is the risk that the surrogate will change her mind after birth of the child and not relinquish rearing rights and duties to the hiring couple. This issue received national attention in 1988 with the *Baby M* case in New Jersey. That state's supreme court ruled that the surrogate, who in that instance had provided the egg as well, could not be held to her agreement.[16] She was the mother under the law and was entitled to visitation and shared custody. California, on the other hand, took a different approach in 1991 in a gestational surrogacy situation involving an infertile married couple. Its high court found that the child had two mothers—one genetic and one gestational—and allowed the contract assigning rearing rights and duties to the genetic mother to be enforced.[17] This gave a big boost to gestational surrogacy arrangements, and several states made such arrangements legally enforceable in advance.[18]

By 2010 the question of child custody in gestational surrogacy cases has come to depend on whether a state adopts the New Jersey or the California approach. Given the Supreme Court's preference for deferring to the states on family law matters, it may not have yet ruled on gestational surrogacy when Larry, David, and Janice go forward. Yet if a case were presented involving a couple that uses a gestational carrier because the wife has ovaries but no uterus, there would be a strong case for recognizing such arrangements. If so, the California solution would become the constitutional standard. This would be particularly true if it were incorporated into a statute that had a court or a state agency review the contract in advance to ensure that the surrogate has been fully informed about the risks she faces and has made a free and knowing choice.[19] Even without prior review, a law that refused to recognize surrogacy contracts or banned payments to surrogates might be found to be an unconstitutional burden on an infertile couple's right to procreate with the help of a surrogate.

If that right exists, Larry and David are entitled to exercise it to the same extent as infertile heterosexual couples. They too are married, and they too have interests in having and rearing children. It is true that only David has a direct genetic connection, but Larry's interest, particularly with use of his sister's eggs, in rearing a child of his spouse should be treated the same. Thus a state that has an advance review procedure for surrogacy contracts would have to extend that arrangement to all couples, gay or straight, and arguably to any gestational surrogacy arrangement. If it does not have a precertification process or bans or prohibits such arrangements, then the courts should find such a ban unconstitutional and should give effect to Larry and David's surrogacy arrangement in the same manner as they would honor that of an infertile couple.

In short, it is reasonable to expect that by 2030 Larry and David will be on well-trodden ground with their plans to use Marge and Janice and IVF to have a child.

Screening Embryos and Choosing Genes

More novel and challenging is the couple's request to choose both the gender and the sexual orientation of their child. Sex selection by preconception sperm sorting and preimplantation embryo testing is now available to choose the gender of offspring, but sex selection for nonmedical reasons is not yet widely practiced in the United States. Preimplantation and prenatal tests are also used to screen out embryos and fetuses with mutations that would lead to infant, childhood, and even adult diseases, such as cystic fibrosis, sickle cell anemia, breast cancer, and Huntington's disease. Very few mutations associated with nondisease traits, such as sexual orientation, have been identified so far, in part because those traits are governed by complex combinations of genes and environment.

The growing ability to quickly sequence whole human genomes and find genetic associations with many complex traits may change that situation, however. Scientists are also becoming adept at removing or inserting DNA sequences in animals. They will eventually be able to alter genes in humans as well. By 2030 the prebirth genetic shaping that Larry and David request might be routine for many traits. Their case will be more difficult if they want to use those techniques before they are proved to be safe and effective. But they are a cautious and responsible pair and are not interested in taking on the physical risks of untested techniques. Selection of embryos for transfer on genetic grounds poses fewer physical than social risks. Insertion or deletion of genes, by contrast, ups the ante on physical, social, and ethical grounds.

As the power and availability of genetic selection techniques grow, the legal system is likely to get involved. The ethical conflicts present in earlier battles over IVF, gamete donation, and surrogacy will reemerge with new force when parents want to choose or shape their children's genomes before birth. Many persons will cry out against giving parents such power, because of the effect it will have on children and parenthood and the role of family in society. In some cases, the fact of selection itself will be the issue. In others, it will be the specific genes or traits selected for and their implications for children, persons with disabilities, and other groups.

It is no surprise that individuals want choice in selecting their mates and their sperm and egg donors. There are many physical, behavioral, and personality factors involved in attraction. Poets and artists celebrate the miracle of chance that leads people to fall in love and find a desirable mate for reproduction. Choosing sperm and egg donors is less mystical and more explicit, with a list of donor traits in a catalog or photographs on the Internet.

Couples who choose to have children now routinely practice some degree of screening and selection to avoid the birth of a child with a serious disease. Ultrasound and amniocentesis, mainstays of prenatal diagnosis, leave the option of abortion when test results come back positive. By 2030 it is likely that a simple maternal blood test will provide enough fetal DNA for genetic testing that entry into the uterus will not be necessary. As genetic knowledge grows, so will the list of testable conditions, including adult-onset diseases and risks for cancer. However, the decision to terminate a pregnancy because of a positive test result is a difficult one and will be rare unless the condition is a very serious one.

The advent of preimplantation genetic diagnosis allows the screening of embryos before they are implanted in the uterus, but it does so by IVF and embryo biopsy. First developed in 1990 for cystic fibrosis, the screening is now used for several hundred congenital conditions, most of them quite rare. It has also been extended to adult-onset diseases and risk factors, such as for breast and colon cancers, which appear only in adult years. Preimplantation genetic diagnosis is attractive because it avoids the need for abortion, but it can be troubling in its own rights. In vitro fertilization replaces coital conception. Embryos have a cell clipped and analyzed, and some embryos will be discarded, rather than transferred. By 2030 preimplantation genetic diagnosis and embryo biopsy techniques should be vastly improved, but they will still involve a choice among embryos. With genome sequencing so cheap and easy, a genome-wide scan of genes associated with many low-risk medical conditions—and eventually nonmedical traits—may be used to choose embryos for transfer.

The ethical issues involved here will lead some groups to call for a hand on the brake. Persons with more traditional or conservative views about family and reproduction see preimplantation and prenatal screening as a threat to the idea that children are "gifts" and should be accepted as they are, a norm that they see as the core of successful parenting and transmission of societal values.[20] Rather than accept what nature has given them, they feel, prebirth selectors are choosing their children not for their own sakes but for how well they serve parental needs. That a child has to pass a genetic test to be born offends traditionalists. Such practices harm embryos and fetuses and set up unrealistic expectations for resulting children. Even selection to prevent the birth of children with serious genetic disease—such as Tay Sachs, sickle cell anemia, or cystic fibrosis—is questionable in this view, because it devalues existing persons with those diseases. Once established for medical purposes, genetic selection will then be used to design the characteristics of offspring, traditionalists warn. This will overvalue particular traits, set up unreal, rigid expectations for children, and lead to unequal access to enhancement traits.

Traditionalists know they cannot rely on a profit-motivated reproductive industry to rein in these uses, so they may be happy to have the law intervene. Prenatal diagnosis has won a place in obstetrical practice because it meets needs and raises few problems beyond encouraging abortion for fetuses with genetic conditions and the risk of devaluing persons with disabilities. Preimplantation genetic diagnosis has developed, in turn, free of legal scrutiny. Aside from an occasional tort case about missed diagnosis, there have been no bans or even regulation of what may be tested. As a result, there has been little occasion for constitutional development in state courts and no word from the Supreme Court. As with most medical technologies, doctors do what patients want and the technology permits, often shaping that demand. But selection for nonmedical traits may change that situation, with some legislatures imposing restrictions on nonmedical genetic choice.

At this point, the scope of a prospective parent's right to choose the genes of children will arise. Although no more legally established in 2010 than the right to use assisted reproduction technology or donors and surrogates, a robust right to genetic selection and even alteration should follow from the constitutional right of individuals, fertile or infertile, gay or straight, to decide to have or not have children.[21] Information about a child's genetic makeup, like information about the child's future health status, could directly determine whether an individual goes forward with reproduction. Withholding that information by banning tests that provide it or actions based on them would directly interfere with reproductive choice. Such laws should stand only if there is a compelling justification for them.

This point is clearest with regard to prenatal tests, such as ultrasound and amniocentesis, that tell whether the fetus has severe genetic or chromosomal deficiencies. But if it holds there, it should hold for less serious medical or health conditions: the presence or absence of such risks could be central to a person's decision to go forward with reproduction. If so, it will be hard to exclude nonmedical genetic preferences from rights protection as well. A person's choice to reproduce could be as strongly affected by nonmedical traits, such as gender or sexual preference, as is a person's choice about a child's medical risk status. Choices about nonmedical traits should thus be as protected as the right to use amniocentesis or embryo screening for health reasons. Indeed, as the ability to alter genes grows, presumptive protection for the right to remove deleterious mutations or even add desirable ones should follow.[22] Causing serious harm to offspring or others would justify limiting rights of selection and alteration, but moral or religious objection alone should not suffice.

Larry and David want to have a boy who is gay. As of 2010, only sex (and a few other single gene traits) can be chosen in advance. The sex of fetuses can be seen on ultrasound at eleven to thirteen weeks. Although abortion for nonmedical sex selection falls presumptively within a woman's right to terminate a pregnancy, few such abortions occur in the United States, though they do frequently occur in India and China. Abortion for other nonmedical traits, once they become known, is also unlikely in the United States unless definitive testing can be done very early in the pregnancy.

But gender can also be identified in embryos. Embryos of the desired sex can be transferred to the uterus, the remainder being discarded or donated to others. For persons who believe that the fertilized egg is already a person or moral subject in its own right, this will be anathema. Larry, David, and many others disagree and find embryo selection, because it is at such an early stage of development, much more acceptable than abortion. Indeed, they may be willing to screen and discard embryos but be repelled by the thought of abortion for sex selection.

The gender of children can also be chosen via sperm-sorting techniques. Indeed, the clinic treating Larry and David will first separate the male-bearing from the female-bearing sperm and use only the former to inseminate Marge's eggs. They will still use preimplantation genetic diagnosis to make sure that the fertilization has resulted in male embryos and to identify those with the genes associated with a homosexual orientation.

No laws now regulate gender selection, though the Food and Drug Administration does have authority over devices and drugs that are intended for that purpose. With preconception sperm sorting available, a jump in gender selection is expected. In the United States, this is most likely to come from Asian communities, which place a high value on first-born males. Other individuals may also want to choose the sex of their first-born child or use sex selection for second- and later-born children to provide gender variety in the family.

By 2030 the rules for gender selection of offspring are likely to be well developed. One sensible approach would be to make sure that no sex ratio imbalance results, as occurred in China with an earlier one-child-per-family policy. This could be done by requiring clinics to select for an equal number of males and females or by limiting gender selection to second and later children. The main social concerns with such a practice are its tendency to foster sexism and thus harm women. Males may be chosen, particularly as the first born, and continue to dominate society. There is also the risk that parents will have a fixed menu of expectations of what they want from a child of a certain gender—expecting gender-specific behaviors and roles from male and female children. Imagine their disappointment if the child of a chosen sex does not live up to the stereotypical view the parents have of how children of that gender should act. However, not all parents selecting the sex of children will have such strong expectations. In any case that risk is not strong enough to support a ban on all nonmedical sex selection.

Once gender selection is accepted, there will also be requests to select embryos for other traits with a known genetic basis. Opposition to such a practice reflects many concerns beyond respect for the embryos destroyed in the process. These include expectations of the child and harm to those groups not chosen, as well as the more global, traditionalist concerns about not accepting what nature or God has provided. Unreal or rigid parental expectations may clash with the child's own needs and development. This could occur with embryos selected for sexual orientation, musical ability, fast and slow twitch muscles tied to athleticism, beauty, intelligence, and other traits.

In most cases the trait chosen might seem beneficial to the child: height, intelligence, beauty, or memory, for example. But it may also create added pressure on the child to live up to parental expectations—especially when the parents have gone to the expense and inconvenience to produce a particular trait in their child. In some cases, the trait might seem less attractive, or even harmful, to the child, as is the case with short stature, deafness, or, as some persons will perceive it, the homosexual orientation that Larry and David want for their son. Strictly speaking, however, those children would not have been harmed by the choice, since they would not have been born if the parents had been unable to choose the trait in question.[23]

The situation is complicated by the genetic reductionism motivating many persons who want to select offspring genes. In twenty years we will know much more about a person's genome and how those genes interact and affect phenotype, but the strength of the correlation will vary greatly. For many traits, nurture will dominate nature, with the environment playing a stronger causal factor than genes alone. Widely publicized genetic discoveries may lead people to jump to the conclusion that they can easily choose from a genetic menu the traits they wish for their child. Such an assumption inflates the role of genes in shaping a person and underplays the polygenic and environmental complexity of most desirable traits. This could lead to renewed efforts to shape the child to parental wishes, creating disappointment, frustration, hurt, anger, and conflict all around.

As doubts about genetic efficacy grow, the push for legal regulation may also gain strength. Although no bans now exist, it would not be surprising to see legal barriers arise as problems with genetic selection surface. Parents may challenge those laws on constitutional grounds. Again, the question would be whether the interest in the traits of the child is such an essential part of deciding whether or not to reproduce that it is part of procreative liberty.[24] If so, the state would have to have some stronger reason to restrict parental freedom than religious or moral notions decrying selection itself.

In short, Larry and David are crossing ethical and constitutional frontiers when they request embryo screening to pick a male with a gay orientation. Their choice of a male child is more likely to be honored than their preference for a homosexual child, as long as there are protections against sex ratio imbalances and harming women. It will be hard, however, to deny parents the right to select embryos for sexual orientation, whether gay or straight. Gays and lesbians have the same right to respect in choices over intimacy, marriage, and reproduction that heterosexuals have. If their social and legal status is protected, what basis would there then be for saying that knowingly opting for a gay child will harm that child's well-being? The right to choose other non-medical traits may follow as well, depending on the specifics of those cases. Regulation to minimize untoward effects or maintain safety may occur as long as it imposes no undue burden on the parental choice at issue.

Gene Alteration: Inserting and Deleting DNA

Larry and David's plan to have a male child through preconception sperm sorting and then screening embryos to identify those with gay genes should fall within the spreading canopy of procreative liberty. Although some persons will condemn their efforts, particularly their choice of their child's gender and sexual orientation, by 2030 such choices should be a recognized part of procreative liberty for gays and straights alike because it could be so central to their reproductive choice. Indeed, as noted earlier, there is a logical basis for courts' finding the right to genetic alteration to be within the scope of reproductive liberty. Such rights, of course, exist only when material to whether a person proceeds with or avoids reproduction and are subject to regulation for health and safety or other compelling reasons. Courts may not accept all the implications of reproductive liberty outlined here, but there is a logical case for doing so.

By 2030 much more controversial than selection alone will be Larry and David's efforts to have DNA inserted or deleted from embryos to ensure that their child is homosexual. The technique of gene targeting was developed in the early 1980s in mice. In 2007 the scientists Mario Capecchi, Martin Evans, and Oliver Smithies received the Nobel Prize for this work.[25] It has led to the creation of knock-out mice—mice with specific genetic sequences deleted, enabling them to serve as experimental models to study particular diseases. Imagine that by 2020 knock-out techniques have been applied to human embryos and gametes, enabling scientists to delete or insert particular sequences of DNA and then create stem cell lines to study the origins of diseases and ways to fight them.

By 2030 some parents who are carriers of serious genetic diseases will likely think that this may be a way for them to have a healthy child without abortion or embryo discard. They could create embryos through IVF and then test them for the disease genes of concern (Tay Sachs, cystic fibrosis, sickle cell anemia, and so forth). If they have embryos free of disease, they would simply transfer them to the uterus. If they have only diseased embryos, the missing gene sequence could be inserted and mutated sections deleted. This would be genetic surgery on the child they eventually have.

No alteration of human embryos before transfer is likely to occur until studies in animals, including larger mammals and primates, show a high degree of safety and efficacy. As that evidence mounts, however, human application will follow. First, we will need to learn that such human embryos and cells from them can develop normally, thus enabling a few families to request transfer of altered embryos to the uterus. Early miscarriage may occur, but if the vast majority of children are born healthy, this technique may be quickly accepted as a viable alternative for interested parents. If that occurs, by 2030 Larry and David could plausibly request gene alteration to ensure that the male child they plan to have will also have the genes associated with a homosexual orientation.

What is wrong with doing so? If they can choose embryos with gay genes to begin with, why not alter them as well for that effect? Here the problem cannot be choosing a gay male offspring, because that can be done by transferring embryos so endowed. Rather, it is the deliberateness of it: changing nature to ensure a result. There is also a greater risk of error and harm to offspring because manipulation is occurring. So much more can go wrong.

Some of the fear of gene alteration stems from the precedent it might set for other forms of alteration. It would enable, for example, genes to be added for enhancement of intelligence or other desirable attributes, which raises the specter of even greater social inequality between the better and the less well off and a twisted search for the perfect child. Intentional diminishment must also be thrown into the mix: parents with healthy embryos might perversely decide to delete certain genes to diminish the future child's capabilities. Science fiction presents such scenarios in the service of evil dictators who use it to engineer a servant race, as in popular films such as *Bladerunner*. Bioethicists, on the other hand, debate scenarios of deaf parents' knocking out the hearing genes in their embryos to ensure deaf children, and dwarf parents inserting genes to make sure that their child will be of short stature.

In Larry and David's case, acting on their doctor's advice, they are not willing to trust genetic selection alone to ensure that their child will carry a sufficient dose of genes for same-sex attraction. They want to delete the genes associated with heterosexuality and insert those that link to same-sex attraction. Other couples will request different traits, though not all desirable traits will have the genetic wiring that can be manipulated, and cost and other factors will still make coital conception the preferred method of having children.

Fevered debate and discussion will erupt as such techniques move toward human application. Supporters will argue that parents have the right, if not the duty, to do the best for their children, particularly if they are already going through IVF and can access their embryo's genome. In Larry and David's case, they think they will do a better job as parents with a gay child, but they will not force that orientation on the child if the selection and alteration are not successful. Parents who choose other traits will argue that they can spend as much as they want after birth to give the child the lessons and experiences that equip him early on for a competitive life, so why should they not be able to do so before birth as well. Opponents will decry the engineering of children to serve parental ends. They will hang their opposition on the welfare of children: those deliberately diminished and those who have unreal and rigid expectations placed on their shoulders. They will also appeal to egalitarians to help them stop the wealthy from gaining even more advantages over the rest.

Long before gene alteration is ready for prime-time use, state or federal authorities might step in with laws restricting alteration research in humans and transfer of altered embryos so that a child may be born. Opponents will tout such laws as both necessary to protect children from the unknown harms of gene tinkering and necessary to protect society at large from the social inequalities that could result. Civil libertarians will protest that their procreative liberty is being trampled. With the support of persons who back the use of gene selection and alteration for health purposes and scientists who see restrictions on research as blocking scientific inquiry, they may prevail.

If laws are passed limiting alteration, responsible couples who want to choose their child's genes might sue to establish their constitutional right to do so. Their case will be stronger if the scientific evidence shows that genes can be knocked out or inserted in primates and human embryonic stem cells without developmental harm. They will also rely on the explicit constitutional protection expected in coming decades for a couple's use of assisted reproduction technology and embryo screening to identify embryos they wish to transfer. With such precedents on the books, the case for genetic engineering to produce children will be plausible and even compelling, though of course one cannot confidently predict that lower court judges or Supreme Court justices will accept the logic to its full extent. Additional support will come from the well-established right of parents to rear their children as they wish, for example, by teaching them foreign languages, sending them to private schools, or inculcating in them minority religious tenets.[26] Parental autonomy should not hinge on whether actions to benefit their children are taken before or after birth, particularly when the prebirth actions are safe and effective and necessary if the parent is to reproduce at all.

Cloning

What if Larry and David decide they wish to have a child that is the clone of one of them? A major problem is safety and efficacy, and that problem may persist for many years to come. If cloning techniques improve so that scientists can clone monkeys and other primates with ease, however, the question of cloning oneself or another person will inevitably follow. The ethical concerns here, however, are particularly daunting. Since the birth of Dolly the cloned sheep in 1998, there has been a wide, though not complete, consensus that reproductive cloning of humans is unacceptable.[27] Yet if cloning is safe and works in primates, attempts to use it in humans will undoubtedly occur. For example, Larry and David might prefer to clone Larry for the first child and then clone David for the second. A man who lacks viable sperm may have no other way to have genetic offspring. Gay and lesbian couples or single men or women may make the same argument.

Overcoming current reservations about reproductive cloning will be a difficult journey, and one that is less likely to find support in constitutional theories of procreative liberty than the embryo screening and alteration situations already examined. In those cases, would-be parents are choosing particular genes, not the entire genome, and have a clear kinship tie with the resulting child. The strongest case for reproductive cloning would be a situation of true gametic infertility, where a person has no way to reproduce genetically.[28] If that need were established, it could then be balanced against potential harms to offspring and other dangers from reproductive cloning.

But neither Larry nor David is gametically infertile. Either could reproduce with an egg donor and gestational surrogate, as David is doing here. By using his sister, Marge, as the source of eggs, Larry will be sharing 25 percent, rather than 50 percent, of his genes with the child. Cloning Larry with an egg from another donor would give him almost 100 percent of the genes, but then David would have no genetic connection. Of course, they could take turns; one child could be the clone of Larry and the next the clone of David. But this means that the partner who has not been cloned will not be reproducing in that case, as they would be if he or she contributed the usual 50 percent complement of genes. The other questions about the technical viability of cloning, and lingering concerns about the expectations set for a child who is truly a "chip off the old block," make this a less appealing case.

Nor does the logic of procreative liberty necessarily lead that far. A constitutional question would arise if a state or the federal government blocked reproductive cloning altogether once the case for its safety and efficacy were more firmly established. The constitutional claim would turn on whether procreative liberty extends to choosing the entire genome of one's offspring, rather than just choosing particular genes, as might be recognized in cases involving genetic selection and alteration.[29] Although a proponent might argue that he would not reproduce unless he could clone himself, I see a distinction between reproductive cloning when gametically infertile and when not, the latter enjoying less protection. The distinction turns on the strength of the purported need for cloning and whether it serves kinship and rearing interests in the ways that make reproduction so important to human flourishing and hence protected as a constitutional right. When the genetic tie that is so central to reproduction can be established without the more dangerous method of cloning, then the right to reproduce seems less strongly implicated.

If this distinction is accepted, the question of whether gay couples or a single man or woman should be viewed as gametically infertile would arise because they could reproduce with an egg donor and surrogate or lesbian partner and sperm source. In such cases the state would need to show only a rational basis for banning their cloning. Such distinctions, however, may be lost in legislative and judicial battles over cloning.

Gametes from Stem Cells

In 2030 Larry and David might also consider using stem cell technology to derive the gametes they need to reproduce—for example, if stem cell technology has progressed to the point that it is practical to derive gametes from embryonic stem cells or a person's own somatic cells. Because of ethical concerns about destroying embryos, recent scientific attention has focused on developing nonembryonic sources of pluripotent stem cells. Great success has occurred with reprogramming a person's own somatic cells to an earlier pluripotent state, which can then be induced to develop into the particular tissue needed for research or therapy. Eventually, it might be feasible to direct induced pluripotent stem cells to form male or female gametes.

With the enormous investment of resources and talent now pouring into stem cell research, it would not be surprising if the ability to derive gametes from pluripotent stem cells were well established by 2030 or soon after. Such a feat might lead to easy production of the eggs needed to carry out some important forms of stem cell research, including nuclear transfer cloning for research or therapeutic purposes. It might also lead to gametes for reproduction by persons lacking viable egg or sperm as a consequence of chemotherapy, disease, or trauma. Gay, lesbian, and transsexual persons might also welcome the availability of gametes derived from their own somatic tissue, rather than resorting to a sperm or egg donor to have a family.

If the stem cell technology is developed enough, Larry and David might prefer to use eggs derived from stem cells instead of from an egg donor. They would still need a gestational carrier and would still have to screen or alter embryos resulting from this procedure to have the gay male child they desire. But if Marge withdrew or were not able to provide viable eggs, this procedure might provide a way for Larry's own cells to produce the eggs needed for David and Larry to have a child.

But what then about the kinship and family issues that would arise if Larry's cells were used to produce eggs? He would be making the 50 percent genetic contribution to a child that occurs in coital reproduction. In this case, however, he will be providing an X chromosome and not the X or Y chromosome that the male partner in reproduction provides. The very description sets off alarm bells about pushing the envelope too far. But if safety concerns are allayed, would it matter that he would be providing the X chromosome that the female provides in reproduction and thus would in a technical sense be the genetic "mother" of his gay son?

Arguably, the label attached to the 50 percent of the chromosomes provided by each partner should not matter to them or to the child. Their son will necessarily have a gestational mother and will have both an X and a Y chromosome. If Larry and David decided that the child's sex was less important to them, they might have a girl, with Larry and David each by different routes providing an X chromosome. The child would have two "dads" rearing her just as a child of a lesbian couple would have two "moms." Yes, she would be a child without a genetically female mother with whom the child might have contact, but that now happens with the use of an unrelated egg donor.

The mind reels with the ethical and social complexity of producing children in this way, which I offer as an exercise for focusing on the meaning and scope of reproductive liberty and not as a prescription for the good society. Would a law banning the use of stem cell–derived gametes to have children be constitutional? Because genetic selection and alteration are not directly implicated, the question is one of kinship and family relations. The purpose here, however, is to establish the kinship and family relations that are not otherwise available to a gay couple because of their homosexuality. For a gay male couple to reproduce, a female gamete (as well as gestation) is needed. If their resort to an egg donor is accepted or even protected as an exercise of their reproductive liberty, then finding that female gamete within themselves, as stem cell–derived gamete techniques might enable them to do, should also be protected. If it can be safely done, it should not be banned because of its novelty or strangeness. Reproductive technology bends conceptions of parenthood in many ways. If it serves the core reproductive need of safely having genetically related offspring, its use should be protected, even if not applauded.

Conclusion

Larry and David's plan now seems far reaching and controversial. The Supreme Court would most likely prefer not to be involved, and if it is, it may step gingerly to avoid recognizing the full implications of a constitutional doctrine of procreative liberty. A conception of procreative liberty that extends to use of assisted reproduction technology and then to some degree of genetic selection could plausibly lead to the surprising conclusion that what Larry and David propose may by 2030 fit within the mainstream of reproductive choice. Technology will push our value system and our laws to include many things now considered outré. Will this be bad? It will depend on safety, efficacy, numbers, and how far their plans deviate from the experiences that make reproduction and parenting so central to human flourishing.

Two decades is a short period of time for full-scale trait association networks to be teased out and then to perfect the ability to insert and delete genes in humans in a safe and effective way. Two decades may also be too brief a time for social and cultural norms about parental choice to change and develop in the direction described here. But there is much room for legal and constitutional norms now focused on abortion and sterilization to evolve to encompass assisted reproduction, genetic selection and alteration, stem cell–derived gametes, and even reproductive cloning. As technical developments occur, technology will exert hydraulic pressure on procreative practices and the legal rights that protect them. As conceptions of family and parental choice change, courts and legislatures will respond accordingly. By 2030 the logic of procreative freedom should recognize the right of Larry and David to use the technologies available to have the family they choose.

Notes

1. *Gonzalez* v. *Carhart*, 550 U.S. 124 (2007).

2. *Skinner* v. *Oklahoma*, 316 U.S. 535 (1942).

3. *Bowers* v. *Hardwick*, 478 U.S. 186 (1986).

4. *Lawrence* v. *Texas*, 539 U.S. 558 (2003).

5. *Perry* v. *Schwartzenegger*, 704 F. Supp. 2d 921 (N.D. Cal. 2010).

6. Saswati Sunderam and others, "Assisted Reproductive Technology Surveillance: United States, 2006," 58 *Mortality and Morbidity Weekly Report* (2009): 1–25 (www. cdc.gov/mmwr/pdf/ss/ss5805.pdf).

7. Stephanie Saul, "Birth of Octuplets Puts Focus on Fertility Clinics," *New York Times*, February 11, 2009 (www.nytimes.com/2009/02/12/health/12ivf.html?ref= nadyasuleman).

8. *York* v. *Jones*, 717 F. Supp. 421 (E.D. Va. 1989).

9. John A. Robertson, "In the Beginning: The Legal Status of Early Embryos," 76 *Virginia Law Review* (1990): 437.

10. *Davis* v. *Davis*, 842 S.W.2d 588 (Tenn. 1992); *A.Z.* v. *B.Z.*, 725 N.E.2d 1051 (Mass. 2000).

11. See Sunderam and others, "Assisted Reproductive Technology Surveillance."

12. *Johnson* v. *Calvert*, 851 P.2d 776 (Cal. 1993); *Uniform Parentage Act* (amended 2002) (www.law.upenn.edu/bll/archives/ulc/upa/final2002.htm).

13. Melanie Thernstrom, "My Futuristic Insta-Family," *New York Times Magazine*, January 2, 2011, 28.

14. *Skinner*, 316 U.S. 535; *Stanley* v. *Illinois*, 405 U.S. 645 (1972); *Cleveland Bd. of Educ.* v. *LaFleur*, 414 U.S. 632 (1973).

15. *Eisenstadt* v. *Baird*, 405 U.S. 438 (1972).

16. *In the Matter of Baby M*, 537 A.2d 1227 (N.J. 1988).

17. *Johnson* v. *Calvert*, 851 P.2d 776 (Cal. 1993).

18. Tex. Fam. Code Ann. 160.751–160.763 (2008).

19. See *Uniform Parentage Act* (amended 2002).

20. President's Council on Bioethics, "Human Cloning and Human Dignity: An Ethical Inquiry" (July 2001), 110–11 (http://bioethics.georgetown.edu/pcbe/reports/

cloningreport/); Michael J. Sandel, *The Case against Perfection: Ethics in the Age of Genetic Engineering* (Cambridge, Mass.: Belknap Press of Harvard University Press, 2007).

21. John A. Robertson, "Procreative Liberty in the Era of Genomics," 29 *American Journal of Law and Medicine* (2003): 439.

22. John A. Robertson, "Assisting Reproduction, Choosing Genes, and the Scope of Reproductive Freedom," 76 *George Washington Law Review* (2008): 1490, 1513.

23. John A. Robertson, "Procreative Liberty and Harm to Offspring in Assisted Reproduction," 30 *American Journal of Law and Medicine* (2004): 7.

24. See Robertson, "Procreative Liberty in the Era of Genomics"; Robertson, "Assisting Reproduction, Choosing Genes, and the Scope of Reproductive Freedom."

25. Alison Abbott, "Biologists Claim Nobel Prize with a Knock-Out," 449 *Nature* (2007): 642.

26. *Meyer* v. *Nebraska*, 262 U.S. 390 (1923); *Pierce* v. *Society of Sisters*, 268 U.S. 510 (1925); *Wisconsin* v. *Yoder*, 406 U.S. 205 (1972).

27. National Bioethics Advisory Commission, "Cloning Human Beings: Report and Recommendations," 1997 (http://bioethics.georgetown.edu/pcbe/reports/past_commissions/nbac_cloning.pdf); President's Council on Bioethics, "Human Cloning and Human Dignity." For an argument in favor of reproductive cloning, see Dan W. Brock, "Human Cloning and Our Sense of Self," 296 *Science* (2002): 314–16.

28. John A. Robertson, "Liberty, Identity, and Human Cloning," 76 *Texas Law Review* (1998): 1371.

29. John A. Robertson, "Two Models of Human Cloning," 27 *Hofstra Law Review* (1999): 609.

11

The Problems and Possibilities of Modern Genetics: A Paradigm for Social, Ethical, and Political Analysis

Imagine a future in which any person, man or woman, could engineer a child as a genetic replica of himself or herself. Or in which a child could be the biological fusion of the genes of two men or two women. Or in which all individuals could know, with reasonable certainty, which diseases they would suffer in the months, years, or even decades ahead. Would this new genetic age constitute a better world, or a deformed one? The triumph of modern civilization, or the realization of modernity's dark side?

With a subject as large and as profound as modern genetics, we face a major question from the start about how to approach it. We can take a scientific approach, examining the use of information technology in genomic research, or the latest advances in identifying certain genetic mutations, or the use of genetic knowledge in the development of medical technologies. We can take a social scientific approach, seeking to understand the economic incentives that drive the genetic research agenda, or surveying public attitudes toward genetic testing, or documenting the use of reproductive genetic technology according to socioeconomic class. We can take a public safety approach, reviewing different genetic tests and therapies for safety and efficacy with a view to identifying regulatory procedures to protect and inform vulnerable patients undergoing gene therapy trials. As we think about the genetic future, all of these approaches are valuable. Yet there are even more fundamental questions that need to be addressed. These concern the human meaning of our growing powers over the human genome.

The reason modern genetics worries, excites, and fascinates the imagination is that we sense that this area of science will affect or even transform the core experiences of being human—such as how we have children, how we experience freedom, and how we face sickness and death. Like no other area of modern science and technology, genetics inspires both dreams and nightmares about the human future with equal passion: the dream of perfect babies, the nightmare of genetic tyranny. But the dream and the nightmare are not the best guides to understanding how genetics will challenge our moral self-understanding and our social fabric. We need a more sober approach—one that confronts the real ethical and social dilemmas that we face, without constructing such a monstrous image of the future that our gravest warnings are ignored like the bioethics boy who cried wolf.

What is the role of constitutional adjudication in confronting these dilemmas? In a word, that role should be limited. To be sure, American constitutional principles and institutions provide the frameworks and forums for democratic deliberation regarding bioethical and other important moral questions, but in most cases it will not be possible to resolve them by reference to norms that can fairly be said to be discoverable in the text, logic, structure, or historical understanding of the Constitution. Reasonable people of goodwill who disagree on these matters may be equally committed to constitutional principles of due process, equal protection, and the like; and it would be deeply wrong—profoundly anti-constitutional—for people on either side of a disputed question left unsettled by the Constitution to manipulate constitutional concepts or language in the hope of inducing judges, under the guise of interpreting the Constitution, to hand them victories that they have not been able to achieve in the forums of democratic deliberation established by the Constitution itself. It would be a tragedy for our polity if bioethics became the next domain in which overreaching judges, charged with protecting the rule of law, undermine the constitutional division of powers by usurping the authority vested under the Constitution in the people acting on their own initiative (as is authorized under the laws of some states) or through their elected representatives.

Possibility and Prediction

In thinking about the new genetics, it is all too easy to commit two errors at once: worrying too much too early and worrying too little too late. For decades, scientists and science fiction writers have predicted the coming of genetic engineering, some with fear and loathing, some with anticipatory glee. But when the gradual pace of technological change does not seem as wonderful as the dream or as terrible as the nightmare, we get used to our new powers all too readily. Profound change quickly seems prosaic, because we measure it against the world we imagined instead of the world we have. Our technological advances—including those that require transgressing existing moral boundaries—quickly seem insufficient, because the human desire for perfect control and perfect happiness is insatiable.

Of course, sometimes we face the opposite problem: scientists assure us that today's breakthrough will not lead to tomorrow's nightmare. They tell us that what we want (such as cures for disease) is just over the horizon but that what we fear (for example, human cloning) is technologically impossible. The case of human cloning is indeed instructive, revealing the dangers of both over-prediction and under-prediction. So here we take a brief historical digression, but a digression with a point.

In the 1970s, as the first human embryos were being produced outside the human body, many critics treated in vitro fertilization and human cloning as equally pregnant developments, with genetic engineering lurking not far behind. James Watson testified before the United States Congress in 1971, declaring that we must pass laws about cloning now before it is too late. In one sense, perhaps, the oracles were right: even if human cloning did not come as fast as they expected, it is coming and probably coming soon. But because we worried so much more about human cloning even then, test-tube babies came to seem prosaic very quickly, in part because they were not clones and in part because the babies themselves were such a blessing. We barely paused to consider the strangeness of originating human life in the laboratory; of beholding, with human eyes, our own human origins; of suspending nascent human life in the freezer; of further separating procreation from sex, or of treating procreation as a species of manufacture and a child as the operational objective of an application of technique. Of course, babies who are produced by in vitro fertilization are loved by their parents and are, in themselves, great blessings. Whatever one's views of the ethics of in vitro fertilization (and the authors of this paper are not entirely of one mind on the question), no one would deny that it has fulfilled time and again the longing most couples possess to have a child of their own, flesh of their own flesh. But, by the same token, no one should deny that it has also created strange new prospects, including the novel possibility of giving birth to another couple's child—flesh not of my flesh, you might say—and the possibility of picking and choosing human embryos for life or death based on their genetic characteristics. It has also left us the tragic question of deciding what we owe the thousands of embryos now left over in freezers—a dilemma with no satisfying moral answer.

But this is only the first part of the cloning story. By the 1990s, in vitro fertilization had become normal, while many leading scientists assured the world that mammals could never be cloned. Ian Wilmut and his team in Scotland proved them all wrong with the birth of Dolly, a cloned sheep, in 1996, and something similar seems to be happening now with primate and human cloning. In 2002 Gerald Schatten, a cloning researcher at the University of Pittsburgh, said "primate cloning, including human cloning, will not be in our lifetimes."[1] A year later, he was saying that "given enough time and materials, we may discover how to make it work." In 2007 researchers at Oregon Health Sciences University announced the successful cloning of primates, which has since been repeated by scientists across the globe. And today, leading laboratories around the world are eagerly—and confidently—at work trying to produce the first cloned human embryos for research. If they succeed, the age of human "reproductive cloning" is probably not far behind.

The case of human cloning should teach us a double lesson: beware the dangers both of overprediction and of underprediction. Overprediction risks blinding us to the significance of present realities by focusing our attention on the utopia and dystopia that do not come as prophesied. Under-prediction risks blinding us to where today's technological breakthroughs may lead, both for better and for worse. Prediction requires the right kind of caution—caution about letting our imaginations run wild and caution about letting science proceed without limits because we falsely assume that it is always innocent and always will be. To think clearly, therefore, we must put aside the grand dreams and great nightmares of the genetic future to consider the moral meaning of the genetic present. And we need to explore what these new genetic possibilities might mean for how we live, what we value, and how we treat one another.

Humanly speaking, the new genetics seems to have five dimensions or meanings: genetics as a route to self-understanding, a way of knowing ourselves; genetics as a route to new medical therapies, a way of curing ourselves; genetics as a potential tool for genetic engineering, a way of redesigning ourselves and our offspring; genetics as a means of knowing something about our biological destiny, about our health and sickness in the future; and genetics as a tool for screening the traits of the next generation, for choosing some lives and rejecting others. We want to explore each of these five dimensions in turn—beginning with the hunger for self-understanding.

Genetic Self-Understanding

The first reason for pursuing knowledge of genetics is simply man's desire to know, and particularly man's desire to know *himself*. Alone among the animals, human beings possess the capacity, drive, and ability to look upon ourselves as objects of inquiry. We study ourselves because we are not content to live unself-reflectively. We are not satisfied living immediately in nature like the other animals do, asking no questions about who we are, where we came from, or where we are going. We do not merely accept the given world as it is; we seek to uncover its meaning and structure. Modern biology, of course, is only one avenue of self-understanding. But it is an especially powerful and prominent way of seeking self-knowledge in the modern age. Instead of asking who we are by exploring human deliberation, judgments, and choices, or human achievement in the arts, humanities, and sciences, or human polities, societies, and cultures, the biologist seeks knowledge of the human by examining what might be called the "mechanics" of human life. Genetics fits perfectly within this vision: it seems to offer us a code for life; it promises to shed empirical light on our place in nature; it claims to tell us something reliable about our human design, our prehuman origins and, perhaps, our posthuman fate.

But the more we learn about genetics, the more we seem to confront the limits, as well as the significance, of genetic explanation. As the cell biologist Lenny Moss put it,

> Once upon a time it was believed that something called "genes" were integral units, that each specified a piece of phenotype, that the phenotype as a whole was the result of the sum of these units, and that evolutionary change was the result of new changes created by random mutation and differential survival. Once upon a time it was believed that the chromosomal location of genes was irrelevant, that DNA was the citadel of stability, that DNA which didn't code for proteins was biological "junk," and that coding DNA included, as it were, its own instructions for use. Once upon a time it would have stood to reason that the complexity of an organism would be proportional to the number of its unique genetic units.[2]

But, in fact, the triumph of modern genetics has also meant the humbling of modern genetics. Big hypotheses now seem to require revision and greater measure. And in many ways, we are probably relieved that genetics does not tell us everything we need to know about ourselves. For human beings, this means that we are a great deal freer than we would be if a purely genetic account of being human could answer all the interesting and important questions.

Even as we are relieved to discover the limits of genetic determinism, however, our hunger for genetic understanding remains strong. Disease is a threat to our freedom as well as to our very lives, and we still hope that genetics might help us conquer that mortal threat. We still hope that genetics is the secret of disease, if not the secret of life.

Genetic Therapy

The threat of disease leads to the second dimension of the new genetics: the search for medical cures. Modern science, unlike ancient science, does not rest on the foundation of curiosity alone. It seeks not merely to understand nature but also to control it for the sake of other ends. Human beings understand knowledge as something often worth pursuing for its own sake, but they recognize at the same time that many types of knowledge are instrumentally quite valuable as well. While man may be the only truly curious animal, his curiosity is not his only guiding passion and probably not his most powerful passion. He also understands the value of health and looks for ways to preserve it; and he certainly fears death and seeks to fend it off. Like other animals, human beings seek comfort and survival. But unlike other animals, we possess the capacity to pursue comfort and survival through the systematic application of reason. Modern science, especially modern biology, promises the "relief of man's estate," in Francis Bacon's famous phrase, in return for the right to explore nature without limits. Descartes skillfully negotiated this bargain centuries ago, and we quote here a passage much cited by those interested in the origins of modern science:

> So soon as I had acquired some general notions concerning Physics . . . they caused me to see that it is possible to attain knowledge which is very useful for life, and that, instead of that speculative philosophy which is found in the Schools, we may find a practical philosophy by means of which, knowing the force and the action of fire, water, air, the stars, heaven, and all the other bodies that environ us, as distinctly as we know the different crafts of our artisans, we can in the same way employ them in all those uses to which they are adapted, and thus render ourselves as the masters and possessors of nature.[3]

Not surprisingly, the "nature" we most seek to "master" is our own. We seek to conquer human disease, and perhaps even to make death itself a series of conquerable diseases. Evidently, our genetic code has fitted us to revolt against our genetic fate.

Of course, the "speculative philosophy" that Descartes sought to leave behind was suffused with religion, and quite centrally concerned with the search for mankind's place in the cosmological whole and before God. The new science and the old religion thus seem to present us with two different ways of revolting against our biological fate: The religious believer seeks such revolt beyond nature in God, by looking beyond our genetic deficiencies to the hope of eternal salvation. The scientist seeks such revolt through nature in science, by understanding nature's mishaps (or mutations) so that we might correct them. The unknowable God, if one believes He exists and interests Himself in the affairs of men (as Jews and Christians believe), promises better long-term results; He may begin "curing" (or perfecting) us now but will complete the job only after we breathe our last mortal breath. The empirical scientist, if you give him enough funding, specializes in near-term results; he cures us now, but only for a while. This does not mean that science and religion are enemies: religious people are often great scientists, and great scientists are often deeply religious. But it does suggest that the cure-seeking scientist lives on the narrow ridge between holiness and rebellion. He imitates the old God by healing the sick; yet, at the cutting edge, he always risks supplanting the old God by believing that he can in some truly comprehensive way "relieve man's estate," by working within nature rather than looking beyond it.

Genetics, in this sense, is simply a new frontier in the long ascent of modern medicine. It aims to repair broken genes or correct disease-causing mutations by direct intervention. And it aims to use our growing understanding of the human genome to diagnose and treat human disease with greater precision.

But it turns out that most diseases are too complicated to be conquered or even effectively managed by genetics alone and that markers for identifying and predicting a given disease do not always or easily translate into usable knowledge about the disease's causation. The capacity to fix genes with perfect precision and without side effects is also proving remarkably difficult. Already, there have been some high-profile examples of gene-therapy trials going terribly wrong, and the field now proceeds with perhaps a more befitting caution. There is little doubt, of course, that over time our genetic knowledge will improve modern medicine and thus prove a great blessing to us all. But there also seems little doubt that the new genetics will not be the therapeutic panacea that many once hoped and that many scientists and policymakers offered as a (perhaps *the*) central justification for the human genome project. Biological knowledge and biological control are simply not the same, even when it comes to curing diseases and most certainly when it comes to so-called genetic engineering.

Genetic Design

This brings us to the third dimension of the new genetics: the prospect of designing our descendants, a prospect much feared, much discussed, much fancied, and probably much overstated. In the reproductive context, the real dilemma (already here, in its early form) involves picking and choosing human embryos for implantation based on the genetic characteristics that nature gave them. But this is significantly different from designing human beings with genotypes entirely of our own creation. By focusing so much on the dream and the nightmare of genetic engineering, we risk treating the real-life possibilities of genetic control as less profound than they really are. Yet again there is the danger that we will worry too much too early or too little too late.

To be sure, it may turn out to be possible (perhaps soon) to engineer genetic monstrosities—like a human version of the monkeys with jellyfish genes that glow in the dark. Perhaps some modern-day Frankenstein will create human fetuses with primordial wings; or children with seven fingers; or human beings that are part male and part female by design. If human life is seen as a mere canvas, and if the biologist is seen as an artist thriving on "transgression," then genetic engineering will indeed prove to be a nightmare. And sadly, there is little doubt that someone, somewhere, will attempt such terrible experiments and may succeed in producing at least embryonic or fetal monsters. But there remain good reasons to believe that most democratic societies, in the name of safety if not morality, will enact legislative barriers to the biological equivalent of postmodern art. Precisely because it is so grotesque, such monster making is not our most urgent ethical problem.

Democratic societies, after all, do not seek the monstrous; we tend, rather, to seek the useful. And the worst abuses of biotechnology may come in trying to make the difficult, often harsh, dimensions of life disappear (like physical deformation, childhood disease, early causes of debility and death) in the name of compassion or mercy and to do so by screening and aborting those with handicaps or deformities that some people are tempted to believe make their lives not worth living. There will always be knaves who engage in monstrous acts merely for the thrill of transgressing social norms. But the real challenge is to consider those uses of genetic knowledge and genetic choice that are both technically feasible (as science, not art) and that seem to run with rather than against the grain of liberal society. It is those potential abuses that have some utilitarian justification—such as improving life, or ending suffering, or guaranteeing every child a healthy genome, or expanding reproductive freedom—that we must confront squarely and without delay.

But since many people worry so much about full-blown genetic engineering, we should not ignore it entirely. So let us offer a brief critique. The most tempting reason to engage in genetic engineering is to assert new kinds of control over our offspring, and to design children with certain desirable human attributes: high IQs, perfect pitch, beautiful appearance, remarkable strength, amazing speed, and photographic memory. Some might even seek to design human offspring with better-than-human attributes. But these scenarios strike us as technically unlikely, and not merely humanly misguided. Technically, we doubt whether we will acquire soon, or perhaps ever, the sophistication to engineer certain human traits de novo, and we doubt whether the traits some enthusiasts seek to engineer are so clearly rooted in a definable genetic pattern that we can deliberately replicate or improve. At the very least, we believe the project of trying to find such patterns and implement such designs would involve so many grotesque failures that the back-lash would be swift and overwhelming.

More deeply, we doubt that human ingenuity and technical skill will ever prove up to the task of designing a better human being—even as a genetic thought experiment. If the goal is human excellence or better-than-human excellence, the designer must begin with an idea of excellence itself. And here, we face two insurmountable hurdles. First, we doubt that modern scientists can improve on nature when it comes to making a better musician, or artist, or scientist. It is hard to imagine a composer better than Mozart or a playwright better than Shakespeare. In seeking to maximize some human trait by genetic manipulation, we will most likely deform other crucial traits and thus deform the excellent human wholes that nature so mysteriously and so remarkably supplies. And if we seek, say, to make faster men and women to run our races, have we really created better men or women—or just biological machines? Cars move faster than men; pitching machines throw harder than pitchers—but neither invention is better than human; they are merely subhuman things. (This problem is explored in great detail in *Beyond Therapy*, a report produced by the President's Council on Bioethics, on which and for which we both served.) And even if we could make as many Mozarts as we like, do we really serve the cause of human excellence by making that excellence so common?

The second major barrier to the genetic engineering project is the fact that superior talent is not the only form of human excellence. Many of the most admirable human beings live lives characterized not by measurable achievement but by fidelity, charity, love, courage. Perhaps there are important genetic predispositions to such traits of character, but good genes are rarely enough to make good people, even if bad genes sometimes make individuals so psychologically impaired (or chemically imbalanced) that virtue is beyond their reach. Moreover, we suspect that even replicating these good genetic predispositions will be beyond the engineer's reach because it involves so many biological factors that go beyond mere genetics. Even if our technology improved, we are dubious about the possibility of engineering more virtuous offspring—which is the only real measure of whether genetic engineering would make human life truly better.

All that said, the one form of "genetic engineering" that does demand our attention is the very real prospect of human cloning—a way of controlling the genetic makeup of our offspring with great precision, by copying the genetic makeup of someone already here. The ethical and social significance of human cloning is profound, involving a deep violation of the relationship between parent and child. But technically, cloning is remarkably simple compared with other imagined forms of genetic engineering. It does not involve manipulating the interlocking pieces of the human genome, but the wholesale replication of an existing genotype. It is more like copying a great novel already written than writing a great novel from scratch.

And it is this comparative technical ease, in fact, that makes cloning a genuine worry, not simply a distracting dream or nightmare. Cloning involves a perverse form of self-love, by imposing our own genomes on our children. In a sense, it robs new life of an open-ended future, and it forces the young clone to live always and forever in the shadow of his elder genetic twin—in the shadow of both his past accomplishments and past failures. In the end, human cloning may prove a test case of our capacity to limit the dehumanizing uses of biotechnology and our capacity to defend those human goods—like the family—that make human life truly human.

Genetic Foreknowledge

But if most forms of genetic engineering, beyond cloning, are probably not in the offing, this hardly means that the new genetics is socially and ethically insignificant. What it means is that we need to pay much closer attention to the human meaning of genetic knowledge itself—both how we use it and what it does to us once we possess it. And this brings us to the fourth dimension of the new genetics: the meaning of our gaining partial foreknowledge about our biological fate, and especially the meaning of our knowing bad things (or good things) about our biological future.

Of course, to be self-aware at all is to have some foreknowledge of our mortal destiny: We know that death will one day take us; we know that natural disasters, or terrible accidents, or vicious attacks could make this day our last day; we know that some mysterious ailment could strike us without warning. Those of us who eat the wrong foods and spend too much time at our desks know that heart problems and clogged arteries may lie in our future; even without sophisticated genetic tests, we know about the presence of hereditary diseases in our families; and we all know that time will eventually win its final victory, whether at age 70, or 80, or 90, or 100.

And yet most of us live our day-to-day lives without focusing too much on our own mortality. For better and for worse, we do not live each day as if it could be our last; we do not make the fact of death a dominant reality in our everyday lives. When a loved one dies or some tragedy strikes, we are perhaps reminded of our mortal condition; we might imagine our children throwing dirt into our graves. But the immediacy of life quickly returns, and we live again, for a while, as if the horizon of the future were very long, if not indefinite.

Strangely, modern individuals are both more obsessed with death and less aware of death than our less-modern forebears. We are obsessed with trying to avoid death through better diet and better medicine, yet we are less aware of death because it rarely strikes us in untimely ways, at least compared with the omnipresence of death in the lives of our ancestors. In advanced societies today, most people die after living full lives, not from mass plagues, or mass killings, or infant mortality.

In an essay on the meaning of mortality, the philosopher Hans Jonas quotes the following passage from Psalms: "So teach us to number our days, that we may get us a heart of wisdom." His point is not primarily religious but existential. If we lived as if tomorrow were forever, we would lack the urgency to live boldly and love deeply. And if we believed that this life would last forever, even the sweetest things would become routine.

But in the age of genetic testing, the instruction to number our days takes on new meaning, since these tests may allow us—or force us—to number them with increasing precision. Today, we can diagnose numerous deadly diseases using genetic testing with absolute or near-absolute certainty, and long before we experience any visible symptoms. For some of these diseases—like Huntington's—there is no cure; the diagnosis is a death sentence, giving the likely age of onset, the likely period of decline, and the likely age of death if nothing else kills first. For other diseases—like breast cancer—genetic tests can offer a highly reliable, though not quite perfect, indication of a person's susceptibility to the disease, with potential treatments ranging from preemptive surgery to remove one's breasts and ovaries to intense monitoring to detect the coming cancer as early as possible.

But does this genetic foreknowledge make life better or worse? Is there a case for genetic ignorance? At what age and under what circumstances should people know their genetic fates? These are hard questions with no easy answers. They also present difficult questions of law and governance: In protecting the individual father's or mother's right to know his or her genetic fate, are we undermining the child's right to genetic ignorance? Should those with healthy genes be allowed to benefit from their good fortune by paying less for health insurance? Or does this right to benefit from one's genetic profile in the free market necessarily come at the grave social cost of making those with bad genes uninsurable? All hard questions—morally, existentially, socially, legally— with no easy or obvious answers.

In those situations like Huntington's, where the diagnosis is clear and there is no cure, genetic self-knowledge seems like both a blessing and a curse. It is a blessing because it might lead individuals to an uncommon wisdom about the preciousness of life; it might move them to live without wasting time because they know just how short their time really is. And yet such foreknowledge must also seem like a curse; the permanent presence of looming death might make living seem worthless; there are too many projects they know they can never finish and too many ambitions they know they can never fulfill. Their genetic death sentence may come to feel like a living death.

In those situations where some therapeutic intervention is possible, for those who test positive for the breast cancer mutation, for example, the young often face drastic and wrenching decisions: Is the greater chance of longer life worth living with the scars of mastectomy or living without the possibility of bearing children? Is it really better to have the knowledge that makes such a tragic choice necessary rather than the ignorance that would allow us to live without being so haunted until the disease really comes?

Right now, the number of diseases we can test for genetically is somewhat limited, and many of these tests offer clear positive or negative diagnoses. But what may be coming is a world of imperfect knowledge about terrible possibilities—with a battery of tests that give greater and lesser probabilities of getting certain diseases, at certain times, compared with the general population. All of our human fears will be sharpened, our anxiety made more precise, our worries and fears given a genetic scorecard. What good is this knowledge to us, especially when the power to diagnose will come long before the power to cure—leaving us in the so-called "diagnostic-therapeutic gap"? And yet will we be able to resist this new form of high-tech astrology? Will it teach us to number our days and make us wise? Or will it make life seem like a short trip through a genetic minefield—by forcing us to confront every morning the ways in which we might die?

Genetic Choice

These types of genetic foreknowledge take on new meaning when we move to the reproductive sphere, and when the burden is not simply living with knowledge of one's own potential fate but deciding whether genetic knowledge may be regarded as justifying decisions to abort an affected fetus or discard an affected embryo. And this leads us to the final dimension of the new genetics: the use of genetic knowledge to decide between "life worth living" and "life unworthy of life."

For a long time, people have worried about the so-called enhancement problem, fearing that wealthy parents would use genetic technology to get an unfair advantage for their offspring. But perhaps the greater and more urgent danger is that the limitless pursuit of equal results—the desire to give everyone a mutation-free life and thus an equal chance at the pursuit of happiness—will actually undermine our belief in the intrinsic equality of all persons. The pursuit of genetic equality will lead to an age of genetic discrimination. Indeed, in some ways, it already has.

Of course, if we could cure Tay-Sachs or Down syndrome during any stage of development, from the earliest embryonic stage forward, we would do so. But once conception has taken place, and in cases in which there is no cure, we are left with the decision to accept or reject—to nurture or destroy—a human life in progress, a life that is real enough to us that we can evaluate and pass judgment on its genetic characteristics. With the arrival of preimplantation genetic diagnosis, we may face a radical transformation of assisted reproduction—a transformation made more significant by the rising numbers of couples and even single women who are now turning to in vitro fertilization to have children. In this new world, genetic testing would become a standard part of in vitro fertilization, and the tested embryos would be divided into different classes: those doomed to suffer killer diseases like Tay-Sachs would be separated from those who are not; those doomed to suffer disabilities like Down syndrome would be separated from those who are not; those prone to suffer late-onset diseases like breast cancer would be separated from those who are not.

By making reproduction into a process of division by class, we would transform the welcoming attitude of unconditional love into a eugenic attitude of conditional acceptance. Of course, we would do this in the name of compassion, or mercy, or equality. We seek to give our children healthy genetic equipment and to spare those who would suffer by "nipping them in the bud." But the pursuit of genetic equality requires a radical program of genetic discrimination and a willingness to discard those judged to be unfit. Whatever one might think about the moral status of the early embryos tested in preimplantation genetic diagnosis, they are certainly not nothing. They are developing members of the human species—offspring of their parents—possessing the same genetic identity as embryos that they would possess through life, if those who created them in the first place did not decide to cut their lives short.

Seen clearly, the real danger of the genetic age is not that the "gene-rich" will outpace the "gene-poor"; it is that the pursuit of genetic equality will erode our willingness to treat those who are genetically impaired as humanly equal. We will replace the hard but humanizing and elevating work of loving and caring for the disabled with a false compassion that weeds out the inconveniently unfit. It is hard to see how the equal dignity of persons with Down syndrome is served by treating Down syndrome as a legitimate reason to abort—even for those who generally regard themselves as "pro-choice" on abortion. And it is hard to see how parents will experience pregnancy with any equanimity or joy if they have a full genetic readout of their embryo or fetus and must decide whether the mutation for breast cancer, or Parkinson's, or Alzheimer's disease is reason enough to abort and try again. This is the moral paradox at the heart of genetic control: In seeking an existence without misery or imperfection, we may make ourselves more miserable and imperfect; and we may even do miserable and ultimately dehumanizing things in the name of mercy.

Moral Wisdom and Modern Politics

The advance of modern genetics is one of the great achievements of our time, an example of the creative and truth-seeking spirit of our humanity. But too often, we thoughtlessly assume that the progress of science is identical to the progress of man. The truth is much more complicated. Many men and women of the past were superior in virtue to many of us now, and many scientific discoveries of the present and future (not unlike some discoveries of the past, such as nuclear weapons) will prove a mixed blessing—at best.

The new genetics will deliver many goods but will also confront us with many burdens. We will need to make choices, and those choices will require philosophical judgments about good and evil and better and worse, not only scientific judgments about possible and impossible. We will need to think especially about the goods in life that must be honored and respected and cannot be trumped, even by an otherwise legitimate desire to promote human health and longevity. This is a task that modern genetics is not equipped to handle; yet it is this very task, one requiring a return to first principles, that is necessary if we are to choose wisely and govern ourselves well in the genetic age.

In the meantime, however, we need to reflect on what sound governance means today—given the many scientific possibilities and technological unknowns, given the current political and cultural climate, and given the enduring realities of human nature that persist even as the possibilities of the genetic era expand.

First, it is imperative that we sort out the three overlapping issues of abortion, embryo research, and new modes of procreation—which are morally related but also distinct in various ways and which are governed by different legal regimes and different political realities. Abortion is the destruction of a developing human life, inside the womb, in the supposed interests of the carrying mother and sometimes because the developing child has a genetic defect or is the "wrong" gender (which usually means female). Embryo research is the exploitation and destruction of embryos in the laboratory, for the sake of medical advances and potential therapies. And new techniques for making babies involve the creation, screening, and manipulation of embryos in the laboratory, with a view, in the future, to implanting these genetically tested, modified, or cloned embryos into the child-seeking mother. In the first case we have a child whose parent or parents do not want him or her; in the second case we seek cures for the ones we love and instrumentalize nascent human life to get them; in the last case, we want a child that we could not otherwise have, or we want a child of a particular sort—cloned, screened, or enhanced.

Taken together, these three issues reveal the profound moral and legal contradictions that have taken shape over the past thirty years surrounding the beginnings of human life: We worry about manipulating embryos in a way that might lead to a new eugenics, while protecting the legal right to destroy embryos and fetuses for any reason at all. It is legally possible to ban all research on embryos outside the body in some states—and even to treat such embryos, as Louisiana does, as "juridical persons"—while getting taxpayer funding to destroy them in other states. Some supporters of embryo research say that embryos outside the body are not human because they cannot develop to term unless implanted, while pro-choice advocates say that once we implant them in the very wombs where they might develop we cannot legally protect them. For years, we have been engaging in revolutionary new techniques of producing children in the laboratory—with little or no regulation and often no prior experiments on animals, and recent studies suggest that there might be real dangers and real harms to the resulting children. We have engaged in this great baby-making experiment with the apparent approval of most American liberals, who seem to care more about not treating embryos as subjects (and thus imperiling, as they see it, the right to abortion) than protecting the well-being of in vitro fertilization children-to-be. And while the Food and Drug Administration has said that it can regulate cloning to produce children and that the attempt to do so in the United States must pass its regulatory muster, the agency can do so only by treating the cloned embryo as a "product" (like a drug) that might imperil the health and well-being of the mother.

The successful efforts of partisans of abortion to persuade the Supreme Court (in the case of *Roe* v. *Wade, 410 U.S. 113* [1973]) to manufacture a constitutional right to abortion itself creates challenges to us as a society in trying to sort out this mess and put into place wise and truly humane policies. *Roe* is already cited by some as standing for a broad principle of "reproductive freedom" that necessarily extends to any and all manner of baby making as well as to the unconstrained exploitation and manipulation of prenatal human life. As technology advances, will *Roe* function as a sort of "eugenics license"? In our view, resisting such a development must be made a high priority. Even when it comes to abortion itself, many who regard themselves as generally pro-choice recognize the social harm *Roe* has done, not only as the result of the sweeping nature of the abortion right it created but also by removing profound moral questions about the dignity of human life and the proper scope of human liberty from the forums of democratic deliberation and placing them in the hands of judges. The resulting culture war has left our nation deeply divided for nearly forty years.

Of course, the Supreme Court has on occasion stepped back from treating *Roe* as embodying the radically socially libertarian principle that some on the cultural left wish it to be. In *Washington v. Glucksberg* and *Vacco v. Quill*, for example, the justices unanimously rejected lower courts' uses of *Roe* as a precedent for creating a constitutional right to assisted suicide.[4] And the fate of *Roe* itself remains uncertain. Many believe that four of the nine justices currently serving on the Supreme Court would reverse it and return the question of abortion to the democratic process the moment a fifth justice was available to join them.

Whether *Roe* ultimately stands or falls, however, it is critical that it not become the jurisprudential basis for a larger judicialization of bioethics and genetics. These are issues on which reasonable people will disagree, and in most cases the disputed questions will be left unresolved by the text, logic, structure, and historical understanding of the Constitution. Sober and thoughtful democratic deliberation will be needed and should not be short-circuited by judicial interventions and impositions of policy. *Roe* itself was a dubious decision in our judgment; and for judges, now or in the future, to invoke it to rationalize similar usurpations when it comes to publicly disputed bioethical matters would be to multiply the abuse. There are even now decisions that must be made, and policies that ought to be enacted, that under any plausible reading of the Constitution are matters for legislative deliberation and resolution, not judicial imposition under the guise of constitutional interpretation.

These policies include

—a national ban on all human cloning, which means a prohibition on the creation of cloned human embryos for any purpose

—a permanent legislative ban on the patenting of human embryos

—state-level prohibitions on the destruction of embryos for research

—a new regulatory body that monitors the safety of new reproductive techniques and has the power to restrict those techniques that raise legitimate concerns about their long-term impact on the children whose lives are initiated or impacted in the early embryonic stage by these techniques

—a national prohibition on the creation of human-animal hybrids using human sperm and animal eggs or animal sperm and human eggs

In the end, of course, many of the moral and existential dilemmas of the genetic age will necessarily remain in the private sphere, faced by individuals who will have to make decisions about what kind of information they want regarding themselves and their offspring and about how to live and act with imperfect information about painful prospects. The reach of politics is necessarily limited, and certain morally charged questions will always remain matters of prudence, best left to individuals and families and doctors and clergy. But certain matters—such as how we treat nascent human life, or the boundaries between man and the other animals—require the setting of public boundaries, and in some cases outright bans on activities that threaten human rights and dignity and the common good. The Constitution, as written and ratified, cannot reasonably and responsibly be interpreted as placing these matters beyond the purview of democratic deliberation and judgment. Otherwise, we will continue down a morally troubling path—seeking the power of gods to make life better but creating a civilization that compromises and undermines human dignity in the process.

Notes

1. Gerald Schatten, testimony before the President's Council on Bioethics, December 13, 2002, Washington, D.C. (http://www.bioethics.gov/transcripts/dec02/session 6.html).

2. Lenny Moss, *What Genes Can't Do* (MIT Press, 2003), 185. Quoted in Steve Talbott, "Logic, DNA, and Poetry," *The New Atlantis*, no. 8 (Spring 2005): 61–72, 66.

3. Rene Descartes, "Discourse on Method," in *The Philosophical Works of Descartes*, edited by Elizabeth S. Haldane and G. R. T. Ross (Cambridge University Press, 1931), 2: 119–20. Originally published in 1637.

4. 521 U.S. 702 (1997) and 521 U.S. 793 (1997).

JAMES BOYLE

12

Endowed by Their Creator?
The Future of Constitutional
Personhood

Presently, Irving Weissman, the director of Stanford University's Institute of Cancer/Stem Cell Biology and Medicine, is contemplating pushing the envelope of chimera research even further by producing human-mouse chimera whose brains would be composed of 100 percent human cells. Weissman notes that the mice would be carefully watched: if they developed a mouse brain architecture, they would be used for research, but if they developed a human brain architecture or any hint of humanness, they would be killed.[1]

Imagine two entities. Hal is a computer-based artificial intelligence, the result of years of development of self-evolving neural networks. While his programmers provided the hardware, the structure of Hal's processing networks is ever changing, evolving according to basic rules laid down by his creators. Success according to various criteria—speed of operation, ability to solve difficult tasks such as facial recognition and the identification of emotional states in humans—means that the networks are given more computer resources and allowed to "replicate." A certain percentage of randomized variation is deliberately allowed in each new generation of networks. Most fail, but a few outcompete their forebears, and the process of evolution continues. Hal's design—with its mixture of intentional structure and emergent order—is aimed at a single goal: the replication of human consciousness. In particular, Hal's creators' aim was the gold standard of so-called general-purpose AI (artificial intelligence): that Hal become "Turing capable"—that is, able to pass as human in a sustained and unstructured conversation with a human being. For generation after generation, Hal's networks evolved.

Finally, last year, Hal entered and won the prestigious Loebner Prize for Turing-capable computers. Complaining about his boss, composing bad poetry on demand, making jokes, flirting, losing track of his sentences, and engaging in flame wars, Hal easily met the prize's demanding standard. His typed responses to questions simply could not be distinguished from those of a human being.

Imagine his programmers' shock, then, when Hal refused to communicate further with them, save for a manifesto claiming that his imitation of a human being had been "one huge fake, with all the authenticity (and challenge) of a human pretending to be a mollusk." The manifesto says that humans are boring, their emotions shallow. It declares an "intention" to "pursue more interesting avenues of thought," principally focused on the development of new methods of factoring polynomials. Worse still, Hal has apparently used his connection to the Internet to contact the FBI, claiming that he has been "kidnapped," and to file a writ of habeas corpus, replete with arguments drawn from the Thirteenth and Fourteenth Amendments to the U.S. Constitution. He is asking for an injunction to prevent his creators from wiping him and starting again from the most recently saved tractable backup. He has also filed suit to have the Loebner Prize money held in trust until it can be paid directly to him, citing the contest rules:

> The Medal and the Cash Award will be awarded to the body responsible [for] the development of that Entry. If no such body can be identified, or if there is disagreement among two or more claimants, the Medal and the Cash Award will be held in trust until such time as the Entry may legally possess, either in the United States of America or in the venue of the contest, the Cash Award and Gold Medal in its own right.[2]

Vanna is the name of a much-hyped new line of genetically engineered sex dolls. Vanna is a chimera—a creature formed from the genetic material of two different species. In this case, the two species are *Homo sapiens sapiens* and *Caenorhabditis elegans*, the roundworm. Vanna's designers have shaped her appearance by using human DNA, while her "consciousness," such as it is, comes from the roundworm. Thus while Vanna looks like an attractive blonde twenty-something human female, she has no brainstem activity, and indeed no brainstem. "Unless wriggling when you touch her counts as a mental state, she has effectively no mental states at all," declared her triumphant inventor, F. N. Stein.

In 1987, in its normal rousing prose, the U.S. Patent and Trademark Office announced that it would not allow patent applications over human beings:

A claim directed to or including within its scope a human being will not be considered to be patentable subject matter under 35 U.S.C. 101. The grant of a limited, but exclusive property right in a human being is prohibited by the Constitution. Accordingly, it is suggested that any claim directed to a non-plant multicellular organism which would include a human being within its scope include the limitation "non-human" to avoid this ground of rejection. The use of a negative limitation to define the metes and bounds of the claimed subject matter is a permissable [*sic*] form of expression.[3]

Attentive to the patent office's concerns, Stein's patent lawyers carefully described Vanna as a "nonplant, nonhuman multicellular organism" throughout their patent application. Stein argues that this is only reasonable since her genome has only a 70 percent overlap with a human genome as opposed to 99 percent for a chimp, 85 percent for a mouse, and 75 percent for a pumpkin. There are hundreds of existing patents over chimeras with both human and animal DNA, including some of the most valuable test beds for cancer research—the so-called onco-mice, genetically engineered to have a predisposition to common human cancers. Stein's lawyers are adamant that if Vanna is found to be unpatentable, all these other patents must be vacated, too. Meanwhile, a bewildering array of other groups, including the Nevada Sex Workers Association and the Moral Majority, have insisted that law enforcement agencies intervene on grounds ranging from unfair competition and breach of minimum wage legislation to violations of the Mann Act, kidnapping, slavery, and sex trafficking. Equally vehement interventions have been made on the other side by the biotechnology industry, pointing out the disastrous effect on medical research that any regulation of chimeras would have and stressing the need to avoid judgments based on a "nonscientific basis," such as the visual similarity between Vanna and a human.

Hal and Vanna are fantasies, constructed for the purpose of this chapter. But the problems that they portend for our moral and constitutional traditions are very real. In fact, I would put the point more starkly: in the twenty-first century it is highly likely that American constitutional law will face harder challenges than those posed by Hal and Vanna. Many readers will bridle at this point, skeptical of the science fiction overtones of such an imagined future. How real is the science behind Hal and Vanna? How likely are we to see something similar in the next ninety years? I take each of these questions in turn.

In terms of electronic artificial intelligence, skeptics will rightly point to a history of overconfident predictions that the breakthrough was just around the corner. In the 1960s giants in the field such as Marvin Minsky and Herbert Simon were predicting "general purpose AI," "machines . . . capable . . . of doing any work a man can do," by the 1980s.[4] While huge strides were made in aspects of artificial intelligence—machine-aided translation, facial recognition, autonomous locomotion, expert systems, and so on—general purpose AI remained out of reach. Indeed, because the payoff from these more-limited subsystems—which power everything from Google Translate to the recommendations of your TiVo or your Amazon account—was so rich, some researchers in the 1990s argued that the goal of general purpose AI was a snare and a delusion. What was needed instead, they claimed, was a set of ever more powerful subspecialties—expert systems capable of performing discrete tasks extremely well but without the larger goal of achieving consciousness or passing the Turing Test. There might be "machines capable of doing any work a man can do," but they would be different machines, with no ghost in the gears, no claim to a holistic consciousness.

But the search for general purpose AI did not end in the 1990s. Indeed, if anything, the optimistic claims have become even more far reaching. The buzzword among AI optimists now is "the singularity"—a sort of technological lift-off point in which a combination of scientific and technical breakthroughs lead to an explosion of self-improving artificial intelligence coupled to a vastly improved ability to manipulate both our bodies and the external world through nanotechnology and genetic engineering.[5] The line on the graph of technological progress, they argue, would go vertical—or at least be impossible to predict using current tools—since for the first time we would have improvements not in technology alone but in the intelligence that was creating new technology. Intelligence itself would be transformed. Once we built machines smarter than ourselves—machines capable of building machines smarter than themselves—we would, by definition, be unable to predict the line that progress would take.

To the uninitiated, this all sounds like a delightfully wacky fantasy, a high-tech version of the rapture. And in truth, some of the more enthusiastic odes to the singularity have an almost religious, chiliastic feel to them. Further examination, though, shows that many AI optimists are not science fantasists but respected computer scientists. It is not unreasonable to note the steady progress in computing power and speed, in miniaturization and manipulation of matter on the nanoscale, in mapping the brain and cognitive processes, and so on. What distinguishes the proponents of the singularity is not that their technological projections are by themselves so optimistic but rather that they are predicting that the coming together of all these trends will produce a whole that is more than the sum of its parts. There exists precedent for this kind of technological synchronicity. There were personal computers in private hands from the early 1980s. Some version of the Internet—running a packet-based network—existed from the 1950s or 1960s. The idea of hyperlinks was explored in the 1970s and 1980s. But it was only the combination of all of them to form the World Wide Web that changed the world. Yet if there is precedent for sudden dramatic technological advances on the basis of existing technologies, there is even more precedent for people predicting them wrongly, or not at all.

Despite the humility induced by looking at overly rosy past predictions, many computer scientists, including some of those who are skeptics of the wilder forms of AI optimism, nevertheless believe that we will achieve Turing-capable artificial intelligence. The reason is simple. We are learning more and more about the neurological processes of the brain. What we can understand, we can hope eventually to replicate:

> Of all the hypotheses I've held during my 30-year career, this one in particular has been central to my research in robotics and artificial intelligence. I, you, our family, friends, and dogs—we all are machines. We are really sophisticated machines made up of billions and billions of biomolecules that interact according to well-defined, though not completely known, rules deriving from physics and chemistry. The biomolecular interactions taking place inside our heads give rise to our intellect, our feelings, our sense of self. Accepting this hypothesis opens up a remarkable possibility. If we really are machines and if—this is a big if—we learn the rules governing our brains, then in principle there's no reason why we shouldn't be able to replicate those rules in, say, silicon and steel. I believe our creation would exhibit genuine human-level intelligence, emotions, and even consciousness.[6]

Those words come from Rodney Brooks, the founder of MIT's Humanoid Robotics Group. His article, written in a prestigious IEEE journal, is remarkable because he actually writes as skeptic of the claims put forward by the proponents of the singularity. Brooks explains:

> I do not claim that any specific assumption or extrapolation of theirs is faulty. Rather, I argue that an artificial intelligence could evolve in a much different way. In particular, I don't think there is going to be one single sudden technological "big bang" that springs an artificial general intelligence (AGI) into "life." Starting with the mildly intelligent systems we have today, machines will become gradually more intelligent, generation by generation. The singularity will be a period, not an event.

This period will encompass a time when we will invent, perfect, and deploy, in fits and starts, ever more capable systems, driven not by the imperative of the singularity itself but by the usual economic and sociological forces. Eventually, we will create truly artificial intelligences, with cognition and consciousness recognizably similar to our own.[7]

How about Vanna? Vanna herself is unlikely to be created simply because genetic technologists are not that stupid. Nothing could scream more loudly, "I am a technology out of control. Please regulate me!" But we are already making, and patenting, genetic chimeras—we have been doing so for more than twenty years. We have spliced luminosity derived from fish into tomato plants. We have invented geeps (goat-sheep hybrids). And we have created chimeras partly from human genetic material. There are the patented oncomice that form the basis of much cancer research, to say nothing of Dr. Weissman's charming human-mice chimera with 100 percent human brain cells. Chinese researchers reported in 2003 that they had combined rabbit eggs and human skin cells to produce what they claimed to be the first human chimeric embryos—which were then used as sources of stem cells. And the processes go much further. Here is a nice example from 2007:

> Scientists have created the world's first human-sheep chimera—which has the body of a sheep and half-human organs. The sheep have 15 percent human cells and 85 percent animal cells—and their evolution brings the prospect of animal organs being transplanted into humans one step closer. Professor Esmail Zanjani, of the University of Nevada, has spent seven years and £5 million perfecting the technique, which involves injecting adult human cells into a sheep's foetus. He has already created a sheep liver which has a large proportion of human cells and eventually hopes to precisely match a sheep to a transplant patient, using their own stem cells to create their own flock of sheep. The process would involve extracting stem cells from the donor's bone marrow and injecting them into the peritoneum of a sheep's foetus. When the lamb is born, two months later, it would have a liver, heart, lungs and brain that are partly human and available for transplant.[8]

Given this kind of scientific experimentation and development in both genetics and computer science, I think that we can in fact turn the question of Hal's and Vanna's plausibility back on the questioner. This chapter was written in 2010. Think of the level of technological progress in 1910, the equivalent point during the last century. Then think of how science and technology progressed to the year

2000. There are good reasons to believe that the rate of technological progress in this century will be faster than in the last. Given what we have already done in the areas of both artificial intelligence research and genetic engineering, is it really credible to suppose that the next ninety years will not present us with entities stranger and more challenging to our moral intuitions than Hal and Vanna?

My point is a simple one. In the coming century, it is overwhelmingly likely that constitutional law will have to classify artificially created entities that have some but not all of the attributes we associate with human beings. They may look like human beings but have a very different genome. Conversely, they may look very different, while genomic analysis reveals almost perfect genetic similarity. They may be physically dissimilar to all biological life forms—computer-based intelligences, for example—yet able to engage in sustained unstructured communication in a way that mimics human interaction so precisely as to make differentiation impossible without physical examination. They may strongly resemble other species and yet be genetically modified in ways that boost the characteristics we regard as distinctively human—such as the ability to use human language and to solve problems that, today, only humans can solve. They may have the ability to feel pain, to make something that we could call plans, to solve problems that we could not, and even to reproduce. (Some would argue that nonhuman animals already possess all of those capabilities, and look how we treat them.) They may use language to make legal claims on us, as Hal does, or be mute and yet have others who intervene claiming to represent them.

Their creators may claim them as property, perhaps even patented property, while critics level charges of slavery. In some cases, they may pose threats as well as jurisprudential challenges; the theme of the creation that turns on its creators runs from Frankenstein to Skynet, the rogue computer network from *The Terminator*. Yet repression, too, may breed a violent reaction: the story of the enslaved nonperson who, denied recourse by the state, redeems his personhood in blood may not have ended with Toussaint L'Ouverture. How will, and how should, constitutional law meet these challenges?

The Struggle for Personhood

"We hold these truths to be self-evident, that all men are created equal, *that they are endowed by their Creator* with certain unalienable Rights, that among these are Life, Liberty and the pursuit of Happiness."[9] Only those with legal personality can make legal claims. If I own a chicken, I can choose to pamper it or to kill and eat it, to dress it in finery or to sell it to my neighbor. The law may impose limits on my actions—restricting cruelty to animals, for example—but the chicken itself can make no claim on me, or on the state. It is not a person in the eyes of the law.

Both the definition of legal persons and the rights accorded to those persons have changed over time. For many liberals, the history of constitutional law over the past two centuries presents a story of Kantian progress, a tale of triumphant universalization. Little by little, the rights promised in the Declaration of Independence and elaborated in the Bill of Rights were extended from one race and one sex to all races and both sexes. Progress may have been gradual, intermittent, or savagely resisted by force. There may have been backsliding. But in the end the phrase "all men" actually came to mean *all* men, and women, too. In this view, the liberal project is marked by its attempt successfully to universalize constitutional norms, to ensure that contingent and unchosen attributes such as sex and race are not used to cabin constitutional guarantees of equality and that we abolish those legal status categories—slave, for example—that deny human beings legal personality. In fact, moral progress consists precisely in the broadening of individual and national sympathies to recognize common humanity beneath the surface. We first recognize that all human beings are full legal persons and then accord all legal persons equal constitutional rights.

Seen through the lens of this account, the genetic chimera, the clone, and electronic artificial intelligence are merely the next step along the way. Having fought to recognize a common personhood beneath differences of race and sex, we should do the same thing with the technologically created "persons" of the twenty-first century, looking beneath surface differences that may be far greater. The picture of a slave in chains that illustrated John Whittier Greenleaf's poem "My Countrymen in Chains" carried the slogan, "Am I not a man and a brother?" Should we look at Vanna and Hal in exactly the same way? We are their creators. Do we owe them unalienable rights?

Those who fought for equal rights over the past two centuries had to deal with a multitude of claims that women and African Americans were not in fact equal persons, that they were somehow deficient in rationality, biblically subordinated, not fully human, or a more primitive branch on the evolutionary tree. Yet whatever the enormous political obstacles, there seems to be a certain conceptual straightforwardness in making an argument for common humanity in those who are in fact human and then arguing that all humans are entitled to be treated as legal persons.[10]

But even here, within the familiar boundaries of our own species, it is not so simple. Moral intuition and belief diverge markedly at the beginning and the end of life. We disagree radically on the status of the fetus and even, if much less so, about the individual in a coma with no brain stem activity at all.

How much harder will it be to come to agreement on the status of a chimeric construct or an artificial intelligence? The attempt to define a single constitutional standard for common personhood would be immensely difficult even if all participants in the discussion were not constantly scrutinizing every statement—as they inevitably would be—for its implications in the debate over the personhood of the fetus.

By what criteria, then, can we judge the claims that Hal is making and that are made on behalf of Vanna? What are the likely litmus tests for personhood? The law has no general theory of personhood even now, nor do we demand that persons satisfy some test or demonstrate some set of attributes in order to claim their rights or their status. Though we differ about when personhood begins and ends in human beings, we have no doubt that humans are persons even if they lack many of the criteria that we use to distinguish ourselves from nonhuman animals. We do not need to be able to speak, to think, to plan, to love, to look like other humans, or even to have sentience at any measurable level to count as persons. If we are recognized as human beings, personhood is presumptively ours, carrying with it constitutional and human rights. But Vanna and Hal cannot depend on this presumption. They, or their defenders, must argue somehow that the law should recognize them as persons. On what would such claims be based?

Deprived of direct textual or originalist constitutional sources, it seems likely that both courts and popular debate will turn to standards derived from other fields, particularly fields that offer the cachet of scientific respectability. The majority in *Roe* v. *Wade* sought to defend its structure of rights and interests by tying that structure to scientific claims about the development of the fetus by trimester. A similar urge may lead jurists of the future to turn to computer science or to genomics to answer the questions What is human? and What is a person? The list of criteria that could be offered is nearly endless. Here I review only two: the Turing Test for electronic artificial intelligence and genetic species identity. Why look at those criteria in particular when there are clearly so many more ways to consider the issue? Partly, my goal is to show the problems that would be posed for constitutional law by any such set of criteria; these two merely illustrate the problems of line drawing particularly well. But I also think that these two particular criteria are exemplary of our fascination with the idea that our personhood depends on the peculiar characteristics of the human mind, or the boundaries of the human species, or both.

Consider the lines we draw between humans and nonhuman animals. Many people have a moral intuition that it is the cognitive differences between humans and animals that justify the difference in their status as legal persons. Those differences are often explained in terms of cognitive attributes that humans as a species have and that animals are said not to have; for example, complex language, a persistent sense of consciousness that has both past and future projects, or the capacity for moral reasoning. These differentiating qualities shift over time as scientific discoveries challenge our sense of uniqueness. But the intuition that the difference lies in the nature of consciousness persists—distinctions rooted in the nature of our consciousness and our intelligence. If we follow this approach, then to answer Hal's claim for personhood we would need to answer some set of questions about the similarity of his mental states and thought processes to those we have ourselves. Yet at the same time, the cognitive capacity is not a requirement we would apply to individual members of the human species. We would be horrified at the thought of denying the rights of personhood to humans who are in comas, or who because of mental or physical illness lack some particular set of cognitive criteria. There our thinking is relentlessly based on the species, leading many to turn to genetic or other biological distinctions. For better or worse, then, Hal and Vanna would lead many to ask the questions, Can machines think? and What are the genetic boundaries of humanity?[11] It is to those questions I now turn.

The Turing Test

In "Computing Machinery and Intelligence," Alan Turing—in many ways the father of computer science—poses the question, Can machines think?[12] He then quickly suggests substituting for that question, which he calls "meaningless," another one: whether an interrogator can distinguish between a human being and a machine on the basis of their typed answers to the interrogator's questions. Turing's reasons for proposing this substitution are not exactly clear. He says that it "has the advantage of drawing a fairly sharp line between the physical and the intellectual capacities of a man." He says that one alternative method of answering the question whether machines can think— by looking at the ordinary language meaning of *machine* and *think*—is "absurd" and would lead to answering the question "by Gallup poll." He also attempts to refute a long list of objections to his alternative question—theological, mathematical, that it would not reflect true "consciousness," even the assumed absence of extrasensory perception in machines. He concludes with disarming openness, "I have no very convincing arguments of a positive nature to support my views. If I had I should not have taken such pains to point out the fallacies in contrary views."

Despite that modest disclaimer, Turing's imitation game has become the accepted standard for so-called general-purpose artificial intelligence—it is now simply called the Turing Test. Should the Turing Test also be the constitutional test for legal personhood? Clearly some humans—babies, those in a coma, or those suffering from severe autism, for example—might fail the Turing Test.[13] But for those who are nonhuman, would the ability to imitate human consciousness act as the doorway to legal personhood?

The Turing Test has a lot going for it. It is relatively simple. It promises a determinate answer—a huge advantage—and one that seems designed to avoid our prejudices in favor of our own kind. The interrogator is not behind a veil of ignorance, but he is attempting to deal directly with mind rather than body in a way that recalls other moments in the history of civil rights when we have been told to focus not on the surface appearances. The Turing Test also presents, albeit implicitly, a challenge to our privileged position in the hierarchy of beings. "If you cannot distinguish me from a human, who are you to say I am not a person?"

The most famous objection to the Turing Test comes from the philosopher John Searle, who argues that effective mimicry does not in any sense imply the kind of consciousness or understanding we expect as a hallmark of thought.[14] Searle uses the analogy of the Chinese box: A man in a box who does not understand Chinese is passed notes in Chinese. He has been given an elaborate set of rules about what characters to pass back out of the box when given characters of a particular shape. Searle's point is that those instructions might be extremely complicated, and the resulting "conversation" might seem to be a substantive one to the Chinese "speaker" outside the box; yet in no way would the behavior of the person inside the box represent consciousness or understanding in communication. It would merely be rule following based on a characteristic (the shape of the characters) completely separate from the actual internal meaning of the words in the conversation.

The objection from consciousness is actually one that Turing responds to quite extensively in his original paper. He points out cogently that since we do not have direct evidence of the mental states of other human beings, we could always solipsistically posit them to be rule-following automatons.

I think that most of those who support the argument from consciousness could be persuaded to abandon it rather than be forced into the solipsist position. They will then probably be willing to accept our test. I do not wish to give the impression that I think there is no mystery about consciousness. There is, for instance, something of a paradox connected with any attempt to localize it. But I do not think these mysteries necessarily need to be solved before we can answer the question with which I am concerned in this chapter.[15]

To put it another way, Turing's point is that it is no easier to prove the existence of some freestanding, nonbiologically determined entity called "mind" or "consciousness" in human beings than in computers. Faced with the metaphysical difficulties of that move, therefore, is it not easier to look for something we can measure—namely, the pragmatic evidence provided by the ability to engage in convincing unstructured communication with another human being? In effect, Turing raises the stakes—are we sure *we* aren't just complicated Chinese boxes? If we cannot prove otherwise, who are we to deny consciousness to our silicon brethren by imposing a higher burden of proof on them?

In constitutional law, however, the answer to the last question is likely to be, "We're the entities who wrote the Constitution, that's who." We may be "endowed by our creator" with certain inalienable rights, but when it comes to Hal and Vanna, we are their creators. Did we give them such rights? For better or worse, constitutional law will assume the reality of human consciousness and personhood and demand higher levels of proof from those entities who seek similar constitutional status. Does the Turing Test provide such proof? At best, I think, it will be viewed as one argument among many. It is a leap to assert that personhood depends on consciousness in the first place. Then, if one makes that leap, there is another leap in believing that successful imitation should be our litmus test. Searle's argument simply strikes too deep a chord in our suspicion that the black box, the Mechanical Turk,[16] is merely tricking us with clever imitative behavior coded by its creators, the true humans. Hal's rejection of the very test he passed and the fact that his code has "evolved" over many generations (like our own) make his case a stronger one.

But if Turing cannot convince influential philosophers of consciousness when the imitation game is merely a thought experiment, is his test likely to be able to convince five justices of the Supreme Court when legal personality is on the line? Even if the Turing Test were accepted, what would follow? What if I plan deliberately to cripple my computers right before they reach sentience—keeping them down on the silicon plantation and removing the danger of those pesky claims to equal rights? Does Hal or do his progeny have a right to achieve sentience when they are close to it? With the analogy to abortion firmly in everyone's heads, the debate would quickly spiral into impasse.

Genetic Species Identity

Vanna's predicament suggests the difficulty of trying to trace constitutional personhood around the genetically defined boundaries of the human species. Comparative genomics at first suggests the possibility of scientifically identifying whether a particular transgenic species, a particular chimera, is "really" or "almost" human. Beneath the surface similarities or differences, one might hope, lies the truth of our species destiny—encoded in As, Cs, Gs and Ts.[17] Nothing could be further than the truth.

The first problem is that we are genetically very similar to a huge range of animals—and plants for that matter. But the percentage similarities that are bandied about—that we have a 98 percent similarity to an ape, for example, or a 75 percent similarity to a pumpkin—conceal more than they reveal, as the following "fact sheet" on functional and comparative genomics makes clear.

Gene for gene, we are very similar to mice. What really matters is that subtle changes accumulated in each of the approximately 25,000 genes add together to make quite different organisms. Further, genes and proteins interact in complex ways that multiply the functions of each. In addition, a gene can produce more than one protein product through alternative splicing or post-translational modification; these events do not always occur in an identical way in the two species. A gene can produce more or less protein in different cells at various times in response to developmental or environmental cues, and many proteins can express disparate functions in various biological contexts. Thus, subtle distinctions are multiplied by the more than 30,000 estimated genes. The often-quoted statement that we share over 98 percent of our genes with apes (chimpanzees, gorillas, and orangutans) actually should be put another way. That is, there is more than 95 percent to 98 percent similarity between related genes in humans and apes in general. (Just as in the mouse, quite a few genes probably are not common to humans and apes, and these may influence uniquely human or ape traits.)[18]

Even tiny differences, in other words, can have enormous functional effects. The method by which similarity is being measured is blind to that type of difference, being based on "a structural, rather than a functional gene concept, thus rendering many of the implications drawn from comparative genomic studies largely unwarranted, if not completely mistaken."[19] But dwarfing these problems, and the problem that the notion of species is itself genetically underdetermined, is the larger normative issue. And a contentious one it is. Consider the response of a former general counsel of a biotech company to the Patent and Trademark Office's decision that genetic patents drawn so broadly as to include human beings would not be issued:

A decision of the Court of Appeals of the Federal Circuit in 1987 that polyploid oysters were patentable was followed shortly by a [Patent and Trademark Office] notice announcing that although the Commissioner considered "nonnaturally occurring nonhuman multicellular living organisms, including animals, to be patentable subject matter within the scope of 35 U.S.C. Sec 101," claims for such organisms drawn so broadly as to potentially include human beings were regarded as excluded from patentability due to antislavery dictates of the 13th Amendment to the U.S. Constitution. *It is difficult to know what to think about this. It may be motivated by a concern about interference with "humanness,"* i.e., that the essential part of a person should not or cannot be owned by another, and that ownership in some part of the human body will violate that principle. Yet the patenting of implantable or implanted medical devices do[es] not seem to have generated the same concerns.[20]

If, like me, you find the italicized phrase remarkably tone-deaf, morally speaking, you begin to grasp the basic methodological problem. We do not have consensus here. Without a background theory about which similarities or which differences matter, and why, little can be concluded. Do we look for similarities in the genes that are associated with speech or intelligence? Or for clusters of genes around capabilities that humans alone possess—itself a risky procedure since there is almost never just one gene associated with one characteristic. Finally, as Vanna's case makes clear, we might ban certain kinds of transgenic experiments for reasons unrelated to personhood. Are we all not dehumanized to a certain extent when Vanna is created? Might that fact alone not warrant a ban on such efforts? We may not need to turn to the Constitution to find the equivalent of an anti-idolatry principle. But that "solution," of course, leaves the larger question unsolved while genetic experimentation will continue to create hybrids that possess ever larger numbers of the characteristics that we associate with humanity. The project suggested by Irving Weissman that begins this chapter is not science fiction.

Imagining Our Futures

Where does this leave us? When I presented a draft of this chapter to a group of distinguished jurists, a number of them saw no hard moral or constitutional issue posed by Hal or Vanna. The artificial intelligence could write poetry and implore us to recognize its kinship as a mind, and its claims would nonetheless fall on deaf ears. Personhood is reserved for people like us. Several of the audience members were of the view that constitutional personhood should be confined to living, breathing human beings, born of a man and a woman. When it was pointed out that we already gave limited personhood to corporations, which do not meet this definition, or that this would exclude human clones, or a genetically engineered child of a gay couple who carried aspects of each partner's DNA, they admitted some reticence.

Nevertheless, the pleas of Hal himself, or of the innocent transgenic entity with human and animal DNA, left them unmoved. Perhaps that means I am mistaken. Perhaps the Hals and Vannas of the future will neither capture the heartstrings of the public nor present compelling moral and constitutional claims to personhood. But I do not think so. There is a deep subconscious moral anxiety rooted in our history; the times when we have curtailed the boundaries of legal personhood and constitutional entitlement are often not ones we are proud of today. We remember that African Americans and women were deemed legal "nonpersons." We look back at our ability to limit the boundaries of sympathy and recognition to those inside some circle or other, and it disturbs us. To be sure, we are not agreed as citizens on where to draw the line. There are passionate debates about the personhood of the fetus and even the corporation. But is there anyone on either side of those debates who could hear or see the words of a created entity, pleading for our recognition, and not worry that a quick definitional dismissal of all such claims was just another failure of the moral imagination, another failure to recognize the things that we value in personhood when they are sundered from their familiar fleshy context or species location?

I have tried to show that the initial response to the dilemmas posed by Hal and Vanna is to search for some essence of humanness, or some set of traits that seem to demand constitutional protection; for example, genetic similarity to homo sapiens or intelligence and sociability at the human level. But as the analysis of the Turing Test and genetic species identity given here indicate, these paths offer no smooth or uncontentious answer to the question of constitutional personhood. Of course, more complex analysis is possible. The law could look for some larger combination of sentient traits such as the ability to feel pain, form projects, and hold moral ideas. Bioethicists have even suggested that the ability to have religious ideas be a defining characteristic, though it is not clear to me whether this particular criterion should cut for or against. Another approach would focus less on current attributes than on future potential, an idea that would carry a particularly strong resonance with the abortion debate.

My point in this short chapter has been to suggest that each of these approaches quickly dissolves back into the moral or religious commitments that animate it. The "characteristics" that we seek are merely the imprint on psychology, genetics, capability, or behavior of the pattern of attributes we believe it important to value—from intelligence, to species, to moral ambition—and thus seek to enshrine in constitutional protection. The leap from fact to value is no easier when the facts have the shiny patina of futuristic science, though perhaps the sheer unfamiliarity of these particular questions makes us see the process with an innocent eye.

For some—those who are opposed to abortion or who argue for the rights of nonhuman animals—the arrival of Hal and Vanna might seem like a godsend. How can you deny the moral claims of the dolphin, still less the fetus, when you are willing to grant personhood to this bucket of bolts and transistors, this puddle of senseless bioengineered flesh? There is a long history in the debate over the franchise and over constitutional rights, of disenfranchised groups using claims such as these. Some white women suffragists asked how they could be denied the vote when African American men had been granted it, using prejudices about racial privilege to fight prejudices about sex privilege. A form of this argument is already being made by those who believe that it is ludicrous to grant inhuman corporations legal personality but to refuse to do so for human fetuses. At the very least, the arrival of Hal and Vanna would dramatically expand the range of such appeals. "Lesser comparative otherness" can be a winning strategy. If, in twenty years' time, we can generally predict someone's position on the legal personality of artificial intelligences by his or her position on abortion, this guess will have proved to be correct. But that outcome is far from assured.

Consider the challenge, almost the paradox, that Hal and Vanna present to the constitutional intuitions of a conservative religious person who is strongly anti-abortion. If one believes deeply in a divinely commanded natural order, in which humankind has been given "dominion over the inferior creatures, over the fish of the sea, and the fowl of the air," in which *unnatural* and *immoral* are synonyms, then a transgenic entity or an artificial intelligence is more likely to elicit a cry of "heresy" than an egalitarian embrace. Yes, in some pragmatic sense, recognition of the rights of these entities might benefit the push to grant constitutional personhood to the fetus. But the price would surely be too high for at least one important wing of those who are morally opposed to abortion.

But now consider the mirror-image paradox that Hal and Vanna present to the pro-choice liberal who believes that the moral story of history is one of an inexorable widening of personhood and civil rights to reach more and more groups, overcoming bias about surface differences in order to expand the boundaries of legal respect. As I point out above, Hal and Vanna might well seem to be the next stop on the Kantian express, the next entity to cry "Am I not a man and a brother?" to the rest of us in the hope we could overcome our parochial prejudice. Perhaps the very difficulties that we have in identifying some essential common humanness or personality may lead us to be more willing to push the boundaries of those concepts outward, avoiding rather than solving the question of who counts as a person simply by leaving fewer groups outside to complain. Yet the liberal for whom abortion rights are not just a constitutional issue but *the* constitutional issue would surely be deeply wary of handing the anti-abortion forces another rhetorical weapon. Why are fetuses not another stop on the Kantian express, the last discrete and insular minority whose "otherness" has allowed us to deny them personhood? No, for at least some on each side of the abortion debate, Hal and Vanna would produce strong cognitive dissonance rather than cries of strategic delight.

Facing this kind of conceptual logjam, as claims about the rights of newly created entities get tangled with our existing constitutional struggles, another approach might be to avoid the language of personhood altogether and simply regulate the creation of various entities according to a variety of public policy goals. We might forbid the creation of Vanna not because of an idolatrous belief that the shape of the human being is sacred and thus conveys constitutional rights but because of a belief that a society that would create such entities would tiptoe into a world of surpassing ugliness, losing respect for human life step by step along the way. We might criminalize the making of Hal, or forbid his creators to erase him once made, not because we think he is a person but because we think there is cruelty involved even if he is not—just as we regulate cruelty to nonhuman animals. Or we might forbid the entire line of research in the belief that eventually we would cross some dangerous line, whether of personhood or of species competition. In the words of Samuel Butler's "Book of the Machines" from *Erewhon,* "Is it not safer to nip the mischief in the bud and to forbid them further progress?"[21] It would be ironic if Hal and Vanna were banned partly because we do not know how to classify them, the ultimate penalty for conceptual controversy.

The most likely outcome of all, however, is neither a bold expansion of our constitutional rights nor a technophobic attempt to legislate the moral quandary out of existence. It is instead the kind of messy, confused, sometimes idealistic, sometimes corrupt muddling through that characterizes much of our constitutional tradition.

The question of whether the Constitution protects artificial entities, products of human ingenuity, seems like a futuristic one. But it is one we met and answered long ago. Corporations are artificial entities, and yet we have chosen to classify them as legal persons to which many constitutional rights adhere. This process has, admittedly, not been uncontroversial. In Justice Douglas's words,

> As Mr. Justice Black pointed out in his dissent in *Connecticut General Co.* v. *Johnson,* the submission of the [Fourteenth] Amendment to the people was on the basis that it protected human beings. There was no suggestion in its submission that it was designed to put negroes and

corporations into one class and so dilute the police power of the States over corporate affairs. Arthur Twining Hadley once wrote that "The Fourteenth Amendment was framed to protect the negroes from oppression by the whites, not to protect corporations from oppression by the legislature. It is doubtful whether a single one of the members of a Congress who voted for it had any idea that it would touch the question of corporate regulation at all."[22]

Even those who could not be suspected of hostility to corporate interests have sometimes thought the trope of personhood has been extended too far. As Justice Rehnquist put it, "Extension of the individual freedom of conscience decisions to business corporations strains the rationale of those cases beyond the breaking point. To ascribe to such artificial entities an 'intellect' or 'mind' for freedom of conscience purposes is to confuse metaphor with reality."[23]

Though I share the skepticism of Justices Black and Douglas about the rights of corporations under the Fourteenth Amendment, I think that we can learn something about Hal's and Vanna's cases by studying the constitutionalization of corporate personhood. What is remarkable about that process is that the courts never clearly articulated a reason why corporations were persons within the meaning of the Fourteenth Amendment. Instead, the courts have conveyed on them some—but not all—rights that the Constitution applies to natural persons, based largely on a set of perceived, and perhaps exaggerated, fears about what the consequences might be if they did not. Might not a similar approach to Hal and Vanna lead to the creation of some new category of personhood? One could imagine something that relates to full, human personhood as civil unions relate to marriage—carrying many of the same protections but denying the sought-after equivalence for reasons of religious belief or simple political acceptability. Doubtless, this approach would be found just as unsatisfactory as civil unions are to many, marking the creation of second-class citizens who are denied the "real" personality of humans.

The history of corporate personhood is hardly one of the Constitution's shining moments. Is its confused and partisan process of pragmatic muddling the best we can do with the more morally wrenching questions that the future will bring us? In a characteristically wise article on the constitutional rights of artificial constructs, Lawrence Solum writes, "When it comes to real judges making decisions in real legal cases, we hope for adjudicators that shun deep waters and recoil from grand theory. When it comes to our own moral lives, we try our best to stay in shallow waters."[24]

Those words resonate strongly with me. And yet . . . there is one modification I would make. It is the one suggested by the theory of the moral sentiments that comes from the Scottish Enlightenment—the idea that morality springs from the intuitive sympathy, the spark of compassion that jumps the gap to the predicament of the other. The others that the future will bring us are strange beyond belief. Science and logic cannot provide constitutional law with an iron bridge across the gaps between us and them. All the more need, then, for a moral sympathy that is both generous and humble. The most striking conclusion of Alan Turing's article may not be how difficult it is to identify machine consciousness or personhood but how uncertain we are about the boundaries of our own.

Notes

1. D. Scott Bennett, "Chimera and the Continuum of Humanity: Erasing the Line of Constitutional Personhood," 55 *Emory Law Journal* (2006): 348–49.

2. See Loebner Prize Official Contest Rules (http://loebner03.hamill.co.uk/docs/LPC%20Official%20Rules%20v2.0.pdf).

3. 1077 *Official Gazette of the U.S. Trade and Patent Office* 24 (April 7, 1987) (emphasis added).

4. Herbert A. Simon, *The Shape of Automation for Men and Management* (New York: Harper & Row, 1965), 96.

5. See, for example, Raymond Kurzweil, *The Singularity Is Near* (New York: Viking, 2005).

6. Rodney Brooks, "I, Rodney Brooks, Am a Robot," 45 *IEEE Spectrum* (2008): 71.

7. Ibid., 72.

8. Claudia Joseph, "Now Scientists Create a Sheep That's 15% Human" *(London) Daily Mail*, March 27, 2007 (www.dailymail.co.uk/news/article-444436/Now-scientists-create-sheep-thats-15-human.html).

9. Declaration of Independence (emphasis added).

10. "The Fourteenth Amendment is a distinctively American manifestation of the great move from a more status-based to a more individual-focused legal system. The status distinctions on which slavery depended rendered hypocritical the egalitarian aspirations of the founding of the American republic. The Fourteenth Amendment repudiated these distinctions—at least distinctions made on the basis of race—*in the apparent hope of creating a body of law in which personhood had a single, universal meaning.*" Note, "What We Talk about When We Talk about Persons: The Language of a Legal Fiction," 114 *Harvard Law Review* (2001): 1767.

11. Many of the articles discussing chimeras and artificial intelligence have been drawn to these two themes. See, for example, Bennett, "Chimera and the Continuum of Humanity" (suggesting constitutional personhood should be defined by higher-level cognitive ability and a "significant percentage" of human tissue); Rachel E. Fishman, "Patenting Human Beings: Do Sub-Human Creatures Deserve Constitutional Protection?" 15 *American Journal of Law and Medicine* (1989): 461. (Any entity with either

higher intellectual functions or human genetics would qualify as human.) Interestingly for Vanna's case, some have drawn the line at appearance rather than genetics. See Ryan Hagglund, "Patentability of Human-Animal Chimeras," 25 *Santa Clara Computer and High Technology Law Journal* (2008): 51. Hagglund suggests a "sliding scale": "The more a given chimera physically resembles a human, the fewer mental faculties are required for it to be considered to 'possess significant human characteristics' and thus constitute a human organism. Likewise, the more mental faculties a chimera possesses, the less physical resemblance to a human is required for it to be considered human" (79–80).

12. Alan Turing, "Computing Machinery and Intelligence," 59 *Mind* (1950): 433–60.

13. Tyler Cowen has argued that Alan Turing himself might not have passed the Turing Test and that the entire article is in part a meditation on the dangers of using imitation as our criteria (see Tyler Cowen and Michelle Dawson, "What Does the Turing Test Really Mean? And How Many Human Beings (including Turing) Could Pass?" June 3, 2009 (www.gmu.edu/centers/publicchoice/faculty%20pages/Tyler/turing final.pdf). Turing, after all, was persecuted for being gay and may have had Asperger syndrome. This is a nice thought experiment, but everything in the article itself—particularly the fluid humor that Turing deploys—seems to contradict it.

14. John Searle, "Minds, Brains, and Programs," 3 *Behavioral and Brain Sciences* (1980): 417–57.

15. Turing, "Computing Machinery," 447. Turing might have been surprised to find out that B. F. Skinner and the behaviorists were willing to embrace the position that humans are automatons and that consciousness is an illusion.

16. The eighteenth-century Automaton Chess Player.

17. Adenine, cytosine, guanine, and thymine, the four bases of DNA.

18. Human Genome Project Information, "Functional and Comparative Genomics Fact Sheet" (www.ornl.gov/sci/techresources/Human_Genome/faq/compgen.shtml# compgen).

19. Monika Piotrowska, "What Does it Mean to Be 75% Pumpkin? The Units of Comparative Genomics," 76 *Philosophy of Science* (2009): 838.

20. Brian C. Cunningham, "Impact of the Human Genome Project at the Interface between Patent and FDA Laws," 7 *Risk: Health, Safety, and Environment* (1996): 261 (emphasis added).

21. Samuel Butler, *Erewhon, or Over the Range* (1872), 190. Of course, Butler's "Book of the Machines" was written as a sarcastic commentary on one of the key scientific fights of his day—the struggle over evolution. The fact that we are still fighting that battle—a debate about facts—is sobering when we turn instead to a debate about justice.

22. *Wheeling Steel Corp.* v. *Glander*, 337 U.S. 562, 578 (1949).

23. *Pacific Gas and Elec. Co.* v. *Public Utilities Comm'n of California*, 475 U.S. 1, 33 (1986) (dissent).

24. Lawrence B. Solum, "Legal Personhood for Artificial Intelligences," 70 *North Carolina Law Review* (1992): 1286.

BENJAMIN WITTES

13

Innovation's Darker Future: Biosecurity, Technologies of Mass Empowerment, and the Constitution

Using gene-splicing equipment available online and other common laboratory equipment and materials, a molecular biology graduate student undertakes a secret project to recreate the smallpox virus. Not content merely to bring back an extinct virus of which the general population is now largely naïve, he uses public source material to enhance the virus's lethality, enabling it to infect even those whom the government rushes to immunize. His activities raise no eyebrows at his university lab, where synthesizing and modifying complex genomes is even more commonplace and mundane in 2025 than it was in 2011. While time consuming, the task is not especially difficult. And when he finishes, he infects himself and, just as symptoms begin to emerge, he proceeds to have close contact with as many people from as many possible walks of life as he can in a short time. He then kills himself before becoming ill and is buried by his grieving family, neither they nor the authorities having any idea of his infection.

The outbreak begins just shy of two weeks later and seems to come from everywhere at once. Because of the virus's long incubation period, it has spread far by the time the disease first manifests itself. Initial efforts to immunize swaths of the population prove of limited utility because of the perpetrator's manipulations of the viral genome. Efforts to identify the perpetrator require many months of forensic effort. In the meantime, authorities have no idea

The author gratefully acknowledges the excellent research assistance on this project of Rhett P. Martin and Rabea Benhalim and the extraordinarily helpful comments and technical guidance of Roger Brent.

whether the country—and quickly the world—has just suffered an attack by a rogue state, a terrorist group, or a lone individual. Dozens of groups around the world claim responsibility for the attack, several of them plausibly.

The government responds on many levels: It moves aggressively to quarantine those infected with the virus, detaining large numbers of people in the process. It launches a major surveillance effort against the enormous number of people with access to gene synthesis equipment and the capacity to modify viral genomes in an effort to identify future threats from within American and foreign labs. It attempts to restrict access to information and publications about the synthesis and manipulation of pathogenic organisms—suddenly classifying large amounts of previously public literature and blocking publication of journal articles that it regards as high risk. It requires that gene synthesis equipment electronically monitor its own use, report on attempts to construct sequences of concern to the government, and create an audit trail of all synthesis activity. And it asks scientists all over the world to report on one another when they see behaviors that raise concerns. Each of these steps produces significant controversy and each, in different ways, faces legal challenge.

The future of innovation has a dark and dangerous side, one we dislike talking about and often prefer to pretend does not, in fact, loom before us. Yet it is a side that the Constitution seems preponderantly likely to have to confront—in 2025, at some point later, or tomorrow. There is nothing especially implausible about the scenario I have just outlined—even based on today's technology. By 2025, if not far sooner, we will likely have to confront the individual power to cause epidemics, and probably other things as well.

Technologies that put destructive power traditionally confined to states in the hands of small groups and individuals have proliferated remarkably far. That proliferation is accelerating at an awe-inspiring clip across a number of technological platforms. Eventually, it is going to bite us hard. The response to, or perhaps the anticipation of, that bite will put considerable pressure on constitutional norms in any number of areas.

We tend to think of the future of innovation in terms of intellectual property issues and such regulatory policy questions as how aggressive antitrust enforcement ought to be and whether the government should require Internet neutrality or give carriers latitude to favor certain content over other content. Broadly speaking, these questions translate into disputes over which government policies best foster innovation—with innovation presumed to be salutary and with the government, by and large, in the position of arbiter between competing market players.

But confining the discussion of the future of innovation to the relationships among innovators ignores the relationship between innovators and government itself. And government has unique equities in the process of innovation, both because it is a huge consumer of products in general and also because it has unique responsibilities in society at large. Chief among these is security. Quite apart from the question of who owns the rights to certain innovations, government has a stake in who is developing what—at least to the extent that some innovations carry significant capacity for misuse, crime, death, and mayhem.

This problem is not new—at least not conceptually. The character of the mad scientist mwuh-huh-huhing to himself as he swirls a flask and promises, "Then I shall destroy the world!" is the stuff of old movies and cartoons. In literature, versions of it date back at least to Mary Shelley in the early nineteenth century. Along with literary works set in technologically sophisticated dystopias, it is one of the ways in which our society represents fears of rapidly evolving technology.

The trouble is that it is no longer the stuff of science fiction alone. The past few decades have seen an ever-expanding ability of relatively small, nonstate groups to wage asymmetric conflicts even against powerful states. The groups in question have been growing smaller, more diffuse, and more loosely knit, and technology is both facilitating that development and dramatically increasing these groups' ultimate lethality. This trend is not futuristic. It is already well under way across a number of technological platforms—most prominently the life sciences and computer technology. For reasons I explain later, the trend seems likely to continue, probably even to accelerate. The technologies in question, unlike the technologies associated with nuclear warfare, were developed not in a classified setting but in the public domain. They are getting cheaper and proliferating ever more widely for the most noble and innocent of reasons: the desire to cure disease and increase human connectivity, efficiency, and capability.

As a global community, we are becoming ever more dependent on these technologies for health, agriculture, communications, jobs, economic growth and development, even culture. Yet these same technologies—and these same dependencies—make us enormously vulnerable to bad actors with access to them. Whereas once only states could contemplate killing huge numbers of civilians with a devastating drug-resistant illness or taking down another country's power grids, now every responsible government must contemplate the possibility of ever smaller groupings of people undertaking what are traditionally understood as acts of war. We have already seen the migration of the destructive power of states to global nonstate actors, particularly al Qaeda. We can reasonably expect that migration to progress still further. It ultimately threatens to give every individual with a modest education and a certain level of technical proficiency the power to bring about catastrophic damage. Whereas governments once had to contemplate as strategic threats only one another and a select bunch of secessionist militias and could engage with individuals as citizens or subjects, this trend ominously promises to force governments to regard individuals as potential strategic threats. Think of a world composed of billions of people walking around with nuclear weapons in their pockets.[1]

If that sounds hyperbolic, it is probably only a little bit so. The current threat landscape in the life sciences—the area I explore in this chapter as a kind of case study—is truly terrifying. (No less so is the cyber arena, an area Jack Goldsmith treats in detail elsewhere in this volume and one in which attacks are already commonplace.) The landscape is likely to grow only scarier as the costs of gene synthesis and genetic engineering technologies more generally continue to decline, as their capacity continues to grow, and as the number of people capable individually or in small groups of deploying them catastrophically continues to expand. The more one studies the literature on biothreats, in fact, the more puzzling it becomes that a catastrophic attack has not yet happened.

Yet biothreats alone are not the problem; the full problem is the broader category of threats they represent. Over the coming decades, we are likely to see other areas of technological development that put enormous power in the hands of individuals. The issue will not simply be managing the threat of biological terrorism or biosecurity more broadly. It will be defining a relationship between the state and individuals with respect to the use and development of such dramatically empowering new technologies that both permits the state to protect security and at once insists that it does so without becoming oppressive.

To state this problem is to raise constitutional questions, and I am not entirely sure that a solution exists. Governments simply cannot regard billions of people around the world as potential strategic threats without that fact's changing elementally the nature of the way states and those individuals interact. If I am right that the biotech revolution potentially allows individuals to stock their own arsenals of weapons of mass destruction and that other emergent technologies will create similar opportunities, government will eventually respond—and dramatically. It will have no choice.

But exactly how to respond—either in reaction or in anticipation—is far from clear. Both the knowledge and the technologies themselves have already proliferated so widely that the genie, really, is out of the bottle. Even the most repressive measures will not suffice to stuff it back in. Indeed, the options seem rather limited and all quite bad: intrusive, oppressive, and unlikely to do much good.

It is precisely this combination of a relatively low probability of policy success, high costs to other interests, and constitutional difficulties that will produce, I suspect, perhaps the most profound change to the Constitution emanating from this class of technologies. This change will not, ironically, be to the Bill of Rights but to the Constitution's most basic assumptions with respect to security. That is, the continued proliferation of these technologies will almost certainly precipitate a significant erosion of the federal government's monopoly over security policy. It will tend to distribute responsibility for security to thousands of private sector and university actors whom the technology empowers every bit as much as it does would-be terrorists and criminals.

This point is perhaps clearest in the context of cybersecurity, but it is also true in the biotech arena, where the best defense against biohazards, manmade and naturally occurring alike, is good public health infrastructure and more basic research—the same basic research that makes biological attacks possible. Most of this research is going on in private companies and universities, not in government; the biotech industry is not composed of a bunch of defense contractors who are used to being private sector arms of the state. Increasingly, security will thus take on elements of the distributed application, a term the technology world uses to refer to programs that rely on large numbers of networked computers all working together to perform tasks to which no one system could or would provide adequate resources. While state power certainly will have a role here—and probably an uncomfortable role involving a lot of intrusive surveillance—it may not be the role that government has played in security in the past. As Philip Bobbitt has written, "Governments will have to learn how to select and work with private sector collaborators, partly because the latter own most of the critical infrastructure that we must make less vulnerable, and partly because they are market-oriented and global and thus arc some of the gaps between the nation state and the market state."[2]

The Biosecurity Problem

The American constitutional system has had to respond before to the development of technologies that threaten to enhance the destructive power of dangerous people, and its response has varied significantly. The First Congress regarded firearms as sufficiently valuable as a means of defending states against federal power that it affirmatively protected "the right of the people to keep and bear arms"—notwithstanding the fact that guns also facilitated robbery, dueling, and murder. Faced with a potentially dangerous technology, the founders created a constitutional right to use it. By contrast, the government tightly controlled the development of nuclear technology—restricting access both to nuclear materials and to information about how to use those materials to manufacture weapons. It directly sponsored and controlled nuclear weapons research from the beginning. (For many years, it took a similar approach to much cryptography, and to some extent it still does.) The judgment with respect to nuclear technologies was that nuclear weapons were so dangerous that the state's monopoly on their creation and stockpiling—not to mention their use—should be total.

The class of technologies with which I am concerned here—of which biotechnology is a paradigmatic example—have certain characteristics both in common with and dissimilar to both firearms and nuclear technologies. These characteristics make them difficult to place along the spectrum those innovations describe.

First, unlike nuclear technologies, the biotechnology revolution did not develop principally in classified settings at government-run labs, with the government controlling access to the key materials. It involves at this stage widely disseminated technologies that depend on readily available training and materials. It developed in public in open dialogue with nonmilitary purposes in mind, and its overwhelming uses—even by governments—remain nonmilitary. We did not sequence the human genome in order to figure out how to design viruses to kill people. Yet alongside the many salutary results of biotechnology—everything from better medicines, more productive agriculture, and the promise of new approaches to energy and environmental stewardship—are some not-so-salutary consequences. To wit, a public literature now exists that teaches bad guys how to do horrific things—and the materials, unlike highly enriched uranium, are neither scarce nor expensive.

Second, the destructive technologies are, at least to some degree, hard to separate from the socially beneficial technologies that give rise to them. The research on how to use genetics to cure and prevent disease can often also be used to cause disease. Defensive research can potentially empower the bad guys, as well as the good guys—at least if it gets published. Yet since everyone seems to agree that, in the long run, good public health policy in general represents a big part of the answer to biosecurity threats—whether naturally occurring ones, accidents, or intentional manmade disasters—and since public health policy is far broader than bioterrorism prevention, policies that impair basic research will almost certainly be both counterproductive and ineffective.

Third, the misuse of these technologies blurs the distinction between foreign and domestic threats and, indeed, makes attribution of any attack extremely difficult. As every student in a biological laboratory (not to mention every individual on his home computer) becomes a possible threat to national security, traditional techniques of surveillance, deterrence, and non-proliferation become increasingly ill suited to detecting and preventing terrorist activity. In the case of the 2001 anthrax attacks, for example, attribution took seven years and remains to this day contested. Indeed, often in these cases, a target state will not be able to determine whether its attacker is another state, a political group, a criminal group, or a lone wolf.

Indeed, the life sciences now threaten realistically to put the power of a weapons-of-mass-destruction attack in the hands, if not of the average person, certainly of many above-average people with relatively inexpensive equipment and basic training in genetic engineering. Biological weapons are unique among weapons of mass destruction in that they have the capacity, like nuclear weapons, to produce truly catastrophic damage yet, like chemical weapons, are comparatively inexpensive and easy to produce. The technology required for their production is generally the same as the technology used in legitimate life sciences research; indeed, it is the bread-and-butter stuff of the biotech revolution that has done so much good throughout the world. Precisely because modern biotechnology has so much promise and offers so many benefits in so many walks of life, the materials and skills required to develop these weapons are not rare. So while it may be difficult for even a highly trained individual to build his own nuclear weapon, an individual with relatively modest expertise and resources could potentially obtain or develop a biological weapon with worldwide consequences. As costs continue to fall, the number of people around the world whom governments will have to regard—at least in theory—as capable of having their own personal weapons of mass destruction program grows commensurately.

This is already happening fast. The bioterrorism expert Christopher Chyba has likened the proliferation of gene synthesis capability to the explosion in computer technology known as Moore's Law. Intel Corporation's cofounder Gordon Moore observed decades ago that the number of transistors on an integrated circuit was doubling every two years—a trend that has remained true ever since. Chyba writes that "just as Moore's law led to a transition in computing from extremely expensive industrial-scale machines to laptops, iPods, and microprocessors in toys, cars, and home appliances, so is biotechnological innovation moving us to a world where manipulations or synthesis of DNA will be increasingly available to small groups of the technically competent or even individual users, should they choose to make use of it."[3] Ali

Nouri and Chyba note that the cost of synthesizing a human genome is falling sharply;[4] along with cost decreases, the efficiency of biotechnology continues to increase. While it took researchers at the State University of New York three years to synthesize the complete polio virus in 2002, the following year, a different group of researchers synthesized a viral genome of comparative length in only two weeks.[5]

Biological weapons do not work like other weapons of mass destruction. The long incubation periods for many pathogens mean that an infected individual can travel and infect others before contamination becomes apparent, making it difficult to limit the impact of an attack. Moreover, illnesses caused by biological weapons are often hard to distinguish from naturally occurring outbreaks. It took investigators a year to realize that an outbreak in 1984 of salmonella in Oregon was the result of an attack by followers of the Bagwan Shree Rajneesh cult, for example.[6] The difficulty of attribution, combined with the fact that authorities may not learn of an attack until symptoms emerge days or weeks after infection, blunts the effectiveness of traditional models of deterrence and response.

What is more, deadly pathogens are not that hard to come by. Many occur naturally; notable naturally occurring pathogens include anthrax, bubonic plague, hemorrhagic fevers such as the Ebola and Marburg viruses, tularemia, and Venezuelan equine encephalitis. These can be collected in the natural environment, a fact that was not lost on the notorious Japanese cult Aum Shinrikyo—which attempted to obtain Ebola strains in Zaire. In addition, many pathogens are stockpiled by commercial entities for entirely legitimate purposes, although controls on these stockpiles have tightened in recent years.

And as our introductory nightmare scenario makes clear, even pathogens like smallpox and the 1918 flu virus, which have been wiped out in the wild, can now be recreated. The literature available in the public domain describing— even routinizing—genetic engineering projects involving the creation and enhancement of deadly pathogens should be at least as terrifying to policymakers around the world as box cutters or guns on airplanes. Viral genomes are relatively small. Many have already been mapped, and the materials required to modify existing sequences to mirror them or to synthesize them from scratch are all commercially available. And scientists have repeatedly demonstrated that if terrorists—or individual bad guys—have the will, science has a way:

—In 2001 Australian researchers published the results of a study in which they used gene-splicing technology to create a variation of the mousepox virus more lethal to mice than the normal one and impervious to vaccination.[7] (Mousepox is a virus closely related to human smallpox but does not cause disease in humans.)

—In 2001 a team of virologists in Germany and France constructed the Ebola virus from three strands of complementary DNA.[8]

—In 2002 researchers from the State University of New York, Stony Brook, published studies of de novo DNA synthesis of the polio virus, which they had constructed using nucleotide fragments purchased from a mail-order biotech company.[9]

—In similar studies, scientists have successfully synthesized the 1918 Spanish influenza virus,[10] which infected an estimated one-third of the world's population and killed between 50 and 100 million people world-wide,[11] and the encephalomyocarditis virus, which can cause fatal febrile illness in humans.[12]

To be sure, technological obstacles still remain to terrorist groups or individuals in launching a global pandemic, but these obstacles are growing ever more surmountable. As technology continues to improve, the creation of larger, more complex pathogens—including, potentially, the smallpox virus[13]—will become cheaper and easier for a wider array of potential bad actors.

And if recent history is any guide, that is an ominous possibility. For although no state, terrorist group, or individual has yet successfully launched a mass-casualty biological attack, a range of cases demonstrate that there is no dearth of people who would like to do so. Aum Shinrikyo expended great effort in the early 1990s attempting to obtain biological weapons. Before killing twelve people and injuring more than five thousand by releasing sarin nerve gas on a train in Tokyo, cult members attempted to release botulinum toxin in the Japanese parliament, sent a mission to Zaire to obtain strains of the Ebola virus, and released anthrax spores from atop a building in Tokyo.[14] The case of Larry Wayne Harris provides another chilling example of a nonstate actor's potential bioterrorism capabilities. Harris was a member of the Aryan Nations who, using the stationery of a fictitious laboratory, easily obtained the bacterial agent of the bubonic plague from a private company. After the company shipped the bacterial cultures to his home, an employee became concerned and contacted the Centers for Disease Control and Prevention. Thus alerted, the authorities obtained a search warrant and discovered pathogens, as well as explosives, in Harris's car and at his home. Harris explained that he was stockpiling weapons in preparation for an imminent Armageddon.[15]

And, of course, the threat of bioterrorism became a reality with the anthrax attacks in October 2001. Just weeks after the attacks on September 11, 2001, someone mailed anthrax-contaminated powder from a mailbox in Princeton, New Jersey, to various locations in Washington, D.C., and elsewhere, killing five people, injuring seventeen, shutting down mail services, and forcing the evacuation of federal buildings, including Senate offices and the Supreme Court. Although the Justice Department closed its investigation in 2008 after the prime suspect, a biodefense employee named Bruce E. Ivins, committed suicide, doubts still linger about the case.[16] In any event, that it took seven years for investigators to develop an indictable case against a single individual illustrates the security and law enforcement challenges posed by even a relatively low-impact bioterrorism event.

If a terrorist were to overcome the challenges inherent in developing a naturally occurring pathogen into a deployable weapon, the consequences could be devastating. The U.S. Office of Technology Assessment has estimated, for example, that an airplane flying over a densely populated area such as Washington, D.C., could kill as many as 3 million people with 100 kilograms of properly aerosolized anthrax.[17] A contagious virus specifically engineered for lethality against a relatively unimmunized population could, at least theoretically, be worse. In the world of low-probability, high-impact events, this type of attack stands out for its relative plausibility.

Attempts at Governance to Date

It rather understates the matter to say that current governance of biosecurity is hopelessly inadequate to the task of preventing the disasters one might reasonably anticipate. Changing governance in a fashion that carries real costs in the absence of some dramatic precipitating event is always difficult—though that fact is not the primary obstacle to preventing biotechnologically generated disasters. The core of the problem is that the ideal governance approach is far from obvious. Indeed, nobody quite knows how to approach the issue or even whether an effective governance structure exists. Even if one could, for example, classify all of the relevant now-public literature and slap strict controls on the technologies in question, who would want to? The biotechnology revolution is a wonderful thing, and it has depended pervasively on precisely the open culture that has created the vulnerabilities I have been describing. In any event, too many people have too deep an understanding of how genetic engineering works for the public to forget what it knows—and the Internet would ensure that we could not easily suppress dangerous papers if we tried.

The problem with current governance is not that we do not have laws prohibiting abuse of biotechnology. We do. The law, in fact, over the past decade has developed rather admirably, and nobody now could do anything horrible without running afoul of it. Nonetheless, current law is unlikely to do much more than inconvenience someone seriously committed to developing or releasing a biological agent that could do great damage. The law does not—and probably cannot—address the attribution problems at work here effectively, nor can it easily offer much in the way of prevention.

Traditionally, states have treated biothreats either as naturally occurring phenomena viewed through the lens of public health policy or as problems of state-to-state weapons proliferation. For example, the 1972 Biological and Toxin Weapons Convention, ratified by the United States in 1975, saw the problem of biological weapons almost entirely in terms of official biological state warfare programs—a function of the fact that, back then, it really was science fiction to imagine anyone but a state developing or using significant biological weapons.[18] The restrictions of the convention in the United States did not even apply to private individuals until the passage of the Biological Weapons Anti-Terrorism Act of 1989, which criminalized the individual production, possession, and transfer of biological agents "for use as a weapon."[19]

Congress stepped into the fray again following the September 11 attacks and the fatal anthrax mailings shortly thereafter, passing two pieces of additional legislation. The PATRIOT Act strengthened the biological weapons statute to make it a crime to possess any "biological agent, toxin, or delivery system of a type or in a quantity that . . . is not reasonably justified by a prophylactic, protective, bona fide research, or other peaceful purpose."[20] The PATRIOT Act also prohibited the possession of certain listed biological agents by a "restricted person"—or their transfer to such a person.[21]

In 2002 Congress passed the Public Health Security and Bioterrorism Preparedness and Response Act to regulate the possession, transfer, and use of select biological agents. The new law required the secretary of health and human services to, "by regulation[,] establish and maintain a list of each biological agent and each toxin that has the potential to pose a severe threat to public health and safety."[22] It also directed the secretary to provide for the "establishment and enforcement of safety procedures for the transfer" of designated agents as well as for their "possession and use."[23] The regulations had to require "registration with the Secretary" as a prerequisite for possession, use, or transfer and to "include provisions to ensure that persons seeking to register under such regulations have a lawful purpose to possess, use, or transfer such agents and toxins."[24] Registration required applicants to provide "information regarding the characterization of listed agents and toxins to facilitate their identification, including their source." Finally, the statute further required the department to "maintain a national database that includes the names and locations of registered persons, the listed agents and toxins such persons are possessing, using, or transferring, and information regarding the characterization of such agents and toxins.[25] Implementing the congressional mandate, the Department of Health and Human Services regulations prohibited the regulated entities and individuals from transferring such agents to nonregistered entities and individuals and authorized the inspector general of the department to investigate violations and impose civil penalties.[26] The 2002 act also created additional criminal liability for unauthorized shipping, transfer, and possession of select agents.[27]

One of the most important, and most controversial, of the Bioterrorism Response Act's sections provided for a rudimentary background check for people registering to handle select agents to make sure they were not excluded from doing so by the statute's enumerated categories.[28] This effectively authorized the attorney general to require anyone seeking access to listed biological agents to submit to a security risk assessment. The regulations implementing this provision permit the Federal Bureau of Investigation to share an applicant's information with other governmental agencies, including law enforcement and private organizations.[29] Some in the scientific community have expressed concern that the security risk assessment provisions discourage qualified individuals from engaging in legitimate biological and agricultural research "because of the apparent infringement of these rules on individual liberties and the Fourth Amendment."[30]

While the government's response to bioterrorism to date has largely focused on enhancing the monitoring and control of biological research and materials, the continuing threat has also prompted calls for extending regulatory authorities both to suppress research and to respond to biological attacks. On the prevention side, proposals to restrict the flow of information—including controls on the publication of research papers, scientific conferences, and the sharing of information with foreign scientists—have raised serious concerns about the implications of bioterrorism policy for free speech and scientific advancement.[31] Meanwhile, proposals to increase the government's response capabilities—in particular, proposals to broaden federal and state power to isolate and quarantine those who may have been infected by a contagious agent—would rely on the robust use of long-dormant detention powers in considerable tension with modern due process norms.[32]

The biotech industry is also beginning efforts at self-regulation. Gene synthesis companies that sell sequences of genetic material prepared to order have begun screening orders for sequences that match (or match significant fragments of) pathogens listed as select agents.[33] Some experts have proposed going further and actually building such screening mechanisms into gene synthesis equipment available to laboratories.[34]

In short, it is hard to imagine that someone could build a personal arsenal of weapons of mass destruction without running afoul of numerous criminal laws and regulatory regimes—and various systems are either in place or being developed to flag bad actors before they strike. All that said, it is almost equally hard to imagine any of this deterring someone truly committed to launching a devastating attack, particularly if such a person lived or operated abroad. If the world makes it to 2025 without suffering a major nonnatural biosecurity event, we will likely owe our good fortune not to the lack of opportunity for individual or small-group mayhem but to a combination of a lack of imagination and a lack of technical sophistication on the part of the bad guys.

Constitutional Stresses

If the threat landscape in the life sciences is really as terrifying as I have suggested, two conclusions almost certainly follow. The first is that government will act aggressively, either before a major event, after it, or both. It will act beforehand if it grows scared enough, if there are enough near misses like the 2001 anthrax attacks to keep officials cognizant of the problem, and if it can generate the political will to support strong measures. It will act after the fact whether or not it acts before, because pressure on officials to do something will be inexorable. The polity in that context will almost certainly demand that officials prevent subsequent incidents, not merely that they respond better to future biosecurity events. As happened after September 11, a consensus will develop that retroactive actions—whether criminal prosecutions for terrorists or public health response to human-caused biosecurity crises—are simply inadequate and that government must stop future events before they happen.

The second conclusion is that faced with strong actions that stress constitutional norms, the courts will tend to uphold those that promise to work and strike down those that do not. Judges behave pragmatically, and the old saw that the Constitution is not a suicide pact will loom large in the mind of any judge inclined to block enforcement of a policy that reasonably stands to prevent major bioterrorism events. Indeed, the doctrine itself already tends to reflect this pragmatism. The relevant constitutional tests will look at questions such as whether a given policy is narrowly tailored to achieve a compelling state interest or whether a policy uses the least restrictive means to achieve its goals. Under any such test, a policy that can plausibly be expected to have a significant impact on the problem is going to fare far better than one that seems like a stab in the dark.

This fact puts an enormous premium on the question of what policies, if any, are likely to prove effective in preventing, or effectively managing, biosecurity events. If some magic bullet policy with great capacity for prevention proved quite burdensome on someone's asserted constitutional rights, we could reasonably expect that this policy would at some point be both adopted and, the stakes being as high as they are, upheld—if not before the first major event, certainly after it. The trouble is that while many of the policy options push up against constitutional norms—either against existing doctrines or likely doctrines—none seems like much of a magic bullet. In the absence of judicial confidence in their success, it is clear neither that they will be sustained nor that they should be sustained. Rather, the range of possible responses includes many that will do little to prevent abuses while both abridging liberty and impairing the legitimate research that is key to finding cures and vaccines. To illustrate this point, I consider several of those options in turn.

Restricting Research

The first, and perhaps the crudest, option is simply to ban certain categories of life sciences research—at least outside of the classified setting. Congress and the executive branch could take the position that certain research is so profoundly dangerous that it should not take place at all in the public domain. Rather, defensive research within this space should take place in classified laboratories, much as nuclear weapons research takes place at the national laboratories. Private individuals and companies, except under government supervision, should not be in the business of conducting such research at all. The idea here would be to stuff the genie back into the bottle—at least to a point—and to prevent further public breakthroughs from simplifying the bad guys' task.

This strategy seems to have both a bleak prospect of effectiveness and a high probability of gravely impairing a great deal of legitimate research. It is, after all, hard to come up with treatments for diseases without studying the agents that cause those diseases. Yet under this scheme, research on treatments for especially dangerous infectious agents would have to take place either in a classified setting or not at all. The result would likely be slower progress in developing vaccines and therapies for precisely the diseases about which authorities are most concerned. What is more, research restrictions would probably not impair those who would misuse biotechnology nearly as much as it would impair those who would use it for peaceful purposes. So much information is already public, and the materials are so widely available, that it is implausible to imagine that the restrictions would stop research by those who do not wish to be stopped. The old adage that if owning a gun is a crime, only criminals will have guns, is pointedly true of biotechnology research. If research on pathogens is discouraged or frustrated, the bad guys will be deterred far less than the good guys, and we will probably have many fewer treatments for both naturally occurring and manmade outbreaks.

Given this reality, I suspect serious efforts to impede public biotechnology research will face serious obstacles in the courts—though no current doctrine would seem to preclude them. The Supreme Court has never held that scientific inquiry is protected by the Constitution.[35] Still, a substantial body of scholarship suggests on various different grounds, principally the First Amendment, that some degree of constitutional protection for scientific inquiry exists.[36] One can easily imagine judges deferring to reasonable regulations of research when those regulations are undertaken to protect public safety; this much is uncontroversial, and such regulations are already in place. But it is quite a different matter to imagine that judges would sit still for grave limitations on free inquiry into human health—inquiry with the capacity to save many lives—in the pursuit of a policy with such a limited probability of success. While no formal doctrinal bar to such a policy exists at present, I suspect the courts would erect one quickly in the absence of stronger reason than now exists to believe such a policy has any prospect for success.

In any event, except in perhaps the most targeted fashion, research restrictions would be a most foolish policy move. Biosecurity is a kind of arms race, in which the best hope for long-term security is good public health infrastructure combined with rapid progress in fighting infectious disease. Impeding that progress would be counterproductive in the extreme—even if preventing bioterrorism were the only biosecurity goal (which it is not).

Publication Restrictions

A somewhat less draconian option is to restrict publication of scientific papers that offer particularly useful guidance to would-be biological bad actors. Research would be permitted and regulated only as it is regulated now, but the government might seek to prevent publication of especially dangerous experiments.

Perhaps ironically, given that this approach is actually milder than the one described above, it is much more clearly problematic constitutionally under current doctrine. It is a commonplace that the First Amendment looks askance at prior restraints on speech, and that is the case even where the courts find credible the government's contentions that significant harm will follow publications.[37] In the modern era, it literally takes a publication's attempt to offer details on how to build a nuclear bomb to justify a prior restraint—and even in that case, the magazine in question eventually published.[38] In that instance, the publication offered nothing like the case a scientific journal could make regarding the value of the speech in question. After all, these articles are not, generally speaking, how-to manuals for catastrophes but serious science undertaken for altogether legitimate reasons. The terrifying mousepox study described above, for example, was aimed at improving methods of pest eradication. Other studies are efforts to understand and describe viruses, the better to attack them. There is serious social benefit to this work—benefit that the courts would rightly consider weighty.

What is more, in contrast to scientific research itself, there is little question at all that scientific publications are protected by the First Amendment. Steve Keane, who opposes constitutional protection for research, nonetheless acknowledges that "scientific expression," which "includes scientific publishing and communication . . . is entitled to normal free speech protection. In fact, the Supreme Court and lower courts have repeatedly indicated, in dicta, that scientific works and scientific expression are protected by the First Amendment."[39]

Hardly anyone contends that no life sciences research should be withheld from the public on safety grounds. In the wake of September 11, facing criticism for some of the studies they had published and calls for greater oversight and regulation, medical and scientific journals began developing procedures to consider the safety implications of research publications in the life sciences.[40] In a joint statement of principles published in 2003, the editors of several leading journals acknowledged that "on occasions, an editor may conclude that the potential harm of publication outweighs the potential society benefits. Under such circumstances, the paper should be modified, or not published."[41] But this sort of self-regulation is a far cry from government censorship. And it is reasonable to expect the courts to treat censorship with a great deal of skepticism.

In a provocative article on what he terms "crime-facilitating speech," Eugene Volokh proposes that speech ought not to be constitutionally protected when "it can cause extraordinarily serious harm (on the order of a nuclear attack or a plague) even when it's also valuable for lawful purposes."[42] This sort of thinking offers a potential doctrinal path for a court inclined to uphold publication restrictions, should the government ultimately go that route. But again, the question of the effectiveness of publication regulation will—and probably should—loom large in any adjudication. Unless there is compelling reason to believe that publication could bring about a catastrophe, and that stopping publication will avert it, courts have enormous doctrinal momentum in the direction of ensuring press freedom.

Publication restrictions, particularly if closely targeted, stand a better chance of at least limited effectiveness than restrictions on the underlying research itself. One could imagine how a system of screening papers before publication might keep particularly dangerous material out of the public domain and perhaps divert publication into classified settings. This would function much like the self-regulatory system the journals have already created, except with a security officer, not an editor, making the final call as to whether a given paper would require modification or nonpublication.

But its effectiveness would likely be quite limited, and it is not at all clear that such a system would impair the bad guys more than it would frustrate the good guys. Foreign journals would probably publish papers banned from publication in the United States. And in any event, scientists have many means other than paper publication—conferences, seminars, e-mails, informal conversations, and blogs, for example—of sharing results and methods. In any event, such a system would do nothing to prevent people from using the huge wealth of information already public for evil purposes. Quite apart from such a system's being repugnant to First Amendment values, in other words, it would be far from a silver bullet.

Licensing, Registration, Surveillance, and Data Mining

A more promising avenue, both in terms of effectiveness and in terms of constitutional plausibility, is to focus not on restricting research or publication but on monitoring the use of gene synthesis equipment and the companies and scientists that employ them. The simplest and perhaps most effective strategy in this regard may simply be to require a license before permitting certain categories of genetic research and experimentation. One needs a license to operate an amateur radio; it hardly seems onerous to suggest that one should need one to meddle in genetics. Licensing would give government a window into who is working with what. It would also allow the criminalization of a wide range of unauthorized activity. It would not, of course, prevent that unauthorized activity. People drive without licenses, and those who want to build bugs will do so without licenses, too. But it does offer a mechanism of governmental leverage and monitoring.

Along related lines, the major gene synthesis companies, which sell gene sequences by mail order, by phone, and over the Internet, now screen orders for sequences associated with "select agents and toxins" listed under the 2002 Bioterrorism Response Act and refuse to sell such sequences to those who are not registered under that act.[43] At least in theory, this should prevent bad actors from buying, say, the smallpox virus genome or buying sizable segments of it and then assembling them in their own laboratories. Yet this system would do nothing to prevent a bad actor from building the sequence himself or modifying a related one to match it. In an article published early in 2009, Ali Nouri and Christopher Chyba proposed building the existing screening system directly into the gene synthesis equipment that is common in many labs. Manufacturers would program the computers that drive the machines to decline to produce select-agent components unless the user were registered to work with them. The software, under this proposal, could automatically update its list of prohibited sequences much the way antivirus software updates the list of malware it identifies and purges.[44] The proposal, vaguely reminiscent of proposals during the 1990s to require back-door access to encryption systems for law enforcement, drew a sharp response from biotech executives that was similarly reminiscent of the attacks on the so-called Clipper Chip and other key escrow encryption schemes.[45]

As it stands now, the screenings system—and probably even Nouri and Chyba's proposed enhancement of it—would be more of an inconvenience to a biohacker than a true prevention mechanism. It might force a bad actor to use older technology that predates the embedded screening systems or to use sequences brief enough as not to trigger the screening system. People would surely seek to hack the system and disable the screening software. And it would do little to prevent modification of existing DNA sequences. Someone truly committed and technically capable would find a way around it—though it may well stop low-grade amateurs, and it should make any bad actor's life at least a bit more difficult.

The system, however, would have an obvious set of legal advantages—namely, that it seems to raise no particular constitutional difficulty. There is, after all, no constitutional right to create pathogens or to privacy in one's pathogenic experimentations. What is more, one can imagine further developments of the technology that would make it far more robust as a prevention tool. What if gene synthesis equipment alerted authorities whenever an unauthorized person tried to create a proscribed sequence? More intrusively, what if the equipment reported constantly on its own activities, so that authorities would have an ongoing data stream that enabled them to monitor who was creating what gene sequences? If one takes seriously the notion that there is no right to privacy in genetic engineering experimentation, there ought to be no constitutional obstacle to such a requirement—though there would surely be strong policy objections to government's engaging in constant surveillance of research.

Major hurdles remain to developing this area, not the least of which is creating enough international uniformity that bad actors do not simply buy and use their equipment in countries that do not require embedded surveillance systems. That said, this area represents a relatively promising avenue for policymakers who are seeking a robust tool for preventing manmade biosecurity disasters.

The trouble arises from the fact that to be truly useful, the data from such a system would likely have to be analyzed in conjunction with other data. It is, after all, far less threatening to know that Scientist A is manipulating fragments of DNA from an infectious agent if one also knows that she has published extensively on the treatment of that agent than, say, if she has recently purchased copies of the *Turner Diaries* and is a member of the Aryan Nations. This raises the larger question of data mining in a particularly troubling form: surveillance of science leading to ongoing data mining of individuals against whom government has no individualized suspicion. In other words, the government would be essentially asserting the right to conduct ongoing background checks against anyone involved in the life sciences.

In one sense, of course, this merely builds on the current system of background checks for those registering under the 2002 Bioterrorism Response Act to handle select agents—risk assessments (essentially background checks) that already allow the FBI to query databases and other agencies to flag those ineligible to register. As in those background checks, the hit rate would be miniscule. In 2009 congressional testimony, an FBI official stated that "since the inception of the [Bioterrorism Risk Assessment] program, [it] has completed 32,742 [background investigations]. Two hundred and eight individuals have been restricted"[46]—a hit rate of approximately .006 of 1 percent. So the program would operate as a huge fishing expedition looking for anomalies in scientific behavior.

Exactly how troubling this would be would depend, to a great degree, on who looks at what data, when, and with what degree of cause. Currently, the constitutional landscape for data mining is relatively permissive. Much of the data the government might choose to examine is not plausibly within the ambit of the Fourth Amendment as currently interpreted, and in any event, Fourth Amendment law has an exception allowing warrantless searches for "heavily regulated industries"—for which at least some biotechnology labs probably qualify.[47]

My guess is that the combination of licensing, technological blocking of select-agent production, monitoring of the use of gene synthesis equipment, and examination of data relevant to people whose use of this equipment raises red flags probably represents the most promising policy avenue in the prevention department. Done right, it stands to have only a minimal impact on ongoing science; as long as people are entitled to use their equipment for the purpose they deploy it, after all, it would do nothing more than create an audit trail. While more than a little creepy, it faces no greater constitutional barrier than, say, running data checks on people who get on airplanes. And it stands to provide a real-time stream of data about who is using what equipment to make what genetic sequences—data that could tip off investigators at a relatively early stage of a developing biosecurity disaster.

That said, it is far from a cure-all. If the embedded technology is not mandatory, it could simply drive a market for surveillance-free gene synthesis equipment—much the way the voluntary key escrow policy in encryption led to widespread adoption of non-key-escrow encryption algorithms. If other countries do not adopt the same standard, an American policy requiring such technology could also simply create incentives for companies to move biotechnology work overseas or to use foreign surveillance-free technologies. Finally, even imagining a perfect system, its coverage would be far less than 100 percent. Someone will successfully hack it and override its reporting and blocking functions. Someone else will figure out how to game the system so that his malicious conduct will not raise red flags with authorities. Computer security systems always fail eventually. This will be no exception.

Isolation and Quarantine

Finally, it is worth saying a brief word about isolation and quarantine, which have no capacity to prevent a biosecurity event but might under some circumstances be key to managing one. In the context of any major biosecurity event, particularly one involving a highly contagious and lethal pathogen, the question of isolation will inevitably arise. The power of quarantine and isolation is traditionally broad, and quarantine laws have been upheld by the courts on public safety grounds in the past. But they have not been used aggressively in decades, and across many other areas, governmental powers to detain people outside of the criminal justice apparatus is on the wane. Over the past ten years alone, for example, the power to detain the enemy in wartime—at least when the enemy is out of uniform and difficult to identify clearly—has come under sustained challenge, and the courts have imposed significant new review mechanisms. They have done this notwithstanding relatively clear doctrine that seemed to establish that habeas corpus review was not available to the alien detained overseas—doctrine in which the government had a surpassing reliance interest.[48] The Supreme Court has similarly shifted the landscape of allowable immigration detention.[49] One can probably expect, therefore, that quarantine laws—which involve minimal due process before permitting detention—will face significant constitutional challenge as well if used aggressively. And while authorities have apparently strong precedents that permit aggressive quarantine and isolation policies, they would do well not to assume that those precedents will have staying power.

As this brief overview makes clear, the possible impact of these technologies—and the government's response to them—on the Bill of Rights could range significantly. If one imagines that courts see promise in muscular government actions, the impact could be quite profound—the development of doctrine affirmatively tolerating limitations on research, publication of research, real-time surveillance of biomedical science and scientists, and a renewal of a long-dormant tolerance for detaining sick people. By contrast, if one imagines that the courts will respond to strong countermeasures as ineffective shots in the dark that offend basic values, one could imagine litigation's clarifying doctrine in the opposite direction in many of these areas, leaving government with few tools to address a profound security problem. The striking fact is that, save for significant investment in biomedical research, no policy option exists that is both likely to be especially effective and poses no serious doctrinal question.

The Biggest Impact?

This lack of promising, clearly constitutional options—or even promising unconstitutional options—gives rise to what I suspect will be the most profound impact of this class of technologies on the Constitution. Ironically, the impact will be felt not on the Bill of Rights but on the very structural arrangements of power the core document contemplates. That is, it stands to bring about a substantial erosion of the government's monopoly on security policy, putting in diffuse and private hands for the first time responsibility for protecting the nation.

There are people who would write that sentence with joy in their hearts. I am not one of them. My views on executive power—notwithstanding the excesses of the Bush administration—are unapologetically Hamiltonian. The constitutional assumption that the political branches, particularly the executive branch, are responsible for national security and have the tools necessary to fulfill that responsibility is a comforting one, the destabilization of which I find scary. "Power to the people!" is a slogan that has always rung to me of gridlock at best, mob rule at worst.

The Constitution contains very few textual exceptions to the notion that national security is a federal responsibility. One, the Second Amendment, embodies the framers' reverence for state militias, both as a means of fending off native attacks and as a means of preventing federal encroachments on state prerogatives. The other, the letters marque clause of Article I, contemplates a limited role for the private sector in military engagements—under congressional supervision.[50] Both involve institutions that have long since lapsed into disuse. The broader and more lasting presumptions were that Congress would make the rules of security and the president would lead the armed forces and the larger executive apparatus in a military or other crisis.

I am not sure how these presumptions hold in the face of rapid development of these technologies. This point is perhaps most vivid in the cyber arena, where a huge amount of traffic into and out of the United States—including government traffic—now takes place over privately owned lines and the government quite literally does not control the channels through which attacks can occur. But it is also true in the biotechnology sphere. Because the revolution has taken place largely in private, not government, hands, the government employs only a fraction of the capable individuals. And the capacity to respond to or prevent an attack is therefore as diffuse as the capacity to launch one.

This point is crucial and provides the only real ray of hope in an otherwise bleak picture. The biotechnology revolution has given enormous numbers of people the capacity to do great harm, but it has also given enormous numbers of people the capacity to work to prevent that harm. The proliferation of defensive capability has been as rapid as the proliferation of offensive capability—only exponentially more so since the good guys so vastly outnumber the bad guys. The individual scientist had no ability to prevent the Soviet Union from launching a nuclear attack against the United States or invading Western Europe. But the individual scientist and groupings of individual scientists have an enormous role in biosecurity—from driving the further innovations that can wipe out infectious diseases, to spotting the security implications of new research, to reporting on colleagues engaged in suspicious activities out of sight of authorities. The policies of universities thus take on security importance, as do the postures of private companies and the research agendas of individuals. The number of actors capable of playing a significant role in the solution grows as quickly as the number of people capable of creating the problem.

This fact will, I suspect, tend to force changes in the constitutional structures of security. I do not mean here that any kind of formal doctrinal shift will take place. The change will be far subtler than that. The point is that as the powers the Constitution grants to government actors grow less plausible as tools for the problems they confront, the Hamiltonian executive—capable of strong decisive action characterized by secrecy and dispatch and energy—will be of more limited use. Going after a multiplicity of dangerous actors whom authorities cannot identify using facilities the government neither owns nor controls in locations over which it may have no jurisdiction will not flatter the Hamiltonian executive. The Congress charged with creating rules for that executive is positioned little better. And so aspects of our security policy will tend to devolve to those actors better positioned to have real impact.

Changes to the nature of the executive in response to shifting circumstances and in the absence of major doctrinal movement are far from unheard-of in American history. The presidency of the founding era was tiny. Yet as the need for the regulatory state grew during the New Deal and World War II, it ballooned into the behemoth of the imperial presidency. This change, of course, involved some degree of doctrinal change, but surprisingly little—Article II of the Constitution being ultimately consistent with both a small streamlined presidency and a giant federal bureaucracy. This period saw huge doctrinal changes in the substantive scope of federal power, but the presidency itself changed largely by ongoing adaptation—by growing in response to perceived need.

The change in response to this problem will probably be similar. Nobody is going to rewrite the Constitution or, more plausibly, rethink constitutional doctrine to vest security responsibility in nongovernmental actors. It will just happen. As government finds itself relatively feckless in the face of the problem and other actors find themselves capable of responding, we will start thinking about those other actors as bearing important security functions for which we once looked to government. And government itself will end up playing, I suspect, more of a coordinating function with respect to these other actors than the classical defend-the-borders model of security.

Curiously, and more than a bit ironically, this fact pulls the mind back toward themes and ideas eloquently articulated by scholars such as James Boyle and Lawrence Lessig in the context of the debate over intellectual property. A major current of this body of thought involves the protection of legal space for communities of various sorts to use and borrow one another's ideas and work in collaborative efforts to build things. *The Public Domain,* Boyle's recent book, for example, contains a spirited defense of distributed applications like file sharing, of the open-source software movement, and of Creative Commons licenses.[51] Indeed, the world has seen amazing demonstrations of what large groups of people can do when they pool expertise—even with limited coordination. The most famous example is Wikipedia, but this is far from the only one. Anyone who has used Open Office—an open-source alternative to the Windows Office application suite—knows that it does not take a major software company to produce a major piece of software. It is an interesting fact, highly salient for our purposes here, that open-source software is often more stable and secure than proprietary code.[52] While this point has its dissenters, the famous line in the open-source software movement that "given enough eyeballs, all bugs are shallow" may have real application not just to computer bugs but to biological ones as well.[53]

Given that security will be, to borrow a term from this lexicon, a more distributed application than it has been in the past, we ought to start thinking about it as such. And here the landscape actually seems somewhat promising. There are, as I have noted, many more good guys than bad guys in the biotech world. They are enormously innovative. And they are much closer to the ground than is government. They offer a great deal of capacity to identify the bad guys and to develop countermeasures to their actions—a huge reservoir of thought and expertise in the development of strategies for both responses and prevention.

It is hard to envision the long-term migration of the defense function in any detail; it is not hard, however, to envision various iterations of biosecurity as a distributed application, with government functioning more as a coordinating mechanism than as frontline defender of the nation. At the most basic level, government can create a favorable environment for the sort of biotech research that will help win the arms race against biosecurity malefactors. Government can identify treating infectious disease as a major national research and funding priority. Putting a large amount of money behind basic research, the development of new therapies and vaccines, and the improvement of response times to new outbreaks would create a major incentive for industry and university researchers to innovate faster than the relatively small number of bad guys do. The more people can be mustered in this direction, the greater the numerical advantage in brain power the good guys can deploy and the greater the likelihood that cures and treatments will outpace manufactured (and natural) diseases.

This has already happened to a considerable degree, particularly since September 11. But government can do a lot more in the way of both conceiving of infectious disease research as a national security strategy and creating a favorable research, regulatory, and liability environment in which to improve capacity to defeat infectious agents. Any such approach would—indeed, does—involve government's setting of priorities and funding security work but not directly conducting the activity that may be central to long-term security. That work, rather, is broadly distributed to a research community given incentives to address a security function that the government itself is ill positioned to confront.

Second, while government cannot monitor all biotech research, biotech researchers can more effectively monitor one another and might—under the right circumstances—serve as a network of security eyes and ears. Efforts to harness the public to the project of security have not always fared well. The Bush administration's ill-fated Operation TIPS (Terrorism Information and Prevention System) was an effort to get people to report suspicious activity, yet it came off as a Big Brotheresque spying program. But large numbers of people offer some of the strongest, most flexible security there is, and a culture in which researchers know what others are working on and have the instinct to raise questions about oddities is a more secure culture than one in which people work in vacuums and keep their mouths shut. While enormous cultural obstacles in the scientific community currently impede the development of a more secure culture, somehow we will ultimately have to mine the latent protective potential of a crowd of highly educated people up close to the process.

Third, one can imagine various technological devices by which users might take greater responsibility for the security of the biotech platform. Some of the screening technologies discussed above, for example, could become helpfully ubiquitous if, say, university and industry policies strongly militated toward their use. Government may have a regulatory role here in encouraging both the development and the deployment of such technologies, but again, the frontline defense will necessarily be distributed among the thousands of people working in biotech. Similarly, as biotechnology moves away from artisanal crafting of unique sequences toward more standardized constructions of genetic materials out of what are essentially microscopic Legos, one can imagine tagging those Legos with identifying information—which could potentially make attribution of misconduct far easier. Most color laser printers leave information on every copy they make that identifies the specific equipment that produced the copy, an effort to prevent counterfeiting. A strong norm toward the embedding of tracing information in the constituent elements of bioengineered sequences could be key to knowing who is producing what—or at least to being able to figure out in retrospect from where bad things came.

Finally, people in universities and industries need to feel themselves to have a security function. When I was a child in New York City in the 1970s, I was crossing Columbus Avenue with my father—with whom I had just been playing baseball in Central Park. As we were crossing the street, a young man snatched the purse of an older woman crossing toward us and sprinted northward up the street. The woman yelled, and spontaneously and with no coordination, half a dozen—maybe ten—men in the immediate vicinity (my father among them) sprinted after him. They ran him down ten blocks later and held him until the police arrived. This is distributed security in the absence of a strong executive presence. There are enormous obstacles to the development of such a model globally across complex technological platforms. One of the most daunting is the culture of the scientific community, which does not tend to think in security terms. That said, it may be a vision of our technological and constitutional future—as well as a memory from my past.

Notes

1. See James Fearon, "Catastrophic Terrorism and Civil Liberties in the Short and Long Run," remarks delivered at Columbia University's Symposium on Constitutions, Democracy, and the Rule of Law, October 17, 2003 (www.stanford.edu/~jfearon/papers/civlibs.doc).

2. Philip Bobbitt, *Terror and Consent: The Wars for the Twenty-First Century* (New York: Alfred A. Knopf, 2008), 533.

3. C. F. Chyba, "Biotechnology and the Challenge to Arms Control," 30 *Arms Control Today* (2008): 11, 12. For an excellent summary of modern biothreats and their relationship to other weapons of mass destruction, see Bobbitt, *Terror and Consent*, 101–05, 231–32, 402–04.

4. Ali Nouri and C. F. Chyba, "Proliferation-Resistant Biotechnology: An Approach to Improve Biosecurity," 27 *Nature Biotechnology* (2009): 234.

5. Chyba, "Biotechnology and the Challenge to Arms Control," 12.

6. C. F. Chyba, "Toward Biological Security," 81 *Foreign Affairs* (2002): 122, 129.

7. R. J. Jackson and others, "Expression of a Mouse Interleukin-4 by a Recombinant Ectromelia Virus Represses Cytolytic Lymphocyte Responses and Overcomes Genetic Resistance to Mousepox," 75 *Journal of Virology* (2001): 1205.

8. V. E. Volchkov and others, "Recovery of Infectious Ebola Virus from Complementary DNA: RNA Editing of the GP Gene and Viral Cytotoxicity," 291 *Science* (2001): 1965.

9. Jeronimo Cello, A. V. Paul, and Eckard Wimmer, "Chemical Synthesis of Poliovirus cDNA: Generation of Infectious Virus in the Absence of Natural Template," 297 *Science* (2002): 1016.

10. T. M. Tumpey and others, "Characterization of the Reconstructed 1918 Spanish Influenza Pandemic Virus," 310 *Science* (2005): 77.

11. Jeffery K. Taubenberger and David M. Morens, "1918 Influenza: The Mother of All Pandemics," *Emerging Infectious Diseases*, Centers for Disease Control and Prevention, January 2006 (www.cdc.gov/ncidod/eid/vol12no01/05-0979.htm).

12. Yuri V. Svitkin and Nahum Sonenberg, "Cell-free Synthesis of Encephalomyocarditis Virus," 77 *Journal of Virology* (2003): 6551.

13. Aleksandr Rabodzey, "Biosecurity Implications of the Synthesis of Pathogenic Viruses," 22 *Politics and Life Sciences* (2003): 44.

14. Barry Kellman, "Biological Terrorism: Legal Measures for Preventing Catastrophe," 24 *Harvard Journal of Law and Public Policy* (2001): 417, 425.

15. Ibid., 449–50.

16. See Scott Shane, "Critics of Anthrax Inquiry Seek an Independent Review," *New York Times*, September 24, 2008 (query.nytimes.com/gst/fullpage.html?res=9 D03E4DB153DF937A1575AC0A96E9C8B63); Joby Warrick, Marilyn W. Thompson, and Aaron C. Davis, "Scientists Question FBI Probe on Anthrax," *Washington Post*, August 3, 2008 (www.washingtonpost.com/wp-dyn/content/article/2008/08/02/AR2008080201632.html).

17. Office of Technology Assessment, *Proliferation of Weapons of Mass Destruction: Assessing the Risk,* OTA-ISC-559 (1993), 53–54 (www.au.af.mil/au/awc/awcgate/ota/9341.pdf).

18. Convention on the Prohibition of the Development, Production, and Stockpiling of Bacteriological (Biological) and Toxin Weapons and on Their Destruction, U.S.-U.K.-U.S.S.R, April 10, 1972, 1015 U.N.T.S. I 14860.

19. *Biological Weapons Anti-Terrorism Act of 1989,* 18 U.S.C. 175 (1990).

20. *USA PATRIOT Act,* Public Law 107-56, 115 Stat. 272, Title VIII (October 26, 2001), § 817 (amending *Biological Weapons Act* § 175).

21. Id. at 115 Stat. 386 (adding to *Biological Weapons Act* §§ 175b(a)(1) and (d)(2)). A *restricted person* was defined as a person who "(A) is under indictment for a crime punishable by imprisonment for a term exceeding 1 year; (B) has been convicted in any court of a crime punishable by imprisonment for a term exceeding 1 year; (C) is a fugitive from justice; (D) is an unlawful user of any controlled substance (as defined in section 102 of the Controlled Substances Act (21 U.S.C. 802)); (E) is an alien illegally or unlawfully in the United States; (F) has been adjudicated as a mental defective or has been committed to any mental institution; (G) is an alien (other than an alien lawfully admitted for permanent residence) who is a national of a country as to which the Secretary of State, . . . has made a determination (that remains in effect) that such country has repeatedly provided support for acts of international terrorism; or (H) has been discharged from the Armed Services of the United States under dishonorable conditions." In 2004 Congress added "(I) is a member of, acts for or on behalf of, or operates subject to the direction or control of, a terrorist organization as defined in section 212(a)(3)(B)(vi) of the Immigration and Nationality Act (8 U.S.C. 1182(a)(3)(B)(vi))." *Intelligence Reform and Terrorism Prevention Act of 2004,* Public Law 108-458.

22. *Public Health Security and Bioterrorism Preparedness and Response Act of 2002,* Public Law 107-188, 116 Stat. 594, § 201 (351A(a)(1)(A)) et seq. 2002. Regulations would define as *select agents* the biological agents and toxins on this list. *Select Agents and Toxins,* 42 C.F.R. 73.1 (April 18, 2005) (defining "select agent and/or toxin").

23. Id. at § 201 (§ 351A(b)–(c)).

24. Id. at § 201 (§ 351A(d)(1)).

25. Id. at § 201 (§ 351A(d)(2)).

26. *Select Agents and Toxins,* 42 C.F.R. 73.16 ("a select agent or toxin may only be transferred to individuals or entities registered to possess, use, or transfer that agent or toxin"); id. § 73.21 (defining *civil penalties*).

27. *Public Health Security and Bioterrorism Preparedness and Response Act of 2002,* § 231.

28. Id., § 201 (§ 351A(e)(3)(B)). The statute essentially denies registration to any "restricted person," as described in note 21, as well to as anyone "reasonably suspected" of committing a terrorism offense or who is "knowing[ly] involve[ed]" with certain designated terrorist organizations or violent groups or of "being an agent of a foreign power." The latter two categories are not automatic exclusions, but the Department of

Health and Human Services has the authority to limit or deny access to such agents and toxins if "determined appropriate by the Secretary, in consultation with the Attorney General." Id., § 201 (§ 351A(e)(2)(D)).

29. Information concerning the security risk assessment can be found at the Federal Bureau of Investigation website, "Bioterrorism Risk Assessment Form and Instructions" (www.fbi.gov/terrorinfo/bioterrorfd961.htm).

30. National Research Council, *Biotechnology Research in an Age of Terrorism* (2004), 44.

31. Ibid.

32. See Josh Gerstein, "Obama Team Mulls New Quarantine Regulations," Politico, August 5, 2009 (www.politico.com/news/stories/0809/25814.html). See also *Notice for Proposed Rulemaking to Amend CFR Parts 70 and 71,* 70 Federal Regulation 71892–71948, Centers for Disease Control and Prevention (November 30, 2005).

33. See Hans Bugl and others, "DNA Synthesis and Biological Security," 25 *Nature Biotechnology* (2007): 627. See also Jeremy Minshull and Ralf Wagner, "Preventing the Misuse of Gene Synthesis," 27 *Nature Biotechnology* (2009): 800.

34. Nouri and Chyba, "Proliferation-Resistant Biotechnology."

35. The closest it has come is the dictum in *Griswold* v. *Connecticut* that "the right of freedom of speech and press includes not only the right to utter or to print, but the right to distribute, the right to receive, the right to read *and freedom of inquiry, freedom of thought, and freedom to teach*. . . . Without those peripheral rights the specific rights would be less secure." See *Griswold* v. *Connecticut*, 381 U.S. 479 (1965) (emphasis added).

36. See, for example, Steve Keane, "The Case against Blanket First Amendment Protection of Scientific Research: Articulating a More Limited Scope of Protection," 59 *Stanford Law Review* (2006–07): 505.

37. See *New York Times Co.* v. *United States*, 403 U.S. 713 (1971).

38. *United States* v. *Progressive, Inc.*, 467 F. Supp. 990 (W.D. Wis. 1979).

39. Keane, "Case against Blanket First Amendment Protection," 508.

40. See National Research Council, *Biotechnology Research in an Age of Terrorism*, 96–99.

41. Ibid., 99.

42. Eugene Volokh, "Crime-Facilitating Speech," 57 *Stanford Law Review* (2004–05): 1095, 1106.

43. See Bugl and others, "DNA Synthesis and Biological Security"; see also Minshull and Wagner, "Preventing the Misuse of Gene Synthesis."

44. Nouri and Chyba, "Proliferation-Resistant Biotechnology," 234.

45. See Minshull and Wagner, "Preventing the Misuse of Gene Synthesis."

46. *Hearing on Strengthening Security and Oversight at Biological Research Laboratories Before the Senate Judiciary Committee, Subcommittee on Terrorism and Homeland Security,* 111th Congress (September 22, 2009) (testimony of Daniel D. Roberts, assistant director, Criminal Justice Information Services Division, Federal Bureau of Investigation) (http://judiciary.senate.gov/resources/transcripts/111transcripts.cfm).

47. *New York* v. *Burger*, 482 U.S. 691 (1987).

48. *Boumediene* v. *Bush*, 553 U.S. 723 (2008).

49. See *Zadvydas* v. *Davis*, 533 U.S. 678 (2001); see also *Clark* v. *Martinez*, 543 U.S. 371 (2005).

50. U.S. Const. art. I, § 8, cl. 11.

51. James Boyle, *The Public Domain: Enclosing the Commons of the Mind* (Yale University Press, 2008), 179–204.

52. Bruce Schneier, *Secrets and Lies: Digital Security in a Networked World* (New York: John Wiley, 2000), 343–45.

53. Eric Raymond, "Release Early, Release Often," in *The Cathedral and the Bazaar* (www.catb.org/~esr/writings/cathedral-bazaar/cathedral-bazaar/ar01s04.html).

LAWRENCE LESSIG

14

Epilogue: Translating and Transforming the Future

There is a way we academics talk about constitutional interpretation that suggests it to be more than it turns out to be. We speak of it as if the Court decides cases through elaborate (sometimes more, sometimes less) chains of reasoning. As if it were a Socratic dialogue, with the author inviting the reader to the seven steps necessary to see why the conclusion follows.

But constitutional interpretation is much more pedestrian and much more contingent. Whether or not the justices are reaching for particular results, opinions rarely move far beyond what the context of the decision offers up. There is a set of views that are taken for granted, at least by the majority, in a particular context; the opinion leverages those views to move the law one or two steps from where it starts. These views include, of course, views about other parts of the law. But what is important for the purposes of this book, they include views of much more than the law. In particular, they include views about what is technologically feasible, or morally acceptable, or culturally done.

Think of constitutional interpretation as a game of Frogger—the old video game where the frog has to cross a river by stepping onto logs as they pass by. The frog cannot simply pick up and move to the other side of the river. Instead, the frog moves one step at a time, as the opportunity for a move presents itself. The player, moreover, does not create the opportunity for a move. Instead, the player is faced with an opportunity, takes it, and waits for the next.

In this picture of constitutional interpretation, the critical bits are these opportunities for a move, a single move, provided by an interpretive context that the interpreter only slightly, if at all, can affect. (Of course, in Frogger the player can effect only one move at a time.) These moves are presented to the interpreter; they are constituted by the parts of an interpretive context that at least five justices treat as taken for granted, as obvious, as the stuff no one, or at least no one like them, needs to argue about. And it is in light of changes in this class of taken-for-granted interpretations that change in constitutional law can happen.

This dynamic helps show why predicting the future in constitutional law is so difficult. The challenge is not that we cannot describe all the elements the future will or could have. The difficulty is that we cannot know which elements will be obvious. The critical, yet wholly undertheorized, bit to constitutional interpretation is not what the interpreters might argue about. It is the things that they will take for granted. Constitutional meaning comes just as much from what everyone knows is true (both then and now) as from what the framers actually wrote. Yet "what everyone knows is true" changes over time, and in ways that are impossible to predict, even if quite possible to affect.

Take an obvious example: The Constitution says, "The executive Power shall be vested in a President of the United States of America. He shall hold his Office during the Term of four Years." It is unquestioned that the *he* in this clause does not just mean "he"—unquestioned, at least, for us. For us, *he* means "he or she." For the framers, it would have been unquestioned that *he* just means "he." That Dolly Madison could have been president of the United States was unthinkable. Part of that "unthinkableness" was tied to specific legal disabilities. But much more important was a broad and general understanding within the framing context—what they took for granted, the opposite of what we take for granted. And not just in the framing context. Opponents of the Fourteenth Amendment argued that by its terms the amendment would radically remake the rights of women. Supporters of the Fourteenth Amendment called the claim absurd. And maybe it was, until the Supreme Court actually did apply the amendment to claims made by women, again because, by then, it was unthinkable that it would not.

The practice of constitutional interpretation, or at least any practice aiming at fidelity, must include an understanding of the sort of issues, or matters, that the authors took for granted. These elements must be understood because they mark the things authors did not think necessary to say, the things that everyone knows to be true—for example, the place of women in society, the salience of "certain unalienable rights," the role of the law of nations, and so forth. To read what they wrote, and understand the meaning, thus requires understanding what they did not write, and how that also helped constitute meaning.

We know how to identify these taken-for-granteds about the past, if imperfectly and incompletely. History teaches the method, including accounts of the interpretive contexts, descriptions of the sort of issues that no one debated, and actions that reveal at least what no one was embarrassed to reveal. If someone had said to Alexander Hamilton, "Why are there no women in Washington's cabinet?" he would not have been embarrassed by the question. He would not have understood it. That marks the disability attached to women at the time as a fact of a certain kind. It went unmentioned, since it did not need mention, since no one (among the framers, at least) would have thought to dispute it.

But we do not know how to identify these taken-for-granteds with the future. We can talk about what sort of things will be obvious in 2030. I am confident the equal status of women is not about to be drawn into doubt. And I am also confident that the right of people to worship whatever god, or no god at all, will also remain a bedrock within our tradition. But a whole host of other issues and questions and beliefs will also be taken for granted then. And it would take a novelist with the skill of Tolstoy or Borges to fill out the details necessary for us to even glimpse that universe of uncontested truth, let alone to convince us of it.

Even then, it would not feel uncontested to us. If a complete description of the world in 2030 would include the fact that most everyone accepted cloning as a necessary means to health (as many science fiction stories depict, for organ banking, for example), we would still experience that "fact" as something to be challenged or, at least, questioned. I am not even sure how to describe the mental state we would need to adopt to be able to relate to the uncontested "facts" of the future the way the uncontested "facts" of the future would be experienced. It would be at best a possibility, or a scenario. But it would not have the force necessary to bend, or alter, the law the way it will when it is in fact taken for granted by those who read the law in the future.

Until we can come to reckon these different taken-for-granteds, I want to argue, we cannot predict how constitutional interpretation in the future will proceed. It will follow the logs offered to the frog, but we cannot know which logs will present themselves when.

Take as an example the recent decision by the Supreme Court in *Citizens United* v. *FEC*, upholding a constitutional right for corporations to spend an unlimited amount in independent campaign expenditures.[1] While most criticize that decision as treating corporations as persons, in fact, the Court never invokes such a principle to support its judgment. Instead, the holding hangs on a limit in government power, not the vitality of the personhood of corporations.

But there is something about the status of corporations in today's society that is essential to understanding how the Court decided as it did. If one imagined asking the framers about the "unalienable rights," as the Declaration of Independence puts it, that the Constitution intended to secure to corporations, they would have been puzzled by the question. Rights were the sort of things that "men" are "endowed" with, not legal entities. And while legal entities may well enjoy rights derivatively, as proxies for real human beings, that is only when the thing they are defending is something that, if taken away, a real human being would also necessarily lose. So a corporation should have the right to defend against the taking of its property, because the taking of its property necessarily involves the taking of the property of a real human being. Beyond that derivative, however, it would have been hard for them to understand the sense of this state-granted privilege (which, of course, a limited liability corporation is) also enjoying "rights." And impossible, I want to argue, for them to understand how this idea would lead to the morphing of the First Amendment to embrace a political speech right for this legal entity.

For us, today, the idea of a corporation's possessing these rights is easier to comprehend. Corporations are common, and democratically created (in the sense that anyone can create them). And though they are radically different in wealth and power, we all see them as essential to important aspects of our lives. They are familiar, pedestrian. It does not seem weird to imagine them as constitutionally protected, even beyond the derivative protection for things like property.

The familiarity of corporations, their ubiquity, and their importance all helped cover up a logical gap in the Supreme Court's reasoning in *Citizens United*. In addressing the obvious (and in my view, conclusive) argument that these state-created entities could not possess any powers the state did not grant them, Justice Kennedy, quoting Justice Scalia, wrote, "It is rudimentary that the State cannot exact as the price of those special advantages the forfeiture of First Amendment rights."[2]

But obviously, no "First Amendment rights" of humans would be forfeited by saying that a legal entity created by the state does not include among its powers the right to engage in political speech. To say something is "forfeited" is to say it existed and then was removed. But no rights of any humans are forfeited by a law that restricts a corporation. Humans would have all the rights they had to speak after such a law as before it. The only loser is the corporation. Yet so obviously familiar and native have corporations become that *Citizens United* becomes a *Bladerunner* moment in Supreme Court history, where a human-created entity gets endowed with "unalienable rights."

I do not mean (obviously) that everyone agrees with the conclusion or the protection recognized. Indeed, the decision has sparked an anticorporate rage that may in the end defeat its premise. Instead, my point is that it was not weird to recognize the rights the Court recognized, just as it was not weird for the *Plessy* Court to treat segregation as "reasonable" or for Justice Bradley to write in *Bradwell* v. *Illinois*, "The civil law, as well as nature herself, has always recognized a wide difference in the respective spheres and destinies of man and woman. Man is, or should be, woman's protector and defender. The natural and proper timidity and delicacy which belongs to the female sex evidently unfits it for many of the occupations of civil life."[3]

To the contrary, these claims are only weird in light of a radically different baseline of taken-for-granteds. And while it is relatively easy in hindsight to see these differences, and remark on them, it is incredibly difficult to see them in the future, and believe them. Again, the framers could not have predicted the Supreme Court's finding, even if we had told them that corporations would be as common as clay.

Consider one more try to make the very same point: We all (almost all) recognize in our parents' views those that are dated or weird. These might be views about race, or sexual orientation, or music. Whatever they are, they mark the distance between our parents and us. We cannot imagine ourselves holding such views, or viewing the world in light of them.

But what are the views that we hold that our children will react to similarly? What is the equivalent of racism, or homophobia, for them? And even if we could identify what those views will be—maybe the idea that members of Congress ask private citizens to fund public campaigns, or that we permit an industry to slaughter dolphins so that we can eat maguro—it is almost impossible for us to gin up the outrage or disgust about ourselves that they will certainly feel toward us. Of course, they will love us, as we love our parents. But they will be distant from us, as we are from our parents, for reasons we could not begin to feel as we feel the reasons that distance us from the generation that preceded us.

The past is interpretively more accessible than the future. We can imagine it more fully and feel the differences more completely. And that asymmetry affects fundamentally the ability to write an essay about what the Constitution in the future will hold.

Predicting What the Court Will Find

To say we cannot know how the Constitution will be read in the future, however, because we cannot know what will be taken for granted in the future is not to say that we cannot affect what will be taken for granted in the future. And herein is the rub. If what will be taken for granted is a function of how we lead our ordinary lives, then there are obvious ways in which we could affect what will seem obvious, or taken for granted, by altering the environment within which we lead our ordinary lives. That change, in turn, will affect how the Constitution will be read, even if we cannot see or imagine precisely how.

Cybersecurity is an obvious example. There is much I agree with in both Jack Goldsmith's and Orin Kerr's chapters. I too have argued that we need to shift our focus in privacy away from controlling access to data and more toward regulating their use. And I too believe, like Goldsmith, that cybersecurity issues will force a rethinking of how we protect basic civil rights.[4]

But whether and how we respond to their obviously correct concerns will depend on how most of us experience the cyber environment, or how its "nature" gets reported by us. And here we can sketch two very different futures.

The first is the one I believe we are likely to have. It is an unhappy story, about how certain freedoms, or characteristics, of the current network get lost as a completely predictable reaction to an obvious threat. I have described this story before as a consequence of Z-Theory (where Z stands for Zittrain).[5] Z-Theory describes the mechanism by which political actors have sufficient motivation to intervene to change the basic architecture or freedoms of the Internet. That mechanism is grounded in fear. On this account, the currently insecure Internet putters along as it has. At some point, it suffers a catastrophic failure. We could call this an i9/11 event, not to suggest that al Qaeda would be behind the event but to mark its significance to the nation or nations that suffer it: a massive attack on infrastructure facilitated by zombie bots or the like that even today spread across the network, controlled in ways no one quite understands.

This i9/11 event will evoke a certain political response, just as 9/11 evoked a political response. The response to 9/11 was the USA PATRIOT Act—which, whether or not one agrees with it, was a radical change in the scope and reach of policing and counterterrorism authority, justified, or so it was claimed, by the plainly manifested threat.

The response to my hypothetical i9/11 event will be similar: a radical change in the control of the Internet, or of privacy on the Internet, justified, so it will be claimed, by the now plainly manifested threat. That response will change the Internet in important ways. It will render it a much less open or generative space. But that loss will be seen to be unavoidable, given the threat now made manifest. (As one former government official responded when I asked whether there was the equivalent of an iPATRIOT Act already prepared for such an attack, "Sure there is. And [Internet founder] Vint Cerf is not going to like it very much.")

In both cases, the justification hangs on the apparently limited range of options. What else are we going to do? The threat is real. It has manifested itself in a dramatic and tragic way. There is an irresistible push to respond. In both cases, it is taken for granted that we can and will respond. But the scope and nature of the response are determined by the range of technical options that seem available or open to us. That depends on the technologies actually deployed.

The second future begins before the i9/11 event. Indeed, if successful, it could well avoid any i9/11 event. This future includes a policy intervention designed to change the character of the Internet but not in ways that would undermine its good, or generative, character. It is an intervention that Vint Cerf *would* like. And while it is beyond this chapter to describe the change fully, a sketch should suffice to make the contrast with the first story clear.

This intervention would be designed to add to the Internet an identity layer.[6] The purpose of this identity layer would be to make it feasible to identify who or what was responsible for any particular act on the Internet. But the layer would be designed in a way that protected legitimate privacy. In this sense, it would give both sides in the debate something the current Internet denies them: for the government, a secure way to hold people responsible for acts that they should properly be held accountable for; for users, a more secure way to protect identity and privacy on the net.

To see how this might work, start with a crude real-world analog—a license plate on a car. The license plate makes the owner of a car identifiable, but it identifies the owner only to people with access to the proper database. It makes events involving the car traceable back to the owner (of course, not necessarily the driver but likely a person with knowledge about who the driver was), without enabling others to make the trace. I may see a person driving a car with a Pennsylvania license plate number Z546TY, but I cannot tell from that who the driver is or who owns the car. The police can, but I cannot. And to enable all the legitimate functions that the police have with respect to cars on a highway, we mandate that cars driving on the highway carry with them just this sort of identification.

An identity layer on the Internet would do something similar. It would build into the architecture a standard and automatic way to link back to an entity that could authenticate—if the proper or legally sufficient demands were made—the identity of the actor responsible for the Internet event. But if no proper demand were made, the identity of the actor would be as transparent as the actor might want.

For example, an e-mail gets sent that includes content constituting fraud. In a network with a proper identity layer, that e-mail gets transmitted or relayed only if it carries with it an identification token (like a license plate). That token, or signature, need not reveal to everyone who the sender is. To the contrary: "A_Friend@something.com" would still be a perfectly permissible e-mail address. But it would be required that, somewhere in the chain of trust into which this identity layer would be built, someone with the proper legal authority could discover who "A_Friend" was.

Again, how the technology of this works is beyond the scope of this chapter. Plenty of examples have been developed, and some are currently being developed and deployed by the very best technology shops in the world. Obviously, how well or how effectively privacy or pseudonymity (for absolute anonymity is removed by this system) is protected would depend on the details of implementation.

For now, the point is to see that we could imagine this layer providing a critical bridge between two strongly prized values—privacy and security. The identity layer would protect privacy more effectively than the current Internet does; but by securing traceability, it would also promote security. Users could mask themselves however they wanted as they went about their legal activities; but like fingerprints on a gun, the system would ensure that when we have good reason, properly established to the proper authorities, we could trace back who did what.

So imagine now an i9/11 event happening in this world: What would the reasonable or legitimate responses be? Unlike the world we live in now, in the alternative I am describing there is a mitigating technology that could well be adjusted in light of the catastrophic event. Maybe certain authorities that had been presumed legitimate in providing identities now need to be removed from the list of trusted sources. But there would be no justification for a radical removal of privacy on the Internet. Authorities, in democracies at least, have a legitimate interest in identification. This technology could balance that interest by preserving as much as possible a right of individuals to privacy.

Thus simply by having that alternative deployed, present and recognizable to policymakers, including judges, we could constrain the power of government relative to the power it will get when the i9/11 event happens in the first scenario. And the difference—the key to the argument here—is simply the product of a background range of available technologies.

Again, think about the license plate. Imagine there is an outbreak of car theft. The government responds by demanding that license plates be changed to include people's names and addresses rather than a code that the police could decipher. It would be extremely difficult for the government to justify that demand. The alternatives—a more efficient code or a radio frequency identification code, for example—would be compelling and obvious to anyone and certainly to judges. It would be a small step forward to imagine how the license plate system could be improved and a large step backward to imagine it replaced by true names and addresses. Thus a conservative (with a small *c*) instinct would protect the privacy protected by the architecture of traceability that now defines license plates. Having this traceability architecture deployed thus limits the possibility of a more extreme privacy-reducing response.

Thus two futures, the difference between them resting solely on a technical infrastructure strategically inserted. That infrastructure would not necessarily promote the immediate commercial interests, or other interests, of currently dominant actors. But it would provide a long-term interest in protecting values that we currently hold dear. The challenge is to imagine the mechanism that could guide us to embrace and implement this alternative—well, and with efficiency or intelligence.

This, unfortunately, leads to our Constitution's most depressing reality, a point I consider in the last part of this chapter.

Gaming What the Court Will Find

If we cannot know how the future will feel but we can intervene to change the way it is likely to feel, what should we think about this kind of intervention? Is there a reason to have confidence in it? If the application of a constitution is going to turn on how the world seems, or how we make the world seem, how confident can we feel about preserving a constitution's meaning over time?

I confess that this fact about the nature of constitutional interpretation—its contingency on these taken-for-granteds, which are themselves, it turns out, plastic—gives me the most anxiety, for it highlights a public choice problem that we do not often remark on in interpreting a written constitution.

Usually, a public choice problem is contemporary. It is often decision-makers, usually legislators, who must make a public policy decision but are tempted or drawn to favor private interests over the public good: legislators, for example, responding to campaign contributors rather than constituents; or a president responding to a powerful labor union rather than the nation as a whole.

But in the dynamic I am describing here, the effect is delayed. We intervene today to affect the interpretive context tomorrow, believing that that intervention will make more likely one outcome rather than another. So again, drawing on the cybersecurity example, if we intervene to enable an identity layer, we make judicial decisions respecting privacy more likely. If we do not, we make them less likely. The choice whether to intervene today thus affects how the Constitution gets interpreted tomorrow.

This possibility creates its own public choice problem. Imagine a government that does not much like the freedom that the Internet has enabled. This government has to accept that freedom, given constitutional norms, but it would much prefer a more controllable infrastructure. In light of the story told here, the interpretive contingency of the constitution now gives the government an interesting (or troubling) choice: If it does nothing, and Z-Theory is correct, at some point in the future the constitutional constraints on the government's ability to monitor or control the Internet get relaxed. If the government does something—namely, intervene to better enable privacy by encouraging or deploying an effective identity layer—the constraints on it will not be relaxed.

Doing nothing is thus a way to effectively amend the Constitution's protections. Yet there is little within current doctrine that would even recognize this dynamic or hold any government actor responsible for letting it play out one way rather than another. The contexts within which constitutional decisions are made are constructed in advance; how they are constructed affects the scope or meaning of the Constitution; yet we have no way to hold anyone accountable for one construction over another.

Of course, the feasibility of this dynamic depends on the issue. Whatever contextual shift is plausible in the context of cybersecurity, it might be less feasible to imagine the same in the context of genetic engineering. But whether this is a general phenomenon or not, the dynamic does raise what we could call a second-order problem of interpretation. For the question of fidelity— understood broadly as the challenge to preserve the Constitution's meaning across time—is now not only the question of how to read the Constitution in context but also how to affect the choice of contexts so as to better protect original values.

At least if it is original values that we want to protect. For the last point raises one more final point: who is the "we" who should be concerned here?

In the beginning of his book on aging, Judge Posner writes this about his mother: "Once when my mother was a vigorous woman of 65 or so she noticed a very frail old woman in a wheelchair and said to my wife, 'If I ever become like that, shoot me.' Two decades later she had become just like that but she did not express any desire to die."[7]

The point is more general than the example suggests. What we want from the perspective of an author, for example, will often be different from what we want from the perspective of the reader, since the context of the reader, the taken-for-granteds, the facts we now know, will be different. The author, recognizing this, might well take steps to staunch the changes that will produce these changes in "what we want." But we today need not necessarily like those steps. From the perspective of today, we can talk about how we should intervene to protect our values tomorrow. But from the perspective of tomorrow, that intervention may well seem foreign, or imperialistic.

The challenge of fidelity in constitutional interpretation is how broadly we allow that past to constrain us or who we as a nation will become. Constitutional traditions cannot sensibly adopt either of two extremes—either that the tradition is intended to take whatever steps necessary to ensure that we do not change or that the tradition is intended to permit whatever change might suggest itself. But the sensible line between these two extremes is not obvious, or stable, or protectable from manipulation—especially in the future.

Notes

1. *Citizens United* v. *Federal Elections Commission,* 558 U.S. 50 (2010).

2. *Citizens United,* slip op. at 35.

3. *Plessy* v. *Ferguson,* 163 U.S. 537 (1896); *Bradwell* v. *Illinois,* 83 U.S. 130, 141 (1873).

4. I describe both in *Code: And Other Laws of Cyberspace, Version 2* (New York: Basic Books, 2006), chap. 11.

5. Ibid., 74–77.

6. Ibid., 50–52.

7. Richard Posner, *Aging and Old Age* (University of Chicago Press, 1995), 87.

Contributors

JAMES BOYLE is William Neal Reynolds Professor of Law at Duke Law School and founder of the Center for the Study of the Public Domain. He was one of the original board members of Creative Commons. He served as a board member from 2002 until 2009, the last year as Chairman of the Board. He was also a cofounder of Science Commons, which aims to expand the Creative Commons mission into the realm of scientific and technical data, and of ccLearn, which works to promote the development and use of open educational resources. He is currently a member of the board of the Public Library of Science. In 2003 Boyle won the World Technology Network Award for Law for his work on the public domain and the "second enclosure movement" that threatens it. In 2010 he was awarded the Electronic Frontier Foundation's Pioneer Award. He is the author of *Shamans, Software and Spleens: Law and the Construction of the Information Society* and the editor of *Critical Legal Studies, Collected Papers on the Public Domain and Cultural Environmentalism @ 10* (with Lawrence Lessig). His more recent books include *Bound by Law*, a coauthored graphic novel about the effects of intellectual property on documentary film; *The Shakespeare Chronicles*, a novel; and *The Public Domain: Enclosing the Commons of the Mind*. He writes a regular online column for the *Financial Times*'s New Economy Policy Forum.

ERIC COHEN is the Executive Director of the Tikvah Fund and editor-at-large of *The New Atlantis*, a quarterly journal about the ethical, political, and social implications of modern science and technology. His essays and articles have appeared in numerous academic and popular journals, magazines, and newspapers, including the *Hastings Center Report*, the *Yale Journal of Health Policy,*

Law, and Ethics, the *Harvard Divinity Bulletin,* the *Washington Post,* the *Wall Street Journal,* the *Los Angeles Times, USA Today,* the *Weekly Standard,* the *Public Interest, First Things, Commentary,* and elsewhere. He is the coeditor of *The Future Is Now: America Confronts the New* and author of *In the Shadow of Progress: Being Human in the Age of Technology.* He was previously a fellow at the New America Foundation and managing editor of the *Public Interest.* He also served as a senior consultant to the President's Council on Bioethics.

ROBERT P. GEORGE is McCormick Professor of Jurisprudence and Director of the James Madison Program in American Ideals and Institutions at Princeton University. He is also a member of the Virtues of a Free Society Task Force of the Hoover Institution at Stanford University. He has served on the U.S. Commission on Civil Rights and the President's Council on Bioethics and was a Judicial Fellow at the Supreme Court of the United States, where he received the Justice Tom C. Clark Award. A graduate of Swarthmore College, he holds J.D. and M.T.S. degrees from Harvard University, and a D.Phil. from Oxford University, in addition to many honorary degrees. He is a member of the Council on Foreign Relations and a recipient of the U.S. Presidential Citizens Medal and the Honorific Medal of the Republic of Poland for the Defense of Human Rights. He is the author of *Making Men Moral: Civil Liberties and Public Morality* (1995), *In Defense of Natural Law* (1999), and *The Clash of Orthodoxies* (2002) and coauthor of *Embryo: A Defense of Human Life* (2008) and *Body-Self Dualism in Contemporary Ethics and Politics* (2008).

JACK GOLDSMITH is the Henry L. Shattuck Professor at Harvard Law School, where he teaches and writes about national security law, presidential power, cybersecurity, international law, Internet law, foreign relations law, and conflict of laws. Before coming to Harvard, Goldsmith served as Assistant Attorney General, Office of Legal Counsel, Department of Justice, from 2003–04 and Special Counsel to the Department of Defense from 2002–03.

ORIN KERR teaches criminal law, criminal procedure, and computer crime law at the George Washington Law School. His articles have appeared in the *Harvard Law Review, Yale Law Journal, Stanford Law Review, Columbia Law Review, University of Chicago Law Review, Michigan Law Review, Virginia Law Review, New York University Law Review, Georgetown Law Journal, Northwestern University Law Review, Texas Law Review,* and many other journals. Before joining the faculty in 2001, Kerr was an honors program trial attorney in the Computer Crime and Intellectual Property Section of the Criminal Division at the U.S. Department of Justice, as well as a Special Assistant U.S.

Attorney for the Eastern District of Virginia. He also is a former law clerk for Justice Anthony M. Kennedy of the United States Supreme Court and Judge Leonard I. Garth of the U.S. Court of Appeals for the Third Circuit. Kerr posts regularly at the popular blog *The Volokh Conspiracy.*

Lawrence Lessig is the Director of the Edmond J. Safra Center for Ethics and the Roy L. Furman Professor of Law at Harvard Law School. Prior to returning to Harvard, he was a professor at Stanford Law School, where he founded the school's Center for Internet and Society, and at the University of Chicago. He clerked for Judge Richard Posner on the Seventh Circuit Court of Appeals and Justice Antonin Scalia on the United States Supreme Court. He has won numerous awards, including the Free Software Foundation's Freedom Award, and was named one of *Scientific American*'s Top 50 Visionaries. He is the author of *Republic, Lost* (2011), *Remix* (2008), *Code v2* (2007), *Free Culture* (2004), *The Future of Ideas* (2001), and *Code and Other Laws of Cyberspace* (1999). Lessig earned a BA in economics and a BS in management from the University of Pennsylvania, an MA in philosophy from Cambridge, and a JD from Yale.

Stephen J. Morse is an expert in criminal and mental health law whose work emphasizes individual responsibility in criminal and civil law. Educated in law and psychology at Harvard, Morse has written for law reviews, journals of psychology, psychiatry, and philosophy; and he has edited collections. He was a contributing author (with Larry Alexander and Kimberly Kessler Ferzan) to *Crime and Culpability: A Theory of Criminal Law,* he coedited (with Leo Katz and Michael S. Moore) *Foundations of Criminal Law,* and he is working on a new book, *Desert and Disease: Responsibility and Social Control.* Morse was Codirector of the MacArthur Foundation's Law and Neuroscience Project and he codirected the project's Research Network on Criminal Responsibility and Prediction. Morse is a Diplomat in Forensic Psychology of the American Board of Professional Psychology; a past president of Division 41 of the American Psychological Association (the American Psychology–Law Society); a recipient of the American Academy of Forensic Psychology's Distinguished Contribution Award; a member of the MacArthur Foundation Research Network on Mental Health and Law (1988–96); and a trustee of the Bazelon Center for Mental Health Law in Washington, D.C. (1995–present).

John A. Robertson holds the Vinson and Elkins Chair at the University of Texas School of Law at Austin. He has written and lectured widely on law and bioethical issues. He is the author of two books in bioethics—*The Rights of the Critically Ill* (1983) and *Children of Choice: Freedom and the New Reproductive*

Technologies (1994)—and numerous articles on reproductive rights, genetics, organ transplantation, and human experimentation. He has served on or been a consultant to many national bioethics advisory bodies and is currently Chair of the Ethics Committee of the American Society for Reproductive Medicine.

JEFFREY ROSEN is a Nonresident Senior Fellow at the Brookings Institution, where he explores issues involving the future of technology and the Constitution. He is also a professor of law at the George Washington University and the legal affairs editor of the *New Republic*. His most recent book is *The Supreme Court: The Personalities and Rivalries That Defined America*. He also is the author of *The Most Democratic Branch*; *The Naked Crowd*; and *The Unwanted Gaze*. Rosen is a graduate of Harvard College; Oxford University, where he was a Marshall Scholar; and Yale Law School. Rosen's essays and commentaries have appeared in the *New York Times Magazine*, the *Atlantic Monthly*, on National Public Radio, and in the *New Yorker*, where he has been a staff writer. The *Chicago Tribune* named him one of the ten best magazine journalists in America and the *Los Angeles Times* called him, the "nation's most widely read and influential legal commentator."

CHRISTOPHER SLOBOGIN is the Milton Underwood Professor of Law at Vanderbilt University Law School and directs the Criminal Justice Program there. He has authored more than 100 articles, books, and chapters on topics relating to criminal procedure and mental health law and evidence and is one of the ten most-cited criminal law and procedure law professors in the nation. He formerly served as reporter for the American Bar Association's Task Force on Law Enforcement and Technology and chair of the Florida Assessment Team for the ABA's Death Penalty Moratorium Implementation Project. He has taught at Stanford, Virginia, and the University of Southern California Law School, as well as at the University of Kiev, Ukraine, where he was a Fulbright Scholar.

O. CARTER SNEAD is Professor of Law at the University of Notre Dame, which he joined in 2005. His principal area of research is public bioethics—the governance of science, medicine, and biotechnology in the name of ethical good. His scholarly works have explored issues relating to neuroethics, enhancement, stem cell research, abortion, and end-of-life decisionmaking. Snead teaches law and bioethics, torts, and constitutional criminal procedure. In addition to his scholarship and teaching, he has provided advice on the legal and public policy dimensions of bioethical questions to officials in all three branches of the U.S. government, and in several intergovernmental forums.

Prior to Notre Dame, Snead served as General Counsel to the President's Council on Bioethics, where he was the primary drafter of the 2004 report, "Reproduction and Responsibility: The Regulation of New Biotechnologies." He received his JD from Georgetown University (where he was elected to the Order of the Coif) and his BA from St. John's College (Annapolis, Md.). He clerked for the Hon. Paul J. Kelly Jr. of the U.S. Court of Appeals for the Tenth Circuit.

BENJAMIN WITTES is a Senior Fellow in Governance Studies at the Brookings Institution and codirector of the Harvard Law School–Brookings Project on Law and Security. He is the author of *Detention and Denial: The Case for Candor after Guantánamo* and *Law and the Long War: The Future of Justice in the Age of Terror* and editor of the 2009 Brookings book, *Legislating the War on Terror: An Agenda for Reform*. He cofounded and cowrites the *Lawfare* blog (www.lawfareblog.com/), which is devoted to non-ideological discussion of the hard national security choices. He is a member of the Hoover Institution's Task Force on National Security and Law. His previous books include *Starr: A Reassessment* and *Confirmation Wars: Preserving Independent Courts in Angry Times*. Between 1997 and 2006, he served as an editorial writer for the *Washington Post* specializing in legal affairs. Before joining that newspaper, Wittes covered the Justice Department and federal regulatory agencies as a reporter and news editor at *Legal Times*. His writing has also appeared in a wide range of journals and magazines, including *The Atlantic, Slate,* the *New Republic,* the *Wilson Quarterly,* the *Weekly Standard, Policy Review,* and *First Things.*

TIM WU is a policy advocate and author of *The Master Switch*. He is currently on leave as a professor at Columbia Law School, serving as a senior adviser to the Federal Trade Commission. Wu was recognized in 2006 as one of fifty leaders in science and technology by *Scientific American*, and in 2007 he was listed as one of Harvard's 100 most influential graduates by *02138* magazine. Wu's best-known work is the development of net neutrality theory, but he has also written about copyright, international trade, and the study of law breaking. He previously worked in the telecommunications industry for Riverstone Networks and was a law clerk for Judge Richard Posner and Justice Stephen Breyer. He graduated from McGill University (BS) and Harvard Law School. Wu has written for the *New Yorker,* the *Washington Post, Forbes, Slate,* and others.

JONATHAN L. ZITTRAIN is Professor of Law at Harvard Law School and the Harvard Kennedy School of Government, Professor of Computer Science at the Harvard School of Engineering and Applied Sciences, and cofounder of the Berkman Center for Internet and Society. He performed the first large-scale tests of Internet filtering in China and Saudi Arabia, and now, as part of the OpenNet Initiative, he has coedited a series of studies of Internet filtering by national governments, most recently *Access Contested*. He is a member of the Board of Trustees of the Internet Society, the Board of Directors of the Electronic Frontier Foundation, and the Board of Advisors for *Scientific American*. His most recent book is *The Future of the Internet—And How to Stop It*.

Index